MYTHS · AND · LEGENDS · OF · ANCIENT · ROME

KENNETH · McLEISH

MYTHS · AND · LEGENDS
OF · ANCIENT · ROME

LONGMAN

LONGMAN GROUP LIMITED
Longman House, Burnt Mill, Harlow, Essex CM20 2JE, England and Associated Companies
throughout the world

© Kenneth McLeish 1987

First published 1987
ISBN 0 582 00288 5

Set in 11/13 Palatino Roman

Printed in Great Britain
by Butler & Tanner, Frome

CONTENTS

INTRODUCTION   vii

In the beginning   1

1   STORIES OF THE GODS   2
    *The beginning of life;   Janus;   Phaethon;   The making of mortals;   Pomona
    and Vertumnus;   Arethusa;   Picus and Canens*

2   SILVER AND IRON   15
    *The Silver Age;   Cupid and Psyche;   The Age of Iron;   Erysichthon;
    Lycaon;   Baucis and Philemon;   The Trojan War*

The story of Aeneas   33

3   TROY   34
    The Wooden Horse;   Destruction;   Flight

4   THE TROJANS AT SEA   44
    Omens;   Monsters;   Storm

5   THE GODS TAKE ACTION   55
    Carthage;   Dido and Aeneas;   Sicily

6   THE UNDERWORLD   66
    The Sibyl of Cumae;   The path to Hell;   Torments;   The Elysian Fields

7   WAR COMES TO ITALY   77
    Latium;   Allecto;   Evander

8   THE SIEGE OF THE TROJAN CAMP   89
    *The siege begins;   Nisus and Euryalus;   Turnus in the Trojan camp;   Aeneas
    returns*

9   THE BATTLE ON THE PLAIN   99
    *The gods in council;   Pallas' death;   The ghost;   Mezentius;   Truce;
    Camilla;   Peace*

v

18063

Stories of Rome   111

10   THE BIRTH OF ROME   112
     Lavinium and Alba Longa;   Wolf-twins;   Women;   The end of Romulus' reign

11   STORIES OF THE KINGS   124
     *Numa and Egeria;   The Horatii and the Curiatii;   Rome and Alba;   Tullus'
     death;   Tarquin*

12   THE LAST KINGS OF ROME   137
     *Tarquin and Tullia;   Who shall take command?;   The rape of Lucretia;   Tarquin
     in retreat*

Additional stories, alternative versions and notes   149

SOME BOOKS TO READ   181

MAPS   182

INDEX   185

INTRODUCTION

The stories

The earliest Roman stories of all – those in the first two chapters of this book – were retellings of Greek myth. The names were often changed, and the setting was usually Italy, but the characters were the same gods, giants, nymphs and spirits as in Greek tales, given additional adventures in Roman style. In later times, and particularly after the coming of the Roman emperors just before the birth of Christ, the Romans began weaving old stories of gods and heroes into accounts of their own past history. They wanted to show how the rulers of Rome were descended in a more or less unbroken line from the gods of Olympus, how the gods had blessed each step in Rome's development, from the moment when Aeneas and his followers left the ruins of Troy to the time when Tarquin the Proud, the last tyrant-king, was expelled from Rome.

Some of the stories in this 'history' of Rome are straightforward fiction, and no one really imagined that they were true. But others are legends rather than myths: that is, although their details are just as fictional, they were probably based on real people or actual events. Janus, the two-headed god who first ruled Italy, is a character from myth; Tarpeia who betrayed the Roman citadel to the enemy, or Horatius who held the bridge, belong to legend. Two Roman writers above all others, Virgil (who wrote about Aeneas' journey from Troy and the first Trojan settlement in Italy) and Livy (who wrote a 'history' of the founding of Rome by Romulus and Remus and of the centuries which followed), expertly blended myth and legend to make ordered accounts, so persuasive that they were even taught in Roman schools as fact. However unlikely some of their events might seem – the constant presence in mortal lives, for example, of giants, witches, and other supernatural beings – the settings were always real places, and the weather and scenery would have been familiar to everyone who heard or read the stories.

This book

Like its companions *Children of the Gods* (myths and legends of ancient Greece) and *Myths and Folk-stories of Britain and Ireland*, this book sets out to tell the stories clearly and simply, without interruption. Where stories have already appeared in *Children of the Gods*, and the Roman version is hardly different – a good example is the tale of the Trojan War – they are mentioned only briefly here. In stories retold by Virgil and Livy, because the way those writers ordered the tales was so important to the Romans themselves, we have followed their sequence of events, and sometimes (for example in *The Story of Aeneas*) adapted their actual words. Additional stories, alternative versions, notes, and maps are in a separate section at the end of the main text. A star * in the text means that there is more information in this section. A dagger † refers to a family tree. Suggestions for further reading are on pages 181, and maps are on pages 182–3.

Acknowledgements

Chapters 3–9 are based on Kenneth McLeish's *The Story of Aeneas*, a translation of Virgil's *Aeneid* published by Longman in 1968 and long out of print. His versions of the stories of Baucis and Philemon and Romulus and Remus appeared, in a different form, in *Mediterranean Folk-tales* (Ginn, 1986), and we are grateful for permission to use them here. The author thanks Anne Nash for typing the manuscript, and, as always, Valerie McLeish for encouragement throughout the writing of the book and for compiling the index.

IN · THE · BEGINNING

1
STORIES · OF
THE · GODS

The beginning of life

The universe began with struggle. There was nothing to separate its elements. Light, darkness, earth, air, sea and fire were lumped together like animals in a bag, and seethed and writhed in the emptiness of space. Even as they struggled, they mated and their offspring swarmed around them: monstrous shapes, born of their mingling.

At last, under the power of their own movement, the elements began to spin apart. Sky freed itself from earth, fire from water, light from dark. From time to time they squabbled – as when air and sea made typhoons, rock and fire made lava, water and fire made steam. But for the most part they lived contentedly together. Earth hung poised in space, and Sea spread his arms from coast to coast, embracing her. Air clothed her like an unseen skin, and Sun and Moon rode in turn above her, flooding her with light. As the ages passed, light bred new life in her, and her plains and hills filled with flowers, grass, trees, animals, nymphs and spirits of every kind.

Janus

Above Mother Earth in the vaults of space, and below her in the Underworld, other creatures lived. The upper world was the home of Titans,* the children of Earth and Sky. They galloped their chariots along the highways of space or visited Mother Earth to revel in her flowers and trees and take delight in her birds, animals and insects. The Underworld beings were monsters, giants, furies and spectres: children of darkness who feared the light. Their queen was Hecate. She had a serpent's body and neck with three faces: horse, dog and boar. All day she lurked in the Underworld, and at midnight she crawled to the upper world to gulp newborn lambs and puppies and to lick honey from wild bees' nests.

One midnight, as Sky was hovering above Mother Earth, admiring his own moonlit reflection in a rock-pool, Hecate surged from a crevice in the ground below him, sniffing the air. As soon as she sensed Sky's presence, she wriggled back underground like a frightened snake – but not before Sky had been smitten with love for her. He called her, he groped on the ground and tried to pull the crevice apart with his fingers. But his efforts produced no more than a wilderness of tumbled, broken rock. At last he decided that the only way to find her was to tempt her out of hiding by giving her a present, a toy made from the elements of creation all around him. He took handfuls of earth, darkness, air and water, moulded them into a ball and sent it rolling down the crack in the earth's crust where she had disappeared.

As the ball rolled, it gradually changed shape. Its sides flattened and its ends bulged, until it was like a cylindrical pillar rumbling on edge through the caverns of the Underworld. The friction of its movement heated it and gave it life, so that by the time it reached Hecate's lair in the lowest depths of Hell, it was a creature able to breathe, think and move for itself. Hecate called it Janus, cradled it in her monstrous coils and tried to feed it puppy's entrails, warm lamb's blood and woodlice plucked from the earth like sweets. Revolted, Janus wriggled off her lap and splashed into the icy river Styx, hoping that his earthy body would carry him to the bottom and drown him.

But Janus' body was made of air as well as of earth, and he had been given immortality by the fingers of his father Sky which moulded him. He bobbed to the surface, and the river-current carried him nine times round the Underworld, washed him to the surface and spewed him out on the bank of an ice-cold, bubbling spring, the headwaters of the river Eridanus in Italy.

Janus lay exhausted on the snow. He had no eyes, no ears, no other sense-organs, but he could feel the sun on his body, the first warmth he had ever known. It worked on him as on a growing plant, and he began to sprout legs, arms, eyes, ears and noses. He jumped to his feet and ran down the hillside beside the river, slipping in the snow, waving his arms and shouting for the joy of existence, while birds and animals cowered in terror and his father Sky beamed from above with serene, unblinking pride.

3

Gradually, as the centuries passed, the creatures of Italy discovered that so far from being a monster, Janus was gentle and kindly. His appearance, with his scores of knotty arms and legs, and the faces all round his head, was more hideous than anything else on earth, but for all that his wisdom and honesty so affected the beings of Italy that they all bowed down to him and respected him as king.

While this was happening on earth, civil war broke out in heaven. The Titans, who had ruled the universe since the beginning of creation, were challenged by Saturn's children, the gods, led by the brothers Jupiter, Neptune and Pluto.* For centuries the power-struggle rumbled across the sky, and neither side could win. But then Mother Earth sided with the gods, and sent her children the Cyclopes to help them. The Cyclopes made gifts for each of the three god-brothers: a trident for Neptune, powerful enough to prise up hills and break open the barriers of the sea; a helmet of invisibility for Pluto; and for Jupiter the power of fire, gathered and stored in thunderbolts. With these weapons the gods at last began to win the power-struggle, and Saturn, king of the Titans, fled from his sky-palace and began roaming Mother Earth for refuge. He found it at last in Italy, among the forests and hills of Latium. Here Janus, mindful that Saturn was his own half-brother, another child of Sky, promised him protection.

The gods searched for Saturn with unsleeping ferocity. Neptune levered whole continents apart, so that fragments spilled into the seas of the world and made islands; Pluto crept about invisibly at night, snatching animals and other living creatures into his dark embrace and so bringing death into the world; Jupiter rolled thunderbolts and hurled lightning-spears till he set the sky ablaze. The gods' fury was destroying the universe; creation cowered. In Italy, Janus watched in despair as, one after another, the hills of his beautiful kingdom were pounded to rubble, the forests were charred to ash, and the rivers were choked with the bloated bodies of his subjects. At last, torn between loyalty to his half-brother and to his country, he went to Jupiter and whispered that if the gods promised mercy to Saturn, he (Janus) would tell them his hiding-place.

Jupiter gave his promise. The giants rounded up Saturn and the other Titans and escorted them to Mount Olympus for judgement. Instead of harming them, Jupiter gave them a new home, the Islands of the Blessed in the far west of the world, on condition that they never again trespassed in the kingdom of the gods. He rewarded Janus by making him an immortal god; but at the same time he punished his

4

treachery to Saturn by making him no more than two-faced and by taking away his power of movement. Janus stood forever as doorkeeper at heaven's gate and the Hours, his children, fed him and cared for him. He was rooted to the spot like the pillar he so much resembled, and one face was fixed to gaze ahead and one behind.*

Phaethon

Phaethon was the son of Phoebus, god of the sun, and the nymph Clymene. His best friend was Epaphus, son of Jupiter and Io. One day the two young men were boasting about their fathers. Phaethon claimed that the Sun was superior to Jupiter, god of the sky, because light ruled clouds; Epaphus retorted by asking who would know about the sun's light if the clouds were not there to support it. Boasting turned to argument, argument turned to quarrel and in the end Epaphus said angrily, 'In any case, how do you know for sure that the Sun really is your father? It could have been anyone, even one of the palace slaves.'

Blushing with embarrassment, Phaethon ran to ask his mother if the Sun was truly his father. Clymene said, 'Of course he is. Go to his palace and ask him yourself.'

Phaethon saddled his horse and galloped without rest to the Sun's palace on the eastern edge of Ocean, the river that girds the world. The palace's blocks and pillars were faced with gold and glowed like fire. Phaethon climbed the steps, hid at the entrance to the throneroom and peeped round the door, shading his eyes from his father's dazzle. The Sun was sitting in state; his light was cloaked (for it was night) and his servants the Days, Months and Seasons stood beside him. He sensed Phaethon at the door and said, 'Phaethon, I see and hear everything on earth: I watched your quarrel and I know your question. I swear to you by Styx, the river of Darkness, that I'm your father, and I'll prove it by granting any favour you care to ask.'

'Father,' answered Phaethon at once, 'let me ride your chariot across the sky, for just one day. Only a child of the Sun will be able to control it. That will be my proof.'

'Oh, Phaethon,' said the Sun. 'Why did I promise to give you anything you asked? Not even Jupiter dares ride that chariot. From dawn to noon the way is steep as the horses pant to the zenith of the sky; the chariot hangs there, poised, till even my head reels with dizziness; then it plunges headlong and sinks into the western sea. My horses' breath is fire; they fight the bit; even I hardly master them. Ask for anything else – or take my care for you as proof that I'm your father, with all a father's love, and leave my chariot for me to ride.'

But Phaethon insisted, and his father had sworn by Styx and had to keep his word. He took Phaethon to the stables, where the chariot stood waiting in the darkness. Vulcan, blacksmith of the gods, had made it long ago, edging the wheel-rims with gold and the spokes with silver, and studding the sides with jewels which glittered in the glow from the Sun's hooded face. Phaethon ran his hands eagerly along the driver's rail and began fingering the reins. His father would have tried once more to deter him – for he knew everything, including that this journey would end in death – but it was almost dawn, and the Morning Star was already gathering the stars to herd them from the sky. The Sun beckoned to his servants to harness the horses: Aethon, Eous, Phlegon and Pyrois. The horses were led out, eyes flashing and nostrils breathing fire, and were yoked to the chariot. The Sun rubbed Phaethon with ointment made from the gods' immortal ambrosia, to protect him from the flames, and gave him some last advice. 'Use your whip sparingly; keep firm hold of the reins. Don't drive straight across the sky. There's a well-marked path, with wheel-ruts in the clouds: follow it.'

He would have said more, would have tried even at this last moment to check his son. But Phaethon leapt into the chariot and seized the reins. The horses whinnied and their golden hooves struck sparks from the cobblestones. The Hours opened the stable doors, and Phaethon, the horses and the Sun's fiery chariot streamed out across the sky.

The horses knew at once that something was wrong. They were used to the weight of an immortal god, and Phaethon's flimsy mortality left the chariot bucking and yawing like a boat on a stormy sea. The horses raced out of control; Phaethon tugged the reins, cracked the whip and shouted orders without effect. He had no idea where the true path lay, and was not strong enough to pull back the eager horses. The chariot swooped to the North Pole and roused the Serpent that sleeps in ice; it soared to the vault of heaven, scorching Olympus' doors; it climbed the sky and hung, poised at the zenith, while Phaethon gazed in panic at the clouds and the earth below.

Until now, Phaethon had heeded his father's instructions, and held hard to the reins. But now, as the horses began their downward plunge, he suddenly saw that the starry plains ahead were filled with monsters: the Scorpion, Boötes, iron-hoofed oxen, the Crab with its pincers poised. Fear loosened his fingers and he dropped the reins. Now the immortal horses were utterly beyond control. They galloped pell-mell across the sky, scattering the stars. They swooped so low across the earth that the soil caught fire. Rivers dried up; plants withered; fissures cracked open and the shades of the Underworld blinked at the unaccustomed light. Deserts appeared where once fertile fields had been; even the Mediterranean Sea began to dry up like a puddle till fish floundered and sea-creatures gasped on the sun-dried ooze.

At last Mother Earth, scorched and anguished, crawled to Jupiter's throne room, high in cool Olympus. Her flesh was baked and fissured; her eyes were smoke-blackened; her clothing of trees and plants hung like withered sacks. 'My lord,' she gasped, 'Is this my reward for nourishing crops and feeding animals throughout the year? Have I endured the wounds of spades and ploughs for this? Even if I deserve it, what has Neptune your brother done to see his kingdom evaporate all round him? Send a thunderbolt. Kill Phaethon – and hurry, for Atlas is shifting his shoulders under the red-hot sky, and if he once lets it slip your palace, your estates, Olympus itself, will crash to ruin.'

She shrank down from Olympus and drew her head for protection far inside herself, into the caverns of the Underworld. Jupiter called the gods to council. 'How can we rescue the universe, except by Phaethon's death?' he asked. 'Look at me; admit that there is no other choice.' One by one the gods agreed; even the Sun bowed his head, tears sizzling on his cheeks. Jupiter wasted no time. He soared to Olympus' highest tower, lifted a thunderbolt and hurled it. It hit the Sun-chariot full on, and smashed it to fragments. The panic-stricken horses galloped wildly in different directions, dragging broken harness about the sky. Chariot-splinters flew like meteorites, and Phaethon himself hurtled, blazing, from sky to earth. He plummeted into the river Eridanus, and the water hissed on his fire-scorched skin, dragged him down and drowned him.

Silence fell on earth. Darkness cloaked the sky. It was as if all life's candles had been snuffed. Then, gradually, cicadas began chirping, birds began to sing, and the lowing of animals, splashing of fish and crying of mortals could be heard once more. The Sun shook the tears from his eyes, and sent his servants to round up the frightened horses.

7

A second chariot was harnessed; the stable doors were flung open a second time; a second dawn began.

The river-nymphs put up a memorial to Phaethon on the banks of the Eridanus, and his mother and sisters gathered to weep for him. Their tears were so bitter and so constant that the Sun at last took pity on them and transformed them into alder-trees, bending low over the water as if to pay their respects to the Sun their master, reflected in the waters that had engulfed his son.

The making of mortals

Although most of the Titans had supported Saturn in his battle with the gods, and had been banished with him, a few remained. They had been loyal to Jupiter, and their rewards were homes in Olympus, respect second only to the gods', and freedom to wander wherever they liked in earth, sea and sky. They still had the power to take on any shape they chose, and made use of it: they became hills, clouds, rivers or forests, settling here or there until their mood and their shape changed and they disappeared as mirages vanish in desert sand.

Most of the Titans were content with this new life, and gave the gods no trouble. But one of them, Prometheus, regarded his freedom as imprisonment. He could go where he chose and do as he pleased – but only because the gods allowed it. He was jealous of Jupiter, and bored. One day he sat idly on a river-bank, in the form of a living hill. He was amusing himself by willing things into existence – stones, twigs, flowers – and then returning them to the elements from which they had sprung. When he tired of it he sat without thought, gazing at the mud of the river-bank – and as often happened when he brooded, the image of Jupiter came into his mind. At once, under his gaze, the river-mud began to roll and squirm, heaving itself into a model Jupiter, with one head, one body, two arms and two legs exactly like the god's. Prometheus was as charmed as a child with a new toy. He conjured up the images of other gods, Minerva, Vulcan, Vesta, and the obedient mud made models at his feet.

Instead of destroying his new creatures, Prometheus let them live. His people could move, speak, feel emotion and reproduce them-selves, exactly like gods. But he had no way of giving them ambrosia, the food of the gods which guarantees immortality, and instead taught them to eat seeds and fruit. Like the food they ate, human beings were

8

short-lived, and the progress of their lives, from birth to withering, seemed to Prometheus their creator no longer than the blinking of an eye. They were also without intelligence: their heads were too small to contain the knowledge of the gods. But ignorance made them happy, and for the short duration of their lives they bustled about on Mother Earth, sharing her riches with the other beings who lived there, and delighting their creator with their laughter and their piping hymns of praise.*

Pomona and Vertumnus

Pomona lived on the Palatine Hill beside the river Tiber. She was a wood-nymph, and her home was an orchard of wild fruit-trees: pear, cherry and above all the apples from which she took her name. She spent her days pruning the trees, grafting them, loading them with blossom in spring and fruit in autumn, and keeping wasps, woodlice and other pests clear of the growing fruit. She was as plump as an apple herself, with apple-blossom skin and pip-brown eyes. All the fauns, satyrs and tree-spirits of Latium were in love with her, and would have courted her if she hadn't turned her back on them and busied herself with her beloved trees.

Pomona's shyest suitor was the wood-god Vertumnus. Each autumn he was responsible for turning the leaves from green to gold, and floating them to the ground to make way for new growth. But for the rest of the year he had nothing to do but watch Pomona bustling about her work in the orchards, and hide behind a tree, blushing, each time she looked his way. A thousand times he plucked up his courage to declare his love, and a thousand times his nerve failed at the last moment and he ducked back, panting with shame, into the shadow of the trees. In the end he asked advice from Pales, the goddess of pastures after whom the Palatine Hill was named. 'It's simple,' she answered. 'You change the leaves in autumn – why not change yourself, from shy to bold, and see what she makes of that?'

Vertumnus spent the rest of the day in a corner of the orchard, practising transformations. That evening he walked through the trees disguised as a ploughman going home from work: muddy boots, ploughshare over one shoulder, oxen shambling ahead of him. As he passed the part of the orchard where Pomona was working, ringing the trees with tar to keep pests away, he tipped his hat and said 'Good evening' in a hearty ploughman's voice. Pomona's only answer was to bend double over her work, slapping tar on the trunks till Vertumnus went away.

Vertumnus sat awake all night, picking tar-splashes from his clothes and wondering what disguise to try next. At the first sign of dawn he put on soldier's boots, a sword and a swagger and marched to see Pomona, who was clearing mud from an irrigation-channel at the orchard's edge. He clicked his heels, saluted and said 'Good morning' – and Pomona answered by bending double over her work and squelching mud till he went away.

That evening Vertumnus disguised himself as a fisherman, with a rod in his hand, hooks in his hat and six trout in a basket. The next day he made himself a beekeeper, with face-net and smoke-can; the day after that he was a fruit-farmer with a ladder and a pruning-knife. And each time, however cheerfully he said 'Good morning' or 'Good evening', Pomona bent double over her work and ignored him till he went away.

Vertumnus' final transformation was into an old woman. He hobbled into the orchard in the heat of noon, with a crystal cup and a jar of water covered with a cloth. But when Pomona sat down gratefully in the shade to drink, Vertumnus' passion overcame him, and he put his arms round her and hugged her in a way no old woman ever would.* Pomona jumped up, furious, and ordered him out of the orchard. He walked dejectedly between the trees, shaking the old-woman disguise from him as a dog shakes water and resuming his old shy shape. But when he reached the orchard's edge and turned for a last wistful glance at Pomona, he found her staring after him with wide-open eyes and a dropping jaw. 'Vertumnus!' she called. 'Where have you been hiding all this time? I'd no idea such handsome gods existed!'

She held out her arms, and Vertumnus threw off his shyness like a last disguise, ran back and took her in his arms. From that moment on they were inseparable, and they have worked together in orchards ever since, so that ripe apples, instead of being just green, are a sunburst of autumn colours: russets, yellows, golds and reds.

Arethusa

One summer day Diana, the moon-goddess, and her nymphs were hunting deer in the forests near Olympia, in Greece. The day was hot and the chase was long, and after a while one of the nymphs, Arethusa, began to lag behind the others. She came to the banks of a stream, and sat down exhausted. She could hear the dogs yapping, the crash of horses' hooves and the excited shouts of her fellow-nymphs fading in the distance. Willows and poplars overhung the river, shading the bank. She dipped her feet in the cool water, then waded into the shallows, and finally hung her clothes on a willow-branch and dived into a deep, clear pool.

As Arethusa floated and duck-dived in the water, she suddenly felt the river gather itself and heave all round her, embracing her as if it were a living thing. She splashed to the bank and stood there shivering with terror. The river-god Alpheus surged out of the water behind her. Enraptured by her beauty, he waded towards the bank with outstretched arms, and Arethusa screamed and ran.

All nymphs, and especially Diana's hunting-nymphs, have strength to run fast and far. But Arethusa was exhausted from hunting, and her pursuer was an immortal god. She fled through the woods of Elis, the foothills of Maenalus, the marshes of Erymanthus – and still she could hear Alpheus close behind her, panting to her to stop. At last she cried, 'Diana! Lady! Help me!', and the goddess swooped to the rescue and covered Arethusa with a cloud that hugged her from head to toe like a foggy cloak. Arethusa stood still, shivering, while Alpheus brushed aside wisps of cloud, trying to find her and declare his love. As she stood there, a cold sweat broke out all over her. Water began to drip from her hair, her face, her limbs, and formed a pool at her feet. She was turning from nymph to stream. At last she was entirely water, and slipped away into a crack in the ground leaving Alpheus reaching out for empty air.

Alpheus, a river himself, was easily able to follow Arethusa underground. But as soon as she slipped below the surface the spirits of the Underworld led her by secret channels all the way from Greece to Sicily. She bubbled up at last in a stream of pure water beside the town of Syracuse, and the Spring of Arethusa has flowed there unceasingly ever since. As for Alpheus, he wandered in despair along the river-channels and streams of the Underworld for a thousand years. In the end the gods took pity on his loneliness, guided him to Syracuse and filled Arethusa's heart with love for him, so that he and she mingled their streams forever. From that day on, when people threw offerings into the river Alpheus in Greece, in the pool where Arethusa bathed, the presents vanished under the surface and reappeared days later in Arethusa's Spring in Sicily, gifts from the river-god to his beloved.

Picus and Canens

When Janus left Mother Earth for Olympus, the gods gave his throne in Italy to Picus, son of Saturn. Picus was a horse-breeder and a huntsman: his pleasures were galloping his thoroughbreds along the Milky Way, and searching Italy's forests and fields for game. He was young and handsome, and every wood-nymph in Italy fell in love with him; even Pomona, the orchard-goddess, languished for him for a whole growing-season, while the fruit hung wizened and untended on her trees. In the end Picus married Janus' daughter Venilia, and the other nymphs had to hide their jealousy. Venilia was a river-nymph, and when Janus was made a god he gave her the gift of beautiful song. Her singing was like a magic spell, taming wild beasts, soothing storms, drawing animals, birds, even rocks and trees to hear her. Her nickname was *Canens*, 'singing', and while Picus her husband was away hunting or horse-riding she spent the time singing, till her maids dropped what they were doing and ran to listen.

One day Picus and his servants were hunting boar in the marshlands of Laurentum, near the river Tiber. Picus rode a prancing horse, wore a purple cloak fastened with a golden chain and carried two boar-spears whose broad blades glittered in the sun. This glitter caught the eye of Circe, the witch-daughter of the Sun. She took it for a signal from her father, and ran to it – and as soon as she saw Picus she was transfixed by his looks as if he were the radiant Sun himself. Her feet felt planted in the ground; she dropped the herbs she had been gathering; passion burned in her veins like fire. As soon as she recovered her wits, her first thought was to draw Picus away from his servants, to a quiet spot where she could declare her love without embarrassment. She moulded a wisp of mist into a boar which only Picus could see or hear. It crashed past him into the undergrowth, and he leapt from his horse and ran after it while his servants gaped. As soon as he was deep in the woods, far from the path, the boar vanished into air. Picus turned to go back to his companions, but Circe uttered a spell which darkened the sun, filled the air with mist and sent him plunging into the woods in the wrong direction, out of reach of rescue. As soon as he was lost and floundering she sprang at him

12

and blurted out her passion. 'Picus,' she said, 'We're both gods' children. Forget Canens; make love with me, and breed immortal sons!'

'No!' said Picus, revolted. 'How can I forget Canens, the apple of my heart? She, too, is a god's child; she and I will breed sons to rule in Italy.'

'Never!' snapped Circe. 'No one scorns Circe, daughter of the Sun!'

She touched Picus with her wand, and froze him where he stood. Then she turned three times east and three times west, muttering spells, and tapped Picus with the wand once more. He felt his feet set free, and turned to run. But even as he ran, he shrank to the size of his own bunched fist. He felt feathers sprouting on his body, purple as his cloak, with a gold band round his neck where the chain had been. His arms widened into wings and his feet into claws. His nose and chin grew longer and formed a sharp, horny beak. He fluttered up to a branch of the nearest tree, and began knocking his head against the trunk in despair. He tried to call out, but he had changed from man to woodpecker, and no words came.

Now, at last, Circe drew the mist from the sky and unveiled the sun. Picus' servants galloped through the woods to find him, shouting his name. But there was no sign of him, nothing but a forlorn woodpecker, tapping unintelligible messages high overhead. As the lords wandered about, calling, Circe capered invisibly round them, howling spells and sprinkling the ground with herb-juice. The earth groaned under their feet, and a grove of dark-leaved trees sprang up. The soil writhed with snakes; the trees dripped blood; the darkness rang with the yap of savage dogs. The terrified servants wheeled their horses, galloped to the palace and told Canens of her husband's supernatural disappearance.

Canens was in despair. She ran to the place where Picus had last been seen, and wandered along the trees, along the banks of the river, through the reedbeds of Laurentum, calling his name. She wandered for six days and nights, neither sleeping nor eating, and at last threw herself on a patch of grass beside the river Tiber, all but dead from grief. Tiber himself, the river-god, took pity on her. As she lay there, sobbing Picus's name, Tiber changed her from a woman to a disembodied spirit, a cloud of air. Her flesh and bones melted away, until all that was left was a voice, hovering and calling, calling and hovering. She has wandered the fields and woods ever since, settling in the throats of this bird or that and lending them her song. Her hope is that one day her calling will awaken an answering song, that Picus will hear and respond to her, and that she will be restored at last to her former shape, able to kiss her beloved husband and hold him in her arms.*

2
SILVER · AND · IRON

The Silver Age

The earliest time of the universe, until Saturn was dethroned, had
been a Golden Age, taking its colour from the sun that warmed the
world. When the gods came to power on Olympus a Silver Age began.
Its colour came from lightning, the dazzle of Jupiter harnessed in
thunderbolts. The Silver Age was one of universal harmony. The
creatures of darkness, giants, furies, illnesses and death, lived in the
Underworld, ruled by Pluto, and never visited the world above.
Heaven was the home of the creatures of light, from the Sun's fiery
horses to the West Wind that warmed the stars. In between, on the
surface of Mother Earth, beings of all kinds, nymphs, satyrs, fauns,
mortals, birds and animals, shared the world's beauty and plenty
without argument. The gods moved at will between all three kingdoms, lords and rulers of creation. Every other being in the universe
accepted their power – and from that acceptance, and that power,
peace was guaranteed.

Cupid and Psyche

There was only one occasion when the harmony of the Silver Age was
threatened, and that was because of jealousy between a mortal girl and
an immortal god. A mortal king and queen of Sicily had three
daughters. The two elder sisters had long had families of their own,
but the youngest, Psyche, lived at home with her parents, longing for
a husband. She was not unmarried for want of suitors; on the
contrary, every young man in the area flocked to her parents' palace to
ask for her hand. But she rejected them all, and the reason was that

15

they were interested in her not for herself but for her extraordinary fame. She was the most beautiful girl that part of the world had ever seen. People compared her with the goddess Venus, at first for a joke and then more and more seriously, taking her offerings, putting her statues in their houses and garlanding them, even claiming that they had seen her in visions or that miracles happened when they prayed to her.

On Olympus, Venus grew more and more furious. Her temples were empty, her statues were dusty, her altars were foul with the remains of months-old sacrifices. All the honours that should have been hers were being paid to a mortal. She knew that very soon it would end, that Psyche would age and die and that all her worshippers would rush once more to Venus's shrines. But in the meantime she was jealous, and she made up her mind to punish Psyche, however undeservedly, for the adoration other people felt for her. She sent for her son Cupid, a handsome young god with the first down of adulthood on his cheeks and the bow and arrows of desire in his hands. 'Go to earth,' she said. 'Find Psyche and transfix her with love. See that she marries the most unlikely person in the universe; see that she never troubles me again.'

Cupid soared eagerly to earth, fitting arrow to bowstring as he flew. No mortal saw him; only Psyche sensed his presence, felt the sting of sudden, irresistible desire and knew that the day of her marriage must be soon or she would die for love. But when her parents went to a hilltop oracle to ask the name of her husband-to-be, the oracle, in riddling, rhyming lines, gave the horrifying answer:

> 'A lord there is whose might
> No power on earth can fight.
> She must be his tonight.'

Psyche's parents were heartbroken. Was their daughter to marry a monster, some pitiless warlord with knives for teeth and flint for heart? Psyche tried bravely to reassure them. 'Don't cry,' she said. 'Leave me here on the hilltop, by the temple, to wait for my husband. The gods will look after me.' Tearfully the people dressed her in bride's clothes and wove fresh flowers into her hair. Then, as dusk fell, they left her on the hilltop, prayed to the gods to protect her, and trudged sadly home.

For all the brave face she'd shown her parents, Psyche was terrified. She sat on the ground in her finery, sobbing and shivering,

16

and at last fell into broken-hearted sleep. As she slept, the West Wind
gathered her up in its soft, warm arms, carried her from the hilltop to a
secret valley and laid her on a lawn sown with daisies as the sky is
sown with stars. When Psyche woke up, she found that she was lying
in the grounds of a palace, a glittering building of marble, ivory and
gold, with its doors wide open to welcome her. She walked inside and
the doors closed gently behind her. She gazed round at the deserted
rooms with their panelled walls, high painted ceilings, mosaic floors
and costly furniture. As she gazed, she felt invisible hands guiding her
to a polished throne, and a table floated towards her of its own accord,
laden with food. Disembodied voices whispered, 'Eat, Psyche. Sit and
eat. Soon it will be bedtime, and your husband will come to you.'

Psyche sat and ate, and food filled her plate and wine her cup of
their own accord. When she'd finished, invisible servants led her to a
bedroom with a huge, canopied bed, undressed her, washed her with
rosewater, rubbed her with perfumed oil and laid her between the
sheets. Sweet drowsiness sealed her eyes, and as she dozed she felt
the weight of someone climbing into bed beside her. A male voice
spoke loving words to her, hands caressed her and her new husband
made gentle love to her in the darkness. She had never known such
tenderness from any man, and her heart, pricked long ago by Cupid's
arrow, swam with love for her unseen husband. She begged him to
call for lights and show himself, but he put his finger to her lips and
said, 'No, Psyche. If you ever see me as I truly am, it will be the death
of you. Enjoy what you have; don't ask for more.'

Psyche fell into a deep sleep, and next morning when she awoke
she was alone. She spent all day wandering in the palace's woods and
gardens and exploring its myriad rooms, and everywhere she went
there were insects, birds and pet animals but no people. That evening
the invisible servants fed her, bathed her and put her to bed as before,
her husband came once again to bed in the darkness and they spent a
rapturous night of love. It was the same for day after day, till Psyche
could not decide whether she was the happiest mortal in the world or
the loneliest and most miserable. That night when her husband came
to bed he found her shoulders shaking with sobs and her pillow wet
with tears. 'O my lord,' she said, 'If you won't ever let me see you, at
least let me see my own family again. Let me show them I'm alive and
happy. Let me talk once more to people I can see.'

The invisible husband sighed. 'If it must be, it must,' he said. 'If I
send the West Wind to carry your sisters here, and let them see my

17

palace, my estates and my riches, will that please you? I ask only one thing in return. Whatever your sisters say, however much they beg you or threaten you, don't agree to try and find out what I look like. If you ever see me as I truly am, it will be the death of you.'

Psyche flung her arms round her husband and kissed him. Next day she ran excitedly round the palace and the gardens, gathering flowers and arranging them in crystal vases in every room. That evening the West Wind wafted her sisters to the secret valley, and they ran across the daisy-starred grass, hugged Psyche and went arm-in-arm with her round the palace, drinking in every detail from the ivory cupboards crammed with jewels to the unseen choirs that burst into song when they walked into each new room.

At first the sisters were glad to find Psyche so happily married, and even gladder when she told them that she was pregnant, and that her invisible husband had promised that the baby would grow up to be one of the immortal gods. But by the time Psyche had loaded them with jewels and bracelets, had sat them down at a crystal table and feasted them on delicious food and wine served by unseen hands, and had never for a moment stopped babbling of her husband's gentle and loving ways, they began to be gnawed with jealousy. They looked at one another, and the same ideas formed in each of their minds: Psyche was far too happy, and it was up to them to destroy that happiness.

'It's perfect, darling Psyche,' said the first sister. 'Except for just one thing. If your husband's as kind and gentle as you say, why does he never let you set eyes on him?'

'If only you knew what people say about him in the world above,' the second sister said. 'They say he's afraid to show himself because he's not a man at all but a shark-toothed snake, and that as soon as the baby's born he'll bite off your head and crunch your bones.'

'Oh no!' wailed foolish Psyche. 'What can I do?'

'Put a lamp and a knife beside the bed tonight,' said the first sister, 'And as soon as he's snoring, light the lamp to see by and slice off his foul snake's head.'

'I will, I will,' cried Psyche. Her heart thudded with dread, both at what she had to do and at the hideous fate that would be hers if she failed. She said goodbye to her sisters on the lawn, and waved as the West Wind wafted them to the clifftop out of sight. Then she fetched a lamp and a carving-knife, bathed and went to bed; for the first time since she'd come to the palace she slammed the door on the unseen servants and refused their help.

That night the invisible husband came to bed as always, and though Psyche felt sick at the thought of his clammy snake's body and the murderous plans he was hiding behind gentle words, she forced herself to make love to him. As soon as he was asleep she slipped out of bed, lit the lamp and took the knife. She turned, holding the knife in one hand and the lamp in the other – and there, stretched sleeping in the bed, was no foul snake but Cupid himself. His golden hair fell in thick curls over his neck; his cheeks were flushed like a baby's; his wings were swansdown-white, and the tiny hairs on each feather quivered as he breathed. His bow and arrows lay at his feet, at the foot of the bed.

As Psyche gazed at him, the most beautiful young man she'd ever seen, she suddenly felt the hardness of the knife-handle in her hand, and realised the dreadful mistake she'd been about to make. She began to sob and shake, and a drop of lamp-oil fell on to Cupid's shoulder and scalded it. He woke at once, calling out in pain, and in an instant took in what had happened. Psyche fell on the floor, terrified; she sensed him surge above her to the full size of an immortal god, filling the room; she felt the rush of his wing-beats and heard his voice, no longer loving but harsh and cruel, saying, 'I warned you, Psyche. If ever you saw me as I truly am, it would be the death of you.' Then there was silence, and Psyche realised that she was no longer in the warm palace bedroom but lying on soaking grass under a drizzly sky. She held out her hands and prayed; she begged for mercy; there was no answer but the sighing of wind in the sodden trees.

Terrified and heartbroken, Psyche picked herself up and began walking. Her nightdress was soaked; her bare feet were chilled by the grass and torn with stones; she had no idea where she was or where her wanderings would take her. She stumbled over the fields in the moonlight, slipping and crying, and every so often the baby kicked inside her womb as if it, too, were trying to punish her. At dawn she found herself on the edge of a village, beside a shrine of Ceres, goddess of harvest. She fell on her knees and cried, 'Ceres, lady, help me!' At once the goddess appeared, hovering overhead in her dragon-chariot. Psyche said, 'Lady, pity me. Save me from Cupid's rage.'

'My poor child,' said Ceres, 'I'd help you if I could. But what can I do? I live down here in Sicily, far from the courts of Olympus. I never see Cupid from one year's end to another. I can't do anything for you now, but as soon as I find a way, you can count on me.'

She faded from sight, and Psyche, even more despairing than

19

before, stood up and wandered on through the village. In a field at the far side she saw what she took to be a scarecrow in the dim light; then she realised that it was Pan, god of flocks and herds. She fell on her knees and begged him to help her. 'My dear child,' said Pan, 'I'd help you if I could. But Cupid's arrows terrify me. What if he pricked my heart with love for a stone, a tree-stump or a compost-heap? I daren't do anything for you now, but if I ever find a way, you can count on me.'

He faded from sight, and Psyche plodded on*. She came to a temple on a hilltop. It was dusty and neglected, and she had no idea which god or goddess was worshipped there. But as soon as she knelt to pray, there was a rush of wings and Venus appeared, frowning and furious. She towered over Psyche and cried, 'How dare you, slut? First you steal the worshippers that should by rights be mine. Then you seduce my darling son Cupid and try to trap him by getting pregnant. You plan to cut his throat; you scald him with boiling oil, and finally you pray to me for help, his mother. Get up! You've earned every second of your suffering; don't expect me to shorten it.'

'O lady,' sobbed Psyche, 'Have pity. I pray to you, radiant goddess. Put aside your anger; help me.'

This prayer threw Venus into confusion. The gods and goddesses of Olympus shared every mortal passion: rage, joy, ambition, jealousy. But they also had one quality denied to mortals: superhuman forgiveness. Whenever they heard prayers for mercy, they had no choice but to listen, no choice but to give way. Venus' heart filled with pity for Psyche, and she came to the very brink of forgiving her. But at the last moment she controlled herself and snapped, 'Very well. This place is littered with grains of millet, wheat and barley, the remains of long-forgotten offerings. Gather them into separate piles by nightfall, one for each kind of grain, and perhaps you'll win me round.'

She disappeared, leaving Psyche wretched on the floor. There were thousands of grains, scattered in the dust on the temple floor. The task was impossible for one pair of hands, and Venus knew it. But this was Ceres' moment, a job only the goddess of harvest could oversee. She sent a column of ants into the temple, with exact instructions, and at nightfall when Venus soared into the temple she found the floor clear of every morsel of litter, every speck of dust, and the grains stacked in piles beside the wall. She bit her lip with rage and said, 'You've had help, my girl. What mortal could have done this on her own? Tomorrow you can find the ram with the golden fleece, and

20

gather enough wool to weave me a headdress. Do that by nightfall, and perhaps you'll win me round.'

Once again she vanished, and once again Psyche was in despair. She'd only ever heard of one ram with a golden fleece, and that had long ago flown to the Sun's palace in Colchis, hundreds of hours' journey from Sicily.* How could she find the way – and even if she did, how could she travel so far over land and sea in a single day? This was Pan's moment, a job for the god who knew every flock and herd on earth. He told Psyche of another golden ram, in a flock in the meadows beside the river Symaethus in Sicily. The flock was guarded by fire-breathing dragons, who would have torn Psyche limb from limb if she'd tried to gather the golden wool in daylight. But Pan told her to wait till nightfall, when the sheep were resting and the cool evening air made the dragons less active, and to gather the wisps of golden wool snagged on briars in the hedge. So Psyche did, and Pan carried her back to the temple just in time before Venus swooped down from Olympus.

When Venus saw the pile of golden wool she stamped her foot, causing an earthquake which shook all Sicily. 'You've had help in this, too!' she shouted. 'There's one more task – see which god will help you now! Take this crystal cup and bring it to me tomorrow, filled with water from the river Styx in the Underworld. Do that if you can, and perhaps you'll win me round.'

This time there seemed no hope at all for Psyche. As Venus well knew, any mortal who ventured alive into the Underworld was doomed to stay there forever, and the gods were so terrified of the river Styx that none of them would dare to steal the water.* But Jupiter himself was watching, and he decided that Psyche had suffered enough, that Venus' jealousy was poisoning the harmony of the universe and that the time had come to end it. He sent his own eagle to snatch the crystal cup from Psyche's fingers, fill it with Styx-water and take it to Venus on Olympus, with stern orders that it was time to end her rage. Then he went to the bedroom where Cupid lay tossing in a fever from the oil-burn. He had with him a box of ointment made from ambrosia, the substance which guarantees the gods' immortality. But before he spread it on the wound, he took one of Cupid's arrows from the quiver beside the bed and pricked Cupid's own foot with it. At once Cupid was filled with love for Psyche as deep as hers for him, and as soon as Jupiter smeared his shoulder with ambrosia and cured his burn, he flew down to Sicily, gathered Psyche in his arms and

21

carried her to Olympus, where the gods' servants tended her torn feet, bathed her and dressed her in saffron robes from Venus' own wardrobe.*

When everything was ready Jupiter called the gods to council. 'The time has come,' he said, 'to put a stop to Cupid's mischief. He's forever flying round the universe, creating havoc in gods and mortals alike. It's time he settled down. He's told Psyche that if she ever sees him as he truly is, it will be the death of her, and a god's word must be kept. I decree, then, that Psyche's mortal self must die. But she will be given ambrosia to eat, will become immortal and will live here on Olympus as Cupid's wife, the mother of his child and Venus's daughter-in-law. If you agree, you gods in council, so let it be.'

One after another, the gods nodded their heads – and Venus saw the look in Jupiter's eye and forced herself to smile. Psyche ate a piece of ambrosia, and at once her mortality fell from her and she became an immortal god. In due course she gave birth to her own and Cupid's child, the goddess Pleasure, and she lived very happily on Olympus ever afterwards. As for her sisters, they were still eaten with jealousy, and were determined to find the magic palace for themselves and plunder its jewel-cupboards. They went to the hilltop oracle, threw themselves over the cliff without waiting for the West Wind to waft them down, and were broken to pieces on the rocks.*

The Age of Iron

The only being in the universe dissatisfied with the Silver Age was Mother Earth. The Silver Age had begun with the dethroning of her son Saturn, and so long as it lasted her other children, the giants, were barred from power. While the children of light, gods, mortals and animals, frolicked in her woods, her vales, her hills, the children of darkness slept in the chasms of the Underworld, with only their mother to remember them.*

Mother Earth endured the light-creatures' happiness as long as she could. Then she began to toss and roll, heaving her giant-children awake in the womb of dark. One by one she gave them second birth, and they crawled to the surface, stretching and blinking in the light. They were as high as hills, and their breath was fire. But they were brainless and lumbering; strength was all they had. Mother Earth told them to take lumps of rock, pieces ripped from her own flesh, and to build a stone-pile as high as Olympus. Then, panting with agony, she began patiently filling each giant's skull with the same whispered, endlessly repeated orders until they were understood: 'Gods . . . kill . . . kill . . . gods . . . .' At first the giants stood stupidly beside their stone-pile, blinking as the words throbbed in their tiny brains. Then, at last, understanding kindled in their eyes and they began swarming up the pile to dethrone the gods. But it had taken them too long to learn: the gods were waiting. Mars, Minerva and Diana led the attack, and the other gods followed with lumps of wood, rocks, furniture from the halls of Olympus and even silver ladles and cauldrons from the kitchens. As the giants wavered, Jupiter dashed them one by one from the stone-pile with thunderbolts, and they were smashed to pieces on the ground below.

So the attack on Olympus failed. The gods bundled the surviving giants down to the Underworld, this time not to sleep but to writhe in eternal torment. The broken bodies of the others lay like boulders on the plains of their Mother Earth. The blood trickled out of them and mingled with dust – and from that mingling Mother Earth created a new race of beings, not monstrous like the giants but small and frail like Prometheus' human dolls. She hoped that the gods would mistake them for Prometheus' mortals and leave them in peace; but she filled their hearts with evil and their minds with intelligence, earth-knowledge from before the era of the gods. Above all, she taught them how to mine ore from her body and smelt it into iron; she taught them to despise their peaceful fellow-mortals as weaklings, to long for power and to defy the gods.

As time passed, the new mortals began to thrive. Their food was no longer seeds or grains but flesh, hunted with iron; they swaggered across the world, killing or enslaving their fellow-beings, enriching themselves with precious metals dug from the ground, and replacing the gods' peaceful government with arrogant new laws of their own. The Silver Age was dead; the Age of Iron was born.

Erysichthon

From Olympus, the gods looked down in dismay as cruelty and war engulfed the earth. They hoped, even now, that with divine guidance the human race could be persuaded to return from evil to good, and they spent their time sending omens, dreams and oracles to point the way. Every warning failed. The more the gods showed their concern, the more human beings laughed at them. In the end mortals began sacking temples, plundering shrines and slaughtering priests, and the gods decided that the time had come to replace warnings with action, to choose the most impious man in the world and to punish him in a way which would terrify every other member of the human race, make them bury their iron weapons deep underground and return to the Silver Age.

The wickedest mortal on earth was Erysichthon, king of Thessaly. His country was a favourite haunt of tree-spirits and river-nymphs. They tended the forests, kept the irrigation-channels clear and freed the crops from weeds. Erysichthon, however, cared nothing for nymphs. He put his country's prosperity down to the fact that it lay at the foot of Mount Olympus, and was hourly scattered with gold by the feet of the gods as they passed to and from Jupiter's court. In the end, in his madness, he planned to build a palace on earth to equal Jupiter's in heaven, and a wall and a toll-gate to charge the gods each time they passed. Barges, ferrying building-stone, soon choked the rivers of Thessaly; the woods rang with axes as the royal workmen felled tree after tree.

Soon Erysichthon's country turned from farmland to desert. The clogged irrigation-channels dried up and disappeared; the crops withered; there were piles of logs beside every path; bonfires of branches filled the sky with smoke. The nymphs and river-spirits clustered for safety in a last stronghold, a copse of trees sacred to the gods. It had stood untouched for a thousand years, and mortals visited it only to worship. Now Erysichthon sent his foresters with axes and wedges to fell the trees. Amid the thump of axes and the crack of splintering wood, shrieks filled the air as the nymphs flew terrified from tree to tree. But the men continued their work, until there was only one tree left: an aged oak whose trunk was as wide as a house and whose branches were a forest in themselves. It was hung with wreaths, garlands and ribbons; prayer-pebbles were lodged in every crack. Erysichthon set his men to fell this tree, and when they superstitiously held back, he snatched an axe and made the first cut himself. On the upswing of the axe, the tree groaned and its acorns and leaves turned pale; when the axe gashed the trunk, the bark bled like flesh. One of Erysichthon's horrified foresters tried to take the axe from his master – and Erysichthon swung it against him himself, lopped his head from his neck and then fell on the tree in a frenzy,

24

striking blow after blow. A voice, faint from pain, began calling from the trunk for mercy, and the madman ignored it. He ordered ropes to be fastened to the tree, and harnessed oxen to them to uproot it from the ground as a tooth is ripped from its socket. At last, in a shower of leaves and a crashing of branches, the huge tree fell. The ground shook as if in an earthquake, and Thessaly's nymphs and wood-spirits fluttered to heaven for safety like startled birds.

From Olympus, the wood-nymphs made their way to Italy to beg Ceres' help. They fluttered in front of her, like a flock of excited geese. 'Erysichthon has blotted out the harvest,' they said. 'He's murdering Thessaly. Punish him!'

'If Erysichthon prefers Starvation to Harvest,' answered Ceres, 'he can have her.' She laid down the wild flowers she had been gathering, put aside the basket of cherries her servants had picked for her, climbed into her dragon-chariot and soared into the sky. At first the journey was through clear, sun-warmed air; but as she went further north, across the hills of Scythia, clouds strewed her path and ice crackled on her eyebrows and finger-nails. She landed at last on bare, frozen earth, in a land where no crops grew. This was Starvation's home. Ceres found the goddess on all fours, tearing ravenously at tufts of frozen grass between the stones. Starvation's skin was like paper; her hair hung like rats' tails; her eyes were wild. She was naked. Her withered breasts flapped from her chest like pouches, and her arms stuck out like twigs. Ceres hovered above her and gave her her orders. 'Go to Thessaly,' she said. 'Find Erysichthon; feed on him.'

As soon as she heard Erysichthon's name, Starvation stood upright and sniffed the air like a rat scenting food. Ceres whipped her dragons and soared away, and Starvation began loping south after her. Wherever she went, people penned their animals and hid their children, as if she were a preying wolf; but she turned her lamps of eyes neither to right nor left, and her pace never slackened till she reached Thessaly, where Erysichthon was snoring in his new palace on a duck-feather bed. Starvation crept into his room and flung herself on him, silent as an owl. She locked her bony arms round him and sank into him, luxuriating in his plumpness as people float in a sun-soaked sea. Satisfied at last, she loped into the darkness and disappeared, leaving Erysichthon still snoring where he lay.

For the rest of that night, Erysichthon tossed and turned uneasily. He dreamed he was at a banquet, but every time he put food into his mouth to chew it, his teeth ground on wood or ash. His flesh, his bones, his veins ached for nourishment: Starvation's embrace had turned him from a man to a hunger-beast. He woke up howling for food, and the more his servants fetched the more he craved. He ate the candles and crammed his mouth with his own bedclothes; his hunger ebbed and flowed like the sea; he was insatiable. As the weeks passed, he consumed every morsel in the palace store-rooms. He fell on the royal flocks and herds and gulped them raw; he stole, lied, cheated, killed. Soon all his people had fled, his palace and kingdom were in ruins and he had nothing left but the rags he stood up in (torn with teethmarks) and his daughter Meara. Meara was a witch, able to turn herself into anything she chose, and for a time she helped her father by letting him sell her to passers-by in exchange for food, then changing into smoke or a blowfly and vanishing from under her new owners' noses. But in the end there was no one left willing to buy, and Meara sat weeping by her father's side while he tossed and raved with hunger. All at once she saw him cram his own fingers into his mouth and begin to chew. She leapt up to stop him, but the hunger-beast had totally overwhelmed the man, and under her horrified gaze Erysichthon began to consume himself. He had a harvest to reap, Ceres' last cruel punishment, and he ripped and gnawed at his own impious flesh till every morsel was consumed.

Lycaon

For a time, it seemed as though the gods' plan had worked. Terrified by Erysichthon's death, the human race abandoned its evil ways, flocked once again to the gods' temples and begged forgiveness. But soon, as surely as the turning tide begins to trickle up the beach, dishonesty and violence reappeared on earth. People lived for greed: friends were not safe from friends, brothers from brothers, mothers from daughters, fathers from sons. The sea, which had once been common to all, swarmed with warfleets eager to snatch all they could; surveyors worked busily on land, marking out borders, kingdoms and protectorates. One by one the gods retreated from earth, leaving it for mortals; Justice was the last to leave.

In the end, Jupiter decided to cleanse the human race from the world forever. To give mortals one last chance, he disguised himself as a human prince and began wandering the earth, to see if any mortals were left who still honoured him in secret, still feared his name. There were none; wild beasts in their lairs were more god-fearing than the human race. In Thessaly, which he visited with a human companion, Jupiter even threw off the disguise of mortality to force the people to acknowledge him – and although the Thessalians fell on their knees to pray, Lycaon, their king, devised a savage test of Jupiter's godly powers. He cut Jupiter's companion secretly into pieces, stewed them and served them up at a banquet. 'If this person truly is Jupiter,' he thought, 'he'll know at once that this is forbidden meat.' When Jupiter kicked back the table and refused to eat, Lycaon devised a second, even more impious test: he crept into Jupiter's bedroom at night and began stabbing the throat and chest of the sleeping god. The iron blade crumpled at the first touch of Jupiter's immortal skin, and the god woke up with a roar of fury that sent thunder crashing across the sky and felled Lycaon's palace in ruins. Lycaon recognised Jupiter as a god at last and held out his hands for mercy. But even as he stood there, howling for forgiveness, the words changed to snarls and whines in his throat. His outstretched arms and his legs and body grew bristling hairs and his nose and mouth stretched into a muzzle. He fell on all fours and loped into the woods, no longer man but wolf. He still craved blood, but now his ferocity was turned from human beings against chickens, lambs and goats. As his people mourned him, or grovelled on the ground for mercy, they too were transformed into wolves and ran into the woods to find their king.

Baucis and Philemon

There was now no doubt: the human race was to be destroyed. At first Jupiter planned to use thunderbolts, to sweep mortals from the earth with fire. But he was afraid of toppling Olympus itself in a sheet of flame. The Fates had long ago prophesied that a time would come when all creation would be engulfed in fire, that sea, earth, sky and the Underworld would be confounded and the era of the gods would end. To avoid this catastrophe, Jupiter laid aside his thunderbolts and chose instead to wash mortals from the world by flood. He gathered the winds and imprisoned them, leaving only the South Wind to marshal its storm-clouds and send rain like iron bars against the trembling earth. He ordered the river-gods to swamp their banks and engulf the fields. He sent the rainbow-goddess Iris, messenger of the gods, to ask his brother Neptune to unlock the floodgates of the sea.

27

Even as the flood began to rise, Jupiter and Mercury set out to roam the world one last time. They hoped to find any mortals still honest, any last remnants of Prometheus' gentle creation, and to warn them in time to escape the flood. Disguised as human travellers, they asked for shelter at a thousand doors, and a thousand householders took them for tramps and set the dogs on them. At last, on a bare hillside rising in mist beside a marsh, they came to a cottage. It was small and poor, with walls of straw and cowdung and a reed-thatched roof; inside lived Baucis and her boatman-husband Philemon. They had married when they were both little more than children, and had made their home in that desolate place for sixty years.

As soon as the gods knocked on the cottage door, still disguised as tramps, Philemon went out to welcome them, shaking their hands as if they were long-lost relatives. They bent their heads to pass through the low doorway, and Baucis laid a cloth and cushions on the old wooden sofa and invited the visitors to sit down and rest after their journey. She stirred the ashes of yesterday's fire, blew them into life and fed the flames with dry reeds and tree-bark. When the fire blazed she piled it with twigs and branches, and put water in a pot to boil. Philemon meanwhile gathered vegetables, chopped them for the stew, and added a slice of salt pork from a leg hanging, soot-blackened and smoky, from the ceiling.

While all this was going on, the old couple chattered as if they'd seen no visitors for years. They filled a beech-wood bowl with water for their guests to wash their hands. They plumped up the reed-mattress on their own bed, and laid over it an embroidered coverlet not seen since the day of their own wedding: they'd kept it in a chest ever since, and treasured it. It was old and moth-eaten, shabby like the bed they put it on, but Philemon gladly spread it out in honour of their visitors.

The cooking was soon finished, and Philemon put a rickety table in front of the gods, with a tile under one leg to balance it. Baucis set out cheese, a plate of cherries pickled in vinegar, another of radishes and endive, and another of duck-eggs roasted in the ashes. There were beechwood cups, and a clay jar of wine. That was the first course; the second was bacon stew, and the third was a basket of nuts, figs, plums and grapes, and a honeycomb on a wooden dish.

All these good things would have kept Baucis and Philemon in food for a week, and they hoped that their visitors wouldn't notice that they'd emptied their larder for just this one meal. But as the meal went

28

on and the wine-jug passed from hand to hand, Baucis and Philemon realised that it never emptied; however much anyone poured out of it, it always filled again of its own accord. They fell on their knees and honoured their visitors as immortal gods. 'Pardon us, your worships,' said Baucis humbly. 'We took you for ordinary folk.'

'Wife,' said Philemon suddenly, 'we must kill the goose and roast it for their worships.'

The goose was their beloved pet, raised in that cottage from the egg. It flapped round the room, hissing and cackling, and Baucis and Philemon panted after it as fast as their aged limbs would let them. At last Jupiter raised a hand and said 'Enough!', and the two old people sat down gratefully to catch their breath. 'There's no need to kill your pet,' said Jupiter. 'What you've done already is quite enough. You've shown us more kindness than a thousand others, and in return you will escape the flood which engulfs the earth.'

Already Neptune had opened the floodgates, and seawater was trickling into every cranny of the world and rising inexorably to drown fields, houses, villages and even fine cities built of marble and domed with gold. The human race splashed in panic, screaming and wailing, but the gods were deaf. Jupiter and Mercury took Baucis and Philemon by the hand up the hill behind their cottage, and as they looked back they could see the whole marsh rise until there was nothing in all directions but glassy sea, and no sound but the gurgle of the flood. All that remained of the mortal world was Baucis' and Philemon's old cottage on the hillside – and even as they watched, it changed into a temple before their eyes, with pillars of painted marble and a roof of gold instead of thatch.

Baucis and Philemon lived as priest and priestess of the temple for many years, honouring the gods who had spared their lives. Then, one day, as the two old people stood hand in hand in the temple yard, Baucis suddenly saw green tendrils sprouting from Philemon's shoulders, and at the same moment Philemon noticed that the skin of her arms was growing brown and hard, like bark. They tried to move their feet, and found that they were taking root in the ground they stood on. Their human lives were ending; they were turning into trees. Baucis became a linden and Philemon an oak, and they had just time to hug each other for the last time, kiss each other with barky lips and murmur 'Farewell, my dear' before the transformation was complete.

The Trojan War

Unknown to the gods, two mortals did escape the flood. Their names were Deucalion and Pyrrha, and they were the last two of Prometheus' doll-creations, the only humans not made from the mingling of the giants' blood with Mother Earth. While the flood-waters covered the ground as skin wraps an apple, they bobbed on the surface in a boat; when Neptune closed the sluices of the sea, rivers returned to their appointed courses and the water-level began at last to fall, the boat grounded on the slopes of a high mountain, and Deucalion and Pyrrha splashed ashore. They looked round in dismay at the sodden trees, the fields slimy with seaweed and the bodies of seals, crabs and fish left exposed by the sinking sea. They listened in terror to the silence, broken only by the gurgle of receding water and empty of all sounds of life. They realised that they were alone, the only beings on the surface of the earth, and fell on their knees, sobbing to the gods to drown them, too. But all at once, all round them, they seemed to hear a voice whispering, 'Earth's bones . . . throw . . . Earth's bones . . . throw . . . .' Themis, Prometheus' mother and their own ancestor, was answering their prayers. Kneeling where they were, they picked up handfuls of pebbles, the moist bones of Mother Earth, and tossed them gently down the hillside. As soon as Deucalion's stones touched the ground, they turned into men; Pyrrha's stones made women; the mountainside filled with a crowd of people, laughing in the sunshine, jumping and splashing in the shallows as the flood-waters disappeared.

So mortals survived even the flood sent to wash them from the earth. But they were reborn not from Prometheus' gentle descendants but from the stones of Mother Earth, and were filled with her ancient wickedness. As the centuries passed the new people built kingdoms everywhere across the world, and thrived. Many remembered the flood and feared the gods; others mocked the flood-story as a foolish myth, snapped their fingers at Olympus and did as they pleased. For many years the gods guided everyone who prayed to them, and sent portents and oracles to warn the others. Some were even attracted to humans, made love with them and produced heroes, beings half-mortal, half-immortal – and for a time the heroes' presence in the world guaranteed goodness in the human race. But as before, the passing of time brought change, and the change was for the worse. Human arrogance swelled like a storm-cloud, until Olympus itself was threatened and it was time once more for the gods to act.

30

This time, instead of trying to destroy humanity, the gods decided to perfect it. They planned to use the whole mortal creation as ore and to forge from it a single god-fearing, noble race. The crucible they chose was war. They sent Prince Paris of Troy to the court of the Greek king Menelaus, and made him steal Helen, Menelaus' queen. The Greeks gathered a huge invasion-force to sack Troy, kill Paris and fetch Helen back. Soon two of the most powerful of all mortal nations were locked in war, and princes, heroes and warriors flocked from every place on earth to join the fight.

The Trojan War lasted for ten mortal years. There were two reasons. The first was that although all the gods agreed that it should end in outright victory, no two gods wanted the same side to win. Jupiter, ruler of gods and mortals, favoured both sides impartially, and Mars the wargod cared nothing about mortal rights and wrongs but simply enjoyed the fighting, helping each side in turn. But many of the other gods fiercely supported either Greeks or Trojans, and gave them all the help they could. In particular, Juno, queen of heaven, favoured Greece, and Venus the love-goddess favoured Troy. Before the war began, three goddesses, Juno, Venus and Minerva, had appeared to Paris on a mountain-top and asked him to say which of them was the most beautiful. Each had offered him a bribe. Juno offered him power; Minerva offered him wisdom; Venus offered him the love of Helen, the most beautiful mortal woman in the world. Paris chose Venus, and set out at once for Greece to steal Helen from her husband. From that moment on Venus favoured the Trojans, and Juno burned with hatred against them and vowed not to rest till the Trojan race was blotted from the world. As for Minerva, she saw that the choice between power, wisdom and beauty was a foolish one to offer any mortal, and that the war would lead only to disaster. She had guarded and protected Troy since its foundation, and her statue, the Palladium, was one of its most sacred relics.* But now she, too, had been offended by Paris' choice of Venus. Accordingly, she supported neither Greeks nor Trojans, but soared above both battlelines equally, her war-shield gleaming in her hand.

The second reason why the Trojan War lasted for ten mortal years was because so many heroes took part in it. No one hero possessed all the knowledge and skills that belong to gods. But each hero had one or other of them, honed to more-than-mortal sharpness. Ulysses' cunning matched that even of Mercury, god of tricksters. Helenus and Cassandra had Apollo's gift of second sight: they could see the future as clearly as the present. Ajax was as brave as Mars. Above all, each side boasted one of the noblest heroes of all those days. Prince Hector fought for Troy; Prince Achilles fought for Greece. They were proud warriors, unbeatable except by one another. For ten years the gods kept them apart, and let them rage through the battlelines like lions, slaughtering lesser men as they hunted each other down. Then, in the tenth year of the war, the Greek commanders insulted Achilles and he withdrew from the fighting. He sat sullenly in his tent, heeding neither orders, prayers nor arguments. The Greeks lost heart, and the Trojans hunted them as wolves hunt sheep. At last Patroclus, Achilles' friend, put on Achilles' own armour and went out to fight – and the Greek army, thinking he was Achilles, ran cheering after him. But Hector challenged Patroclus to a duel and killed him. This, at last, ended Achilles' sulk. He killed Hector in a duel, lashed his corpse to a chariot and dragged it three times round the walls of Troy. The Trojan king Priam, Hector's father, begged Achilles to give him Hector's corpse for burial, and Achilles arrogantly refused. Then Paris, skulking in the shadows, shot a poisoned arrow at Achilles and killed him too.

The deaths of their greatest heroes disheartened both sides equally. Would the war never end? Doggedly, despairingly, the ordinary soldiers buckled on their armour for another weary battle. The leaders met in grim-faced council to discuss the future. And now, at last, the gods whispered to Ulysses, wiliest of the Greeks, the trick of the Wooden Horse. It was a trick that would topple Troy; it would end the war and give birth at last to the noble race the gods had planned. This race was to be the Romans, and they would rise, after great suffering, from refugees led by Prince Aeneas from the sack of Troy.

THE · STORY · OF · AENEAS

3
TROY

The Wooden Horse

The Horse stood alone on the windy plain. Last night, when sentries peered out from the Trojan battlements, there had been a thousand Greek camp-fires winking in the darkness, and the air had been filled with the murmur of an encamped army, incessant as surf on a distant shore. Now the army was gone and the Horse stood alone, facing into the rising sun as if poised to gallop up to Troy's walls and leap over them. It was enormous. Its body was made of pine-planks, overlapping and pegged like the sides of a ship. Its legs were like tree-trunks, stubby pillars ending in solid wooden wheels as high as a man. It was covered all over with magic symbols: the zig-zag lightning-flash of Jupiter, Neptune's whirlpool-whorls, the moon-sickles of Diana the Huntress, and above all the wide-eyed owls of Minerva, goddess of wisdom and protector of Troy.

To the gods, the Horse was a stratagem, a trick to get the Greeks into Troy and end the war. But the Trojans, safe in their high-walled town, suspected nothing. All they knew was what the rising sun showed them: that the enemy who had besieged their city for ten weary years, slaughtering Trojan soldiers and glutting the ground with blood, had disappeared. The plain was deserted. They poured out of the city and began exploring their own countryside like tourists. There were furrows on the foreshore, and mooring-stones with the cut ropes of the Greek ships still tied to them. Pieces of splintered wood and broken bowls and jars lay everywhere; the shore was littered with crates where provision-ships had been unloaded every day for the last ten years. Further in, across the whole plain and right up to the city walls, were circles of ash where the Greeks had built their watch-fires, and discarded tent-poles and weapons half-buried in the sand. In the centre of the plain, near where the Greek leaders Agamemnon and Menelaus had pitched their tents, there was a mound where the commanders had stood to address the army, and the ground had been trodden hard by countless feet. There were hitching-posts and fodder-bins, and half-finished spears still lay on the flat rocks the smiths had used as anvils. Everywhere the plain was littered with the debris of an army; only Ulysses' camp-site was empty, and his servants had taken away everything of value and levelled the sand where the tents had stood.

But of all the objects on the plain, none caused more amazement than the Horse. People seethed round it like ants, and while children clambered over its axles and jumped from its wheels their parents stood in groups discussing what to do with it. Some suggested breaking it up and burning it on the spot, as a symbol of triumph over the hated Greeks. Others wanted to drag it into the city and leave it as a thank-offering in Minerva's temple. Discussion was at its height when Laocoön, priest of Neptune, came hurrying from the city with his half-grown sons beside him. His eyes were blazing with anger, and before he reached the Horse the Trojans could hear him shouting, 'Fools! Do you really imagine that the Greeks are gone? Is that all you know of them? Either the horse is hollow, pregnant with soldiers, or it's a siege-weapon to peer into our homes and spy out our defences. Whatever it is, distrust it! We should fear the Greeks most when they give us gifts.'

So saying, he hurled a spear hard into the Horse's flank. The blade jarred home, and the wooden framework boomed as if the animal was groaning. If the Trojans had been listening to omens, if the gods had not made them deaf, that would have been enough for them. They would have ripped the Horse apart, discovered its secret and saved their city. But before anyone could make a move there was a fresh distraction. A group of shepherds from the hills ran up, dragging a Greek prisoner. He stood beside the Horse, his face grey with fear and his hands bound behind him, while some of the Trojans drew back in terror, plucking their children to their sides, and others ran into the city to fetch King Priam. At last Priam came out, a white-bearded old man surrounded by counsellors and priests – among them his own daughter Cassandra, the wild-eyed prophetess everyone took for a madwoman. The prisoner ran and grovelled at Priam's feet. 'Where can I go?' he sobbed. 'Is nowhere safe? The Greeks have disowned me – do the Trojans, now, want my blood as well?'

'Stand up, Greek,' said Priam. 'Tell us: who are you, and why have the others sailed and left you?'

The Greek licked his lips, and looked this way and that among the crowd like an actor taking stock of his audience. Then, in a voice trembling with self-pity, he told a tale which confirmed every Trojan suspicion about the Greek commanders' treachery. His name, he said, was Sinon, and he had sailed for Troy in the service of his relative Palamedes. Palamedes had rashly boasted that he was a better man than Ulysses, and Ulysses had retaliated by accusing him of spying for the Trojans and having him stoned to death. After that, Sinon said, it was only a matter of time before he, too, fell to Ulysses' fury – and sure enough, when the Greek commanders asked Calchas the prophet why they were making no headway in the war, Calchas (bribed by Ulysses) answered that the gods were angry because the Greek expedition had begun with human sacrifice, the murder of Agamemnon's daughter Iphigenia, and that Olympian anger could only be soothed by another death: Sinon's. That same night, Sinon said, before he could be trussed and slaughtered, he had escaped to the reeds by the river and hidden there, shivering, till the Greeks struck camp and sailed for home, certain that they would never win the war. Now he supposed that they would revenge themselves by butchering his innocent wife and children. He was cursed by the gods; there was no hiding-place left for him on earth.

It was an easily-believable tale. When Sinon began the crowd was muttering and hostile, but by the end they were open-mouthed with pity and credulity. When Sinon mentioned his wife and children a wave of horror ran round the Trojans, and they applauded warmly when Priam promised Sinon and his descendants a home in Troy for as long as the city stood. Then one of Priam's counsellors asked Sinon about the Horse. 'It was built as a peace-offering to Minerva,' answered Sinon. 'From the moment of Achilles' death we were surrounded by bad omens. The sky blackened with thunder, and storms shattered our ships against the shore. In the end Calchas advised us to build this offering to appease the gods, horse-shaped to delight horse-loving Neptune, god of the sea, and covered with magic owl-signs to win Minerva's favour. He told us to make it far too big to be dragged inside Troy. If it ever entered the city, he said, the gods' fury would fall on the Greeks at sea, and drown them all.'

At this a shout went up from the crowd. 'The Horse! Take it into Troy! Drown the Greeks!' Some of Priam's counsellors nodded agreement; but others shook their heads, claiming that Sinon was a liar, and that the Horse should be broken up and burned where it stood. At last Priam ordered Laocoön to go to the foreshore and sacrifice to Neptune, asking for omens to prove Sinon's story one way or the other. Laocoön and his sons made an altar on the shore, and set about lighting a sacred fire while servants fetched a white bull for the offering. Their backs were to the sea, and the other Trojans were crowding round Sinon and the Horse, up at the city gates. No one noticed the sea-monsters until they were close inshore. There were two of them, arching through the water like gigantic snakes. Their heads were huge, with sharks' teeth and fiery eyes; they were crested like newts and scaled like fish. They glided to shore, wrapped themselves round Laocoön's sons and began, soundlessly, to crop their flesh. The children's screaming was the first Laocoön knew of what was happening. He began clawing at the monsters, trying to free himself and his sons from the choking coils. He was a strong man – he could pole-axe a bull-sacrifice with a single blow – but he was no match for the monsters. They finished their meal, slithered into the city and vanished inside Minerva's sanctuary. Where Laocoön and his sons had been, there was nothing but a patch of bloodstained sand, washed by the waves.

There was a long silence. Then Priam said, 'We have our omen. Laocoön hurt the Horse with his spear-cast, and has paid the price. We must drag the horse into Troy and offer it in Minerva's shrine.' At once the people's panic changed to delirious joy. They fetched logs and levers, and fastened ropes to the Horse's axles to drag it into the city. Since it was too wide for the city gates, they tore a gap in the wall to make room for it. Children swarmed over it as the cheering crowd dragged it through the streets to Minerva's temple, stroking it for luck and shouting for joy that the war was won at last. Four times the wheels stuck on the uneven ground, and each time there was a clatter of weapons from inside the Horse. But the gods blocked the Trojans' ears. Only Cassandra heard the warnings, and capered round the Horse shrieking prophecies of which no one took the slightest heed. The Trojans left the Horse in the courtyard of Minerva's temple, and went skipping home to make a victory-feast.

Destruction

That night, there was singing in every house in Troy. Even the gate-guards, now that there was no enemy to watch for, left their posts and ran to join their families. Bonfires and torchlight processions lit the sky; there would have been no night if Jupiter had not put an end to the celebrations at last, blanketing the city in darkness and pouring sleep over every Trojan's eyes. And in the darkness Sinon crept through the streets to Minerva's sanctuary, unbolted a secret trapdoor in the Horse's flank and let his cramped companions out. Acamas, Achaemenides, Agamemnon, Epeus,* Machaon, Menelaus, Pyrrhus, Sthenelus, Thessander and last of all Ulysses, Lord of Lies, swarmed down rope-ladders in the gloom. They set a pine-torch blazing on the walls, and from far out to sea saw an answering signal. The Greek ships, moored out of sight behind the island of Tenedos, had turned and were beating back to the city as fast as their oars could row. The ships beached in the shallows, and armed men darted across the plain and into the city through the gap the Trojans had torn in the wall with their own bare hands.

It was the hour before dawn. In his quiet villa Aeneas, son of Anchises* and prince of Troy, tossed in an uneasy dream. It seemed to him that the ghost of Hector stood beside him. Its hair was blood-caked, its eyes were wild and the death-wound gaped in its chest. 'Get up, Aeneas!' it cried. 'The Greeks are toppling Troy. Get up! Lead our people to a new Troy far away.' Aeneas sprang from sleep and ran to the flat roof of the house to gaze out over Troy. The air was heavy with the baying of Greeks, the shouts of startled Trojans and the wailing of women and children snatched to slavery. The Greeks were like fire advancing through a forest, fanned by the wind, and Aeneas stood like a shepherd on a hilltop, aghast at destruction he could do nothing to halt. The roof of the next-door mansion had already fallen in, and the house was blazing. Flames filled the sky and sent reflections like spears across the straits, till it seemed as if the sea itself was on fire.

Aeneas ran down to the street. Fugitives streamed past him, clutching their children, their household gods, whatever valuables they had snatched up in the confusion. Aeneas shouldered his way against the crowd to the heart of Troy, the hub of the fighting, and as he ran other warlords joined him: Coroebus, Dymas, Hypanis, Iphitus, Pelias and Rhipeus. They ranged through the dying city, implacable as wolves; they hugged the shadows, alert for Greeks. A band of plunderers met them, led by Androgeus, and in the darkness the fool took them for fellow-countrymen. 'Come on!' he shouted. 'What kept you so long in the ships? Hurry up, or there'll be nothing left!' Then he realised who they were, and stepped back as if he'd trodden on a snake. His men dropped their loot and snatched their swords. But they were too late: the Trojans stabbed them where they stood, stripped the bodies and buckled the hateful Greek armour round themselves. The trick worked: band after band of Greeks took them for fellow-countrymen in the gloom, and died without discovering their mistake.

Then, in a quiet city square in front of Apollo's temple, they found a dozen Greeks guarding prisoners doomed to be sold as slaves. They were about to jump on them, slit their throats and free the prisoners when there was a yell of triumph from the temple, and a gang of Greeks ran out dragging Cassandra by the hair. Her hands were tied, her clothes were torn, and she fought like a cat in a bag. The soldiers threw her down among the other prisoners, and when Coroebus (who loved Cassandra, for all her craziness*) saw that, he ran forward in fury and began stabbing at the bewildered Greeks. At first they took him for a madman and fell back, cursing. But when Hypanis, Dymas and the others ran out to help him, they realised that they'd been tricked and swarmed to defend themselves. Even then Aeneas' men would have won if a group of Trojan defenders in the shadows had not seen their borrowed armour, taken them for Greeks and begun exultantly firing arrows and hurling rocks. Aeneas' men were caught between their own side and the enemy: there was no escape. Coroebus fell with a Greek spear through the throat; Hypanis and Dymas were crushed by Trojan rocks. The Greeks made a sudden rush, trampled Rhipeus to death and separated Aeneas, Iphitus and Pelias from the others. The three men pelted into a side-street, tearing off their Greek armour as they ran. Iphitus was old, and Pelias was injured: they soon fell to the pursuing Greeks. But Aeneas escaped and made his way alone, despairing and unseen, to Priam's palace in the centre of the city. There was a secret gate, known only to a handful of Trojans and so far undiscovered by the Greeks. He slipped inside and ran to help the defenders on the roof.

Priam's palace was a fortress: a windowless, oak-gated tower of stone. The Greeks swarmed round it like ants. They were laying siege to it in formal, textbook fashion. Some locked their shields over their heads to form a 'tortoise', while sappers burrowed under cover of the shields to weaken the wall. Other Greeks fetched a battering-ram, a tree-trunk bound with bronze, and began pounding their way into the palace: the walls shuddered with every blow. Still others brought siege-catapults, and began lobbing rocks and fire-arrows at the defenders on the roof. Up here, on a parapet twenty metres above the ground, was a throng of Priam's servants, palace guards, Aeneas and a handful of other princes, all working grimly to deter the Greeks. They hurled down whatever missiles came to hand: roof-tiles, stones from the parapet, even the gold-encrusted joists and beams that had been the pride of the kings of Troy for generations. On one corner of the roof was a wooden watch-tower, where Priam and his family had often climbed to watch battles on the plain outside the city or to gaze at the Greek anchorage and sea beyond. Aeneas led a gang of men to it, and they began hacking at the struts, levering and heaving until the whole structure collapsed into the street with an enormous roar, burying the ram and its bearers in splintered beams.

But it was too late: at the very moment of the tower's collapse the ram breached the gate. The Greeks swarmed over their comrades' corpses into the palace. Pyrrhus led them: a giant of a man, with crisp yellow hair and viper-eyes.* He carried a broad, two-handed axe, and used it to hack down the door to Priam's private apartments. The Greeks flowed after him like a river, engulfing everyone in their path. The defenders ran down from the roof, and stabbed and chopped till each was overwhelmed by a dozen enemies. The palace women shrieked and screamed, hugging the roof-pillars as if they offered some protection. And all the while the Greeks advanced, through door after door, down passage after passage, burning, looting, murdering, led by Agamemnon, Menelaus and the grim figure of Pyrrhus the Destroyer.

Priam was a very old man: he had ruled Troy for eighty years, since he was a child in arms,* and his grandchildren had children of their own. But now, when he saw that Troy's last hour had come and there was no hope left for his people, he covered his trembling limbs with the armour he had not worn for a generation, took in his shaking hands the weapons he was scarcely strong enough to lift and went to face certain death. In the heart of the palace, in a courtyard open to the sky, there was an ancient laurel-tree sacred to Apollo, and next to it the shrine of the household gods. Here, cowering like doves before a storm, were Priam's aged queen Hecuba and her daughters. When Hecuba saw Priam bent under the weight of his armour, she cried, 'My lord, what use is that? Not even Hector, our own dear son, could save us now. Put down your weapons and sit with us here. Pray to the gods to protect us.'

She pulled him down among the women. But just at that moment a warrior ran gasping and bleeding into the courtyard. He was Priam's son Polites – an elderly man, well past fighting age. Wounds like open mouths bubbled in his neck, and he staggered to the altar for protection. But before he could reach it Pyrrhus ran in behind him and felled him with a spear-throw, leaving him to cough out his life at his parents' feet. The sight fanned the last embers of Priam's royal rage. He gathered his strength and hurled his spear. But there was no force in the cast: the spear rattled against Pyrrhus' shield and dangled uselessly from the centre. Pyrrhus took Priam by the hair and dragged him, slipping and staggering in his own son's blood, over to the altar. He plunged his sword into the feeble body and shouted for his companions. They swarmed out of the shadows, carried Priam's corpse to behead it on the shore and drove Hecuba and her daughters, like terrified sheep, to be hauled into slavery with the other prisoners.

Flight

All this time, from the moment when the Greek battering-ram first smashed the palace gate to the death of Priam, Aeneas had been allowed to play no part but that of a helpless spectator. He had burned to help his people, to hurl himself at Greeks and die for his dear city. But the gods knew that his destiny was not to save this city's bricks and stones but to found a new Troy far away. They froze him where he stood, helpless as a statue. He could weep for everything that happened but was unable to move or shout, and they cloaked him in invisibility so that the Greeks brushed past without seeing him. It was not until Priam was dead, Hecuba and her daughters had been dragged to slavery, and the only noises in the palace were the moans of the dying and the distant shrieks of the captured, that they thawed him and sent him along the dark corridors to his people. He still understood nothing; he ran wild-eyed through the shadows, his knuckles white on his sword-hilt and tears pouring down his cheeks. In the end his mother Venus took pity on him and sent omens to teach him his destiny. She put Helen herself in his path – Helen the traitress, whose love-affair with Paris had kindled the whole war and spawned so many deaths. Then, even as Helen cringed at Aeneas' feet and he pulled back her head to cut her throat, Venus sent a second vision: Aeneas' father Anchises, his wife Creusa, his son Iulus and a band of refugees, all waiting for him with fear in their eyes and all they owned in their arms. He left Helen sobbing where she lay, and hurried through the blazing streets to his father's house.

Here a terrible discussion now began. Anchises refused to leave. He was too old, he said, to sail into exile and search for some new homeland; he was a cripple and would be nothing but a burden; his heart was in Troy, and all he asked was to die with it. Aeneas refused to leave him. He said that if Anchises stayed they would all stay: the entire Trojan race would die together. He drew his sword and was about to rush back into battle when Creusa clutched his arm and begged him to take her with him, so that she might die beside him and not wait till the Greeks burned the house about her. Aeneas lifted his hands to heaven and begged for guidance. At once flames flickered on the head of the child Iulus. They licked his skin like a blazing halo, and the servants scurried to the fountain for water. But the little boy merely laughed and held up his hands to play with the fire, entirely unharmed by it. Anchises fell on his knees and said, 'Great Jupiter, if the gods still heed mortal prayers, if they still respect mortal decency, show that this is a good omen, sent to help us not harm us.' In answer there was a clap of thunder, and a lightning-flash soared overhead, trailing sparks like a shooting-star, and furrowed the forests of Mount Ida. The flames died on Iulus' head of their own accord, leaving the child untouched, and Anchises said to Aeneas, 'The gods have spoken. Lead the way: I'll go with you.'

Even as he spoke there was a roar of falling masonry. The house was blazing round them, and unless they left at once the roof would fall in and bury them. 'Hurry!' shouted Aeneas. 'Father, let me carry you. Iulus, take my hand; Creusa, keep close behind. The rest of you, go to Ceres' temple at the edge of the city. Wait for us where the single cypress stands.' The servants hurried away, and he covered his shoulders with a lion-skin, bent and lifted his father's weight, then took Iulus' hand and strode off through the streets. The child ran to keep up with him and Creusa hurried behind. They chose the darkest alleys, the safest short cuts, and although a moment before Aeneas would have faced a thousand Greeks and laughed at the danger, now the slightest breeze terrified him and he froze at the smallest sound. They came to Ceres' temple at last, and found a crowd of refugees waiting. Aeneas handed Anchises and Iulus into their care and looked round for Creusa.

She was not there. Somewhere along the way he had lost her. His heart thudding, he shouted to the others to wait and ran back into the city to look for her. He searched the walls, the battlements, the blazing streets, and saw no one but Greeks and the bodies of the dead. He found his own home a ruin, Priam's palace a heap of rubble, Juno's temple a bazaar crammed with loot, manacled prisoners and Greeks licking their lips at the thought of their share of spoil. But Creusa was nowhere to be found. He was so desperate that he shouted her name above the fire-roar, and heard no answer but the echo of his voice and the crackling of the flames. Then the gods sent him a third vision. He felt Creusa's presence all round him, filling the air, and her voice said gently, 'Go, Aeneas. Your people are waiting. Your destiny lies with them, not here with me. Forget Creusa: save Iulus and Anchises; save your people!' Tears filled his eyes. Three times he tried to take the phantom in his arms, to hug his dear, dead wife, and three times it fluttered through his fingers like a summer breeze. At last it disappeared, and he stumbled heartbroken back to his waiting companions. By now there was a vast gathering at Ceres' temple: the terrified old men, wailing women and children and exhausted fighting-men who were all that was left of Troy. They clutched the Palladium and the other holy statues, cradling them in their arms like babies. Aeneas bent to pick up his father,* took Iulus' hand and gave the order to move. The refugees picked their way along the shore, across the dunes and towards the mountains east of the city. By the time dawn crept over the hills they had left Troy far behind, and were slipping along quiet mountain-tracks like ghosts in the morning mists.†

4

THE · TROJANS
AT · SEA

Omens

For days the Trojans hid among the ridges and gullies of Mount Ida. They had no hope, no idea what the future might bring. Several of the older refugees died of exposure, for it was winter and the mountain was veiled in ice and fog. The survivors came down at last to the town of Antandros on the coast, well out of reach of Greeks. The town had been founded by Trojan settlers years before, and its king was amazed to hear that Priam's proud city had fallen. He gave Aeneas' followers shelter for the winter and all the materials they needed to build a fleet. The work took six months, but by early summer twenty ships stood at anchor in a bay below the town. The Trojans loaded provisions and water-jars, and the Antandrans lined the shore to watch them leave. Aeneas sacrificed to the gods of the sea and his people bent to the oars, setting out on a journey whose end they did not know.

Aeneas' plan was to sail north to Thrace, the lonely mountain kingdom of the Edonians. Its people had been ruled, years before, by the mad king Lycurgus,* and their reputation for human sacrifice had long kept visitors away. But at the beginning of the war they had declared themselves loyal to Troy, and Priam had so much trusted them that he sent them his youngest son, Polydorus, for safe-keeping while the fighting lasted. Aeneas planned now to sail to Thrace, beg land for settlement and rule it jointly with Polydorus, under Edonian protection. The need for such protection was clear as soon as the Trojan ships came on what the Greeks had left of Troy. With tears in their eyes the Trojans explored the plain. Everything had been destroyed. What would burn had been burned. The stones of the walls had been knocked to the ground and smashed. The fields had been ploughed up and sown with salt. The place was deserted, and the gods' curse hung over it like a poison-cloud; what had been the greatest city in the world was now a wilderness, tenanted only by the wind. Sadly the Trojans re-embarked and spread their sails to travel north.

The ships beached in Thrace, and the Trojans stepped out on a deserted shore. While his followers gathered wood for cooking-fires and set about building wind-breaks of piled stone, Aeneas went inland to sacrifice. He found a mound ideal for an altar, an earth-hummock surrounded by wild cherry-trees. On its flat top grew a myrtle-bush, a thicket of shoots stuck in the ground like spears. But as soon as Aeneas began tugging shoots out of the ground to make room for his altar-fire, the ground groaned, scarlet drops oozed out and soaked the soil, and bark stripped from the central stem like skin from a body. Needles of panic stabbed his face and neck. He fell on his knees and begged the gods to turn the omen from bad to good. Then he tried again to wrench the branches from the ground. This time the whole mound split open under him, and a voice cried 'Aeneas, let me lie in peace! My enemies spiked me here with spears; why must you, now, disturb my corpse?'

'Who are you?'

'Polydorus, sent to the Edonians for safety, and butchered by them to please the Greeks. Let me lie in peace!'

Aeneas ran for his most trusted companions: Achates, Ilioneus, Sergestus and the prophet Pantheus, priest of Apollo. They piled fresh earth over Polydorus' mound and sacrificed a lamb above it, cutting a trench for the blood so that the ghost could drink its fill. Then, when the blood had soaked away, Pantheus explained the omen. The Edonians had abandoned their loyalty to Troy, and their murder of Polydorus* proved it. If the Trojans stayed in Thrace overnight, they too were marked for death. They should set sail at once, and visit the holy island of Delos to ask Apollo's oracle for guidance. There was no time to lose: even as they spoke, the Edonians were planning a surprise attack.

Aeneas ran back to the beach, hustled his astonished followers on board ship and cut the mooring-ropes. The Trojans rowed till their hands were blistered. Soon there was nothing to be seen of Thrace but the smoke of their own cooking-fires, still blazing on the beach. A warm wind filled their sails, Neptune spread the sea flat before them, and with these signs of the gods' favour to gladden them they passed an uneventful four days' journey and came at last to Delos. This had once been a floating island, driven from sea to sea at the winds' whim.

But Neptune had anchored it long ago, snug between Mykonos and Rhenea, to be the birthplace of the god Apollo.* Now it was Apollo's main shrine on earth, and its ruler was the soothsayer-king Anius. The Trojans reached the island at evening, and at first kept their distance, not wanting to land in darkness in case the Delians took them for enemies.* But Anius rowed out in person to meet them. He invited them to a feast of welcome in his own palace, and next morning took Aeneas, Ilioneus and the others to consult the oracle. In front of a stone temple was a goats'-horn altar, the oldest object on the island. Apollo himself had built it, legend said, of horns from goats he and his sister Diana the hunting-goddess had killed on Mount Cynthus when he was only four years old. Blood-sacrifice was forbidden, but Aeneas and the others watched in the clear morning air as Anius sprinkled incense on the flames of the altar-fire, made offerings of corn and milk, and prayed to Dragon-Apollo to come down from Olympus and answer their prayers. Priests moved round the altar in a high-stepping, sacred dance, and when it was over Aeneas lifted his eyes to heaven and prayed, 'Lord Apollo, take pity on us. Grant us a resting-place, a home to call our own. We are Troy's last survivors – where are we to go?'

Before his prayer was finished, Apollo answered it. The leaves tossed on the sacred laurel-tree, the ground heaved and the temple shuddered as if a giant were shaking it. A dragon-roar bubbled from the heart of the shrine, till the Trojans covered their ears and cowered. For a moment silence fell, and then the air filled with whispers, eerie voices hissing and muttering in the stillness. Gradually, in the midst of it, the Trojans thought they heard Anius giving the god's answer in a clear, calm voice. 'Trojans, the gods hear you. You will end your wandering in the land where the ancestor of your race was born. You will build cities there, and your children's children, generation after generation, will rule the world.'

The sound died away. The air cleared; birds began to sing again. The god had passed. Eagerly the Trojans discussed the oracle. What had Apollo meant? What was the name of their new homeland, the place ordained for them to settle in? At last Anchises, Aeneas' aged father, suggested an answer. He told them that the Trojan race had been founded by Scamander,* a prince from the island of Crete where Jupiter himself was born. He said, furthermore, that news had reached Delos that Idomeneus, the Cretan king who had fought on the Greek side at Troy, had been driven out by his people,* and that the island was leaderless and ripe for settlement. Fired by this news, the Trojans launched their ships and sailed for Crete. They found the island leaderless, exactly as Anchises had said, and set about building a town. They laid out fields and farms, made friends with the local people and began to plan a peaceful life at last. But the information they trusted to was false. Anchises was mortal, with a mortal's feeble understanding, and his interpretation of Apollo's oracle was wrong. Two summers after the Trojans first set foot on Crete, the gods sent plague to blight the land. The trees dripped slime; dust swirled; the fields shimmered under a vicious sun, littered with the mouldering bodies of cattle and barren of all but graves. The surviving Trojans begged Aeneas to hurry back to Delos and ask Apollo's help before they, too, died of plague. That night, the gods sent Aeneas a final omen, a dream-vision to explain the oracle more clearly and to empty his mind of Crete. He was lying in a bedroom open to the night air and the sounds of the town below. Nocturnal animals mewed and chittered outside, and on the ceiling geckoes scuttled after their prey with tiny scrabblings in the darkness. There was bright moonlight, and a shaft of light flooded across the room. Aeneas tossed and turned uneasily, and in his sleep he thought he saw movement in the corner of the room. There was a shrine there, a wooden box built for the Palladium and the other gods of Troy, and he saw, or dreamed, that the gods' statues had left it and were floating in the moonlight across the room. They were hardly recognisable: their faces had been worn smooth by time and the handling of countless generations. But now in his dream lipless mouths appeared in their featureless faces, and they began to speak in hollow, feeble voices, as if they barely remembered how to make words at all. 'Aeneas,' they whispered, 'hear, and learn! Crete is not for you. Anchises misunderstood the oracle. You must sail west, to the country Greeks call the Evening Land. Where the sun sets we were born, in a land whose oldest inhabitants were your ancestors, the people not of Scamander but of Dardanus.* Latins rule it now; they call their district Latium and their country Italy. Forget Crete. Italy is to be your home; set sail for Italy!'

Monsters

It was one thing for the Trojans to know the name of their new home at last; reaching it was quite another. The journey meant weeks of

travelling through uncharted waters, either beating before unpredict-
able winds or rowing through flat calm under blistering sun. There
was no way of navigation except by the sun and stars; the ships were
too small to stay long at sea without landing for water, and every piece
of land, whether island or mainland, was inhabited by Greeks sworn
to blot out the Trojan race. As for the sea itself, there were grim
travellers' tales of the monsters who patrolled it: Scylla and Charybdis;
the Harpies; the Cyclopes who gorged on human flesh. As Aeneas
tried to plan the best course past all these dangers, Juno put into his
mind the idea of sailing not directly across open sea, but north along
the Greek coast as far as Epirus. From there the crossing to southern
Italy, the heel of the Trojans' new homeland, would be short and
swift. This was the plan she planted, and its purpose was the Trojans'
deaths. They were plague-weakened and dispirited; those who
survived starvation and the strain of rowing would be picked off by
Greeks or torn apart by monsters; none would reach Italy alive.

Of the twenty ships the Trojans had brought to Crete, less than a
dozen were still seaworthy. The others had been broken up for
ploughshares or roof-beams, or had been left to rot. Even so, the fleet
was ample for the Trojan survivors. Wearily they loaded their
belongings, and the few farm-animals not yet dead from plague; then
they sat down on the benches and bent thin arms to the oars. Juno
waited until they were well out to sea, in open water with no land
visible in any direction, and then poured black fog over them. The
daylight vanished; they could see nothing, and wallowed blindly in a
soundless, lifeless desert. They drifted for three days, but on the
fourth day the fog lifted as suddenly as it had fallen, and in the
distance they could see the beaches and hills of a pair of islands, with
fingers of smoke from cooking-fires. They fell to the oars and dragged
the fleet to land.

If the Trojans had known the islands' names, they would have
turned and fled at once. For Juno had brought them to the Strophades,
the Whirling Islands where the Harpies lived. The Harpies were
monstrous vultures with bronze talons and human faces, spewed from
the earth's gullet a million years before:* Aello, Ocypete and Celaeno.
Wherever they landed they smeared the earth with filth; their talons
were deadly to every living thing. They roosted out of sight while the
Trojans landed on a shelving beach with a grove of trees behind it.
Sheep and goats were feeding quietly in a meadow. There was no sign
of the inhabitants whose cooking-fires they had seen from the sea, no

indication that the animals were anything but wild, and the starving Trojans eagerly built fires and began slaughtering beasts for supper. That was when the Harpies appeared, screeching in fury and with their wings blanketing the sun. They swooped on the Trojans, scattering their fires and snatching the meat from the spits. They carried off all they could, tearing it as they flew, and covered the rest with slime. The Trojans built new fires, in the shelter of an overhanging rock, and the same thing happened: the Harpies swooped down and snatched or fouled the meat before they could be driven off. This time, while the women and children rebuilt the fires, Aeneas and his warriors hid spears in the grass, and as soon as the Harpies appeared Misenus, high on the cliff-top, blew a warning trumpet-blast. The men snatched their weapons and prepared to fight. But their spears splintered and their sword-blades buckled against the Harpies' bodies, and the bird-women flew off with angry cries, scattering lumps of meat and blood-soaked fleeces across the shore. One of the Harpies, Celaeno, perched on a needle of rock out of Trojan reach, and screeched at them, 'Fools! Will you murder us as well as our animals? Will you attack even creatures of the Underworld? Even if you reach Italy – for Apollo has decreed it, and no other god can prevent it – your punishments for hurting us are war, famine and disaster. You will find no peace!'

The Trojans ran to their ships and rowed for open sea as fast as their exhaustion would let them. They set course north, counting off the landmarks as they passed them: Zacynthus, Dulichium, Same, Neritus and the rocky shores of Ithaca, where the implacable Ulysses was king. They cursed each Greek stronghold as they passed it, and dared not land. If it had not been for fish caught over the side, and for their own farm animals slaughtered on board and eaten raw, starvation would have killed them all. It was not until they passed the steep headland of Leucate,* and saw sunlight-beams reflected from the white rocks like a beacon from the gods, that they felt it safe to land. They anchored in a quiet bay by a fishing-village, and they were so ragged and feeble that the people pitied them and left them in peace to bury their dead, restore their strength, patch up and restock their ships. Aeneas sacrificed, and the fleet set off with a following wind along the coast, between the mainland of Epirus and the long island of Corcyra, until they came to Buthrotum in Chaonia and beached their ships. The people of Buthrotum were Trojan settlers, and Aeneas' amazed followers recognised their king and queen as Helenus, Priam's son, and Andromache, Hector's wife, whom they had last heard of dragged out of Troy as slaves.* The settlers welcomed them with joy, and gave homes to as many as wanted to stay. But Aeneas, Ilioneus and many others were mindful of Apollo's oracle on Delos, and decided to continue their journey to Italy. They spent the winter in Buthrotum, and set sail at the first sign of spring, laden with gifts. The gods once again sent favourable winds, and the Trojans sailed easily across the narrow straits to Italy and along the heel and instep of their promised homeland. They passed Tarentum, Croton, Caulonia and Rhegium. These were all Greek towns, so that the Trojans sailed only by night, navigating by the stars, and hid in coves and bays by day.

Unknown to the Trojans, Juno had watched every moment, every oar-beat of their journey. She was leading them to the straits of Messina, the narrow funnel of sea between Italy and Sicily, the most dangerous place on earth. There were rock walls on each side, sheer as glass, and the sea raced like a cataract between them. The right-hand side was guarded, from a high cave, by Scylla,* a flesh-eating monster with a woman's body, a fish's tail and six snarling, shark-toothed heads. While the straits were empty she dozed in her lair, her heads whining and growling like dreaming hounds. But as soon as she heard the beat of oars or the flap of sails below, she leaned over the cliff-edge, snatched sailors from their boats as easily as fishermen flick their prey to land, and crunched their bones. The left-hand guardian was Charybdis. Her lair was underwater, and three times each day she opened her jaws and drank the sea, filtering out every living thing and spewing back empty water, dark with sand. There was no way of escape except steering arrow-straight through the channel, looking neither to right nor left, for the monsters had power to charm human beings as snakes charm rabbits, and to lure them to certain death. This was what Juno planned for the Trojans, and she guided their ships inexorably into the channel's jaws. Soon the Trojans could see nothing but towering rock, with a strip of sky overhead and white water underneath; they could hear nothing but the rumbling of Mount Etna in the distance, the Sicilian volcano which pins down the giant Enceladus,* and the hiss of water scything past solid stone. Palinurus, the most reliable man in Aeneas' crew, was steering the lead-boat, and the other Trojans stood by with oars and boathooks, keeping their eyes fixed on the pinhole of daylight at the channel's end. Three times Charybdis gulped the sea to the left of them, and it was all they could do not to gaze, fascinated, at the naked sand below, and be sucked into her lair and drowned. As it was, the ships veered each time towards the whirlpool, and they had to shake their minds free of Charybdis' spell and pole their way clear with oars. Each time, as they swung back to the centre of the channel, Scylla leaned out overhead and snatched at them, her jaws snapping on empty air. If the current had not been so fast, that journey would have been their last. As it was the sea vomited the entire fleet suddenly out of the channel's maw, and the ships floundered in open water, in a bay overshadowed by the bulk of Mount Etna. The sailors flung the mooring-stones overboard, splashed ashore and fell exhausted on the beach.

The night was dark, and the forest near the shore was hung with mist. Beyond it the land rose to a flattened peak, plumed with smoke. Every few minutes there was a rumble and flash of fire as Etna grumbled in its sleep. It was an eerie place, and the Trojans spent the night shivering in terror. As soon as it was dawn they hurtled on board ship and bent to the oars. They were well clear of the shore and were raising their sails when a gaunt figure appeared among the trees. It was a man. His hair straggled to his waist; his body was caked with filth and covered with torn rags pegged with thorns. The Trojans rowed inshore, and found the man crouched on his haunches on the beach, whimpering and pouring handfuls of sand over his head. 'Ships . . . ' he mumbled. 'Ships . . . sail home again . . . please take me home . . . ' Aeneas stepped ashore, and when the stranger saw Trojan clothes he started up, his nostrils wide with fear and his arm over his face as if to ward off a blow. It took food, soft words and the kind of stroking and handling people give a frightened animal to soothe him, and gradually the Trojans pieced his witless ramblings into a story which made them loosen their knives in their belts and stare at each other with fear-filled eyes. The man's name, he said, was Achaemenides. He was a Greek, one of Ulysses' men. After Troy's fall he had sailed with Ulysses in triumph. But storms had blown Ulysses' crew to Sicily, to this same shore, and to their horror they had found it the home of one-eyed, flesh-eating giants: the Cyclopes. Polyphemus, king of the Cyclopes, kept Ulysses' crew prisoners in a cave on Mount Etna, and every night and morning killed two of them for food, gulping down their flesh and spitting out the bones.* It was not till Ulysses blinded him with a sharpened pole that the Greeks were able to escape from the cave and sail away – and in their haste they had left him, Achaemenides, behind. For three months he had dragged out his life in terror, lurking in holes and hollow trees and only daring to come

51

out at night. For as well as blind, pain-maddened Polyphemus there were a hundred other Cyclopes, and each had sworn vengeance on the human race. The forest and volcano blocked escape by land; Achaemenides' only hope was to wait till ships put in to shore and beg their crews, whoever they were, to take him on board or kill him where he stood.

That was Achaemenides' story, and even before it was finished the Trojans saw Polyphemus himself on the hillside: a vast, blind giant with a flock of woolly sheep. They splashed to their ships, dragging Achaemenides with them, and rowed for deep water. Polyphemus came down to the shore, feeling his way with a pine-trunk, muttering and growling. He waded into deep water only a stone's throw from Aeneas' ship, and the sea barely reached his thighs. Grinding his teeth with pain, he began to bathe the festering socket where his eye had been. Aeneas gave a sign, and the Trojans leaned to their oars. They rowed as quietly as they could, hoping that Polyphemus would be too wrapped in agony to hear them. But he turned his face in their direction like a hound sniffing the air, then gave a shout which echoed round the bay and made Etna itself growl in answer. At once the whole tribe of Cyclopes began running from their lairs: it was as if a forest had grown legs. They danced and howled on the beach, while the ground shook and the sun hurled their shadows across the sea. The Trojans were too far out for them to reach, and hauled up their sails to make their escape till the masts bent like bows before the wind. In the nick of time they saw the rock-wall ahead of them, with its gorge like an arrow-head flecked with foam: the wind was driving them straight back towards Scylla and Charybdis. With great difficulty, straining at ropes and oars, they put about and tacked upwind along the coast, past the rocky estuary of the river Pantagia, the Bay of Megara and the Plain of Thapsus – Achaemenides gibbered the names as they passed, for they were retracing his and Ulysses' voyage along the Sicilian coast.

Storm

The Trojans had now survived enemy fury, starvation, plague, the offer of an enticing new homeland far from Italy, even the deadly monsters Juno put in their way. She had no power to kill them – Jupiter had forbidden the gods to take direct action on either side – and

52

though she could strew their path with dangers, she had to leave the Trojans to cope or not, each time, and dared not intervene. There was a moment, in Drepanum in Sicily, when events seemed to favour her. The Fates at last snipped the thread of life they had been spinning for Aeneas' father Anchises, and stretched him dead on the shore at the Trojans' feet. But not even this turned Aeneas from his destiny. He buried Anchises' body, heaped a mound of sand above it and vowed to hold funeral games in his honour, and to sacrifice to the gods of the Underworld, as soon as the Trojans reached safe anchorage at last. Then, with tears in his eyes, he gave the order to sail.

Juno watched in fury as breezes began carrying the Trojan fleet across open sea towards Italy. Then, swooping like a seabird, she flew to Lipara, home of the windlord Aeolus. Here, imprisoned in a vast underground cavern, all the world's stormwinds seethed and billowed. King Aeolus sat on a high, bright throne, while all about him his subjects roared round the windowless walls, looking for a crevice, a crack, a pinhole that would lead them through solid rock to freedom. This was their punishment, long ago, for piracy.* Jupiter pinned them underground, piled ton after ton of rock above them to keep them in place and set grim Aeolus over them, to check their fury till the moment came to release them briefly into the world outside, then funnel them back again and pen them when their work was done. To Aeolus Juno now said, 'Help me, my lord! A Trojan fleet is sailing from Sicily, carrying their accursed country's gods. Savage them! Sink the ships; drown the crews, and I will send Deiopeia, the prettiest of all my nymphs, to sleep with you.'

'Lady,' answered Aeolus, 'you have only to state your wishes, and they are obeyed. I owe everything I have to Jupiter: my power, my immortality, my favour with the gods. What you ask is done.' He took his sceptre and struck the cavern wall. The solid rock split apart, and the winds shouldered their way through the gap and burst out exultantly across the earth. East, North and West joined hands, sending storm-clouds billowing and stacking the sea like hills. Screams and howling filled the sky, and a black cloud engulfed the Trojans. There was no way of telling where the storm-clouds ended and the swollen sea began. Gales bowed the masts; rain fell like iron; death loomed.

Aeneas fell on his knees to pray. But the gods were deaf. The North Wind hurled his ship full in the path of a frowning wave. The mast snapped; the steering-oar splintered; the ship wallowed beam-ends on. On one side the terrified sailors saw a wall of water advancing to crush them; on the other was a precipice, a chasm gaping to sand and black rocks below. The South Wind spun three ships round and sacrificed them on the jagged rocks known ever afterwards as 'the altars'; the East Wind grounded three others in quicksand, buried their crews in tons of choking sand while the men's companions watched in horror. A huge wave crashed snarling on Orontes' ship. The helmsman screamed as the water tossed him overboard, and the sea's jaws gaped and swallowed ship and crew together. The heads of swimming men bobbed briefly among the wreckage, but soon men, spars and cargo vanished in the heaving sea. Ilioneus, Achates, Abas and Aletes all had their ships sunk under them. The storm howled, the ships' seams gaped and water poured in to swallow them.

Far below, in calm water on the ocean floor, Neptune, king of the sea, was sitting in peaceful majesty. Long ago, when three brothers divided the universe between them, Jupiter took the sky to rule, and Pluto the Underworld; Neptune chose the vast, cold empire of the sea. Now, as he sat in his sunken palace, he felt the storm's commotion far overhead, and a litter of debris and corpses floated down even as far as his quiet throne-room. Swiftly he climbed to the surface, and with one glance took in the storm, the splintered ships, the waves and the swollen sky. As soon as he recognised the Trojans, victims of Juno's savagery, he understood the whole plan. He called the East and West Winds to him – they had no choice but to obey – and said, 'Who told you to disturb my kingdom? Who said you could rouse my waves, stir up my storms? Go to Aeolus; remind him that I rule the sea, not he. In his tunnels and caverns he can do as he likes, but on the open sea I control the storms.' So saying, with the speed of thought itself he silenced the storm, untangled the clouds and released the sun. His sea-nymphs and Tritons began levering wreckage from the rocks, and Neptune prised the sand apart with his royal trident; then he skimmed above the waves in his chariot, and soothed the sea. Sometimes, in the midst of a rioting crowd, when anger has improvised weapons from stones and blazing torches, the fighting suddenly stops and all people's eyes are fixed on one man, some dignified speaker who calms their anger and ends their snarls. So the sea hushed now, in deference to its king; he turned his horses and drove his chariot smoothly above the waves until all was calm.

5
THE · GODS · TAKE ACTION

Carthage

Dazed and exhausted, Aeneas' crew rowed for the nearest land, and beached in an inlet protected from the sea by an arm of rock and a sunken reef. On one side a cliff reared to the sky, and while Aeneas' companions built driftwood fires and rummaged through the food-sacks to see if anything was still dry enough to eat, he climbed to the summit and gazed out to sea, looking for survivors. There were neither ships, wreckage nor men: the sea rolled bare to the horizon. Sadly he climbed down the cliff and turned inland. There was a herd of deer grazing among the thorn-bushes, led by a magnificent, royal-antlered stag. Aeneas crept close, downwind, set arrow to bow and fired. The shot laid the king-stag low, and Aeneas divided the meat and called to his crew to fetch it to the shore. They opened wine from the royal store, and spent the long night feasting, forgetting for a time their lost friends, their exhaustion and the dangers both past and still to come.

As soon as it was dawn, Aeneas left his sleeping followers and set off to explore. He was anxious to know if the country was inhabited or merely the home of wild beasts (for there were no signs of cultivation), and whether they should stay where the winds had carried them or risk open sea again. Accompanied by Achates, he left the shore and plunged into the scrubland beyond the dunes. As they picked their way along a dry river-gully shaded by palm and thorn, Aeneas' mother Venus suddenly appeared before them. She had disguised herself – for no mortal can see a god face to face and live – and wore the clothes and carried the bow and quiver of a hunting-girl. But Aeneas recognised her easily. He fell on his knees and said, 'Lady, help us! Tell us where we are; protect us; let us honour you as a god deserves.'

55

Venus giggled, exactly like an embarrassed girl, and said in a shy mortal voice, 'This is Libya, my lord. We are Carthaginians, exiles from Tyre* in Phoenicia. Queen Dido brought us here, and Iarbas sold us land to settle on. Follow this path to Carthage; Dido will welcome you.'

As she spoke, she disappeared like smoke on a summer breeze, and Aeneas cried bitterly after her, 'Why do you always play games with me? Why do you always wear disguise? Am I never to see my own mother face to face? Am I never to embrace you, never to hear you speak in your own dear voice?' But there was no answer, and sadly he stood up and set off with Achates along the path. As they walked Venus sent a mist-cloud to shroud them, to make them invisible until it was time to reveal themselves. Then she flew to Paphus, her favourite place in all the world, where she sings and dances with her worshippers, and the air swoons with the scent of flowers.

Aeneas and Achates continued on their way. They walked all day, and saw no one. Then, at evening, when the sun was low in the sky, they came to the top of a hill and caught their breath in astonishment. Below them, as unexpected in the desert as if some god had conjured it from empty sand, stood a magnificent city. Its walls gleamed yellow in the sunset; they were built from sun-baked bricks, with wooden gates and a paved road leading out across the desert. In the centre was a temple. Incense-smoke rose from the sanctuary and gold inlay glinted on the walls. In front of the temple a crowd of people stood facing a throne on which sat a woman in white, flowing robes, with a crown of golden oak-leaves. She was talking quietly, and the people hung on her words as if she were a god. After a moment guards led a group of men and women from the city gates towards her, and Achates gripped Aeneas' arm in astonishment. The people were Trojans: Antheus, Sergestus, Cloanthus and all the others the sea had snatched. Aeneas longed to run forward, to embrace his companions and hear their adventures. But the gods held him back, and he waited, hidden in the mist-cloud with Achates, to hear what they had to say. Their leader, Ilioneus, stepped forward and bowed to the queen. 'Lady,' he said, 'the gods have favoured you. They have given you a city, a home and a people to call your own. Help us! We are Trojans; we were shipwrecked as we sailed to Italy. Our leader was Aeneas, respected by gods and mortals alike. Let us anchor and repair our ships; see us safely on our way.'

Queen Dido answered, 'Trojans, we are exiles too: you have

nothing to fear. While you repair your ships, I shall send search-parties to find Aeneas. He may be sheltering further along the coast, or he and his crew may be lost in the desert, wandering among the dunes.'

As if these words were a signal, Venus lifted the mist-cloud from Aeneas' and Achates' shoulders, and the crowd gaped. Aeneas stepped forward, handsome as a god, and said, 'Dido, send out no search-parties. I am Aeneas, safe from the sea. You have pitied us; you have offered us shelter, and wherever we go, while rivers still run to the sea, while shadows darken the mountains and the sky still feeds the stars, your praise will be always on our lips.'

With these words he ran to greet his companions, Cloanthus, Gyas, Ilioneus, Sergestus and the others. Dido sent servants to fetch Aeneas' followers from the ship, while others set up tables in the palace courtyard and began slaughtering beasts for a banquet: twenty bulls, a hundred ewes, a hundred lambs and a hundred bristly hogs.

High in Olympus, Venus' heart soared to see her son's good fortune. But she was still not satisfied. She was afraid that Juno might even now turn Dido against the Trojans, that the Carthaginians' welcome might be no more than the prelude to a massacre. There was only one answer. She must fill Dido with a passion for the Trojans so powerful that no influence, mortal or immortal, could ever turn it to hate. She called to her son Cupid, whose love-magic no mortal can withstand, and said, 'Fly down to earth, to Aeneas' ship on the Libyan shore. Aeneas has sent Achates to fetch presents for Dido – bracelets, rings, jewels, the kind of pretty things mortals delight in. Disguise yourself as Iulus, Aeneas' son, and give Dido the presents yourself. Let her kiss you and embrace you – and set her heart on fire for Troy.'

Laughing with glee, Cupid took the golden wings from his shoulders and began marching round the room in imitation of Iulus' childish walk. Meanwhile Venus took Iulus himself in her immortal arms, poured sleep over him and laid him gently on the peak of Mount Idalus, far from mortal sight, on a bed of lilies and yellow primroses. Cupid joined Achates' party in his place, looking exactly like Iulus and carrying Dido's gifts. When they came to the palace Dido, Aeneas and the other leaders had taken their seats on purple cushions and the banquet was beginning. Servants brought water for them to wash their hands, soft napkins and wicker baskets full of bread. There were lords and ladies from all over Carthage, and when Achates' party entered they gasped at the royal gifts, and most of all at Iulus, whose flushed face and piping voice the god mimicked to perfection. At the sight of the gold and jewels Dido was filled with longing, and when she saw Aeneas' son her heart turned to water, and love for the Trojans swept every other thought from her mind. Cupid hugged Aeneas, making everyone smile to see his love for his supposed father; then he ran to kiss the queen. It was as if Dido were drunk with him. She hugged him as if he were her own dear son; gradually even the memory of her Phoenician husband Sichaeus, so cruelly murdered by her own brother, began to fade, and her mind burned with the fire of a new and utterly unlooked-for love.

Dido and Aeneas

As soon as Juno saw Dido's growing passion, she began plotting to make use of it. Carthage was under Juno's protection. If she could only make Aeneas marry Dido, make him Prince Consort where she was Queen, the Trojans would give up all thought of Italy, stay forever in Carthage and make it the most powerful city in Africa, the hub of the mortal world. She sent for Venus and said, with a show of anger, 'Why stop now, you and that boy of yours? Why leave the job half done? Help me! Tomorrow Dido and Aeneas have planned to go hunting, as soon as the sun is up. Before the day is done, I shall pour a rainstorm over them, and scatter their servants. When the rain begins, you lead Dido and Aeneas to the same cave for shelter, and I shall throw them into each other's arms.'

Next morning, as soon as dawn streaked the sky, the Carthaginian and Trojan lords began assembling in front of the palace, their horses stamping and snorting in the crisp morning air. Servants carried hunting-nets and broad boar-spears; dogs whined and strained at their leads; Dido's charger pawed the ground. At last Dido came out in a hunting-dress of purple and gold. Aeneas went to join her, handsome as Apollo when he leads the dance on the hills of Delos, and together they led the party out for the hunt, up to the thickets of the coastal hills. They disturbed a flock of mountain goats, and sent them leaping from rock to rock ahead of them. Further down deer fled as they advanced, down to the grasslands where young Iulus (now safely back from Idalus, and restored to the palace in Cupid's place) was longing for a boar to charge, snorting with rage, or a lion to snarl from the shadows and challenge him.

But soon a low rumbling filled the sky. Clouds gathered; rain and hail began. As the storm increased, and streams began rolling like torrents from the hills, the Trojans and Carthaginians scattered. Venus sent Dido and Aeneas to the same cave for shelter, and Juno hurled them into one another's arms. Torches flared as if for a marriage-ceremony, the sky shook, and high in the mountains nymphs began to sing.

So Juno's plan for Carthage began – and in the weeks that followed Rumour, deadliest of goddesses, darted through every town in Libya, telling her story. Rumour was Mother Earth's child, a monster. She throve on movement: however small she began she soon grew so huge that she could walk on the ground and veil her head in cloud. Every feather on her body hid an eye, an ear and a babbling tongue. Her delight was to perch on roofs or city towers and screech bad news for all to hear. Now she ran joyfully from town to town, spreading her story. Dido and Aeneas were sleeping together. They had forgotten their people and their destiny; all they cared about was lust. Rumour carried this tale all over Libya, and whispered it at last to King Iarbas, who had planned to marry Dido himself and unite their kingdoms.

There were one hundred stone temples of Jupiter in Libya, and Iarbas ordered sacrifices at every one of them. He stood with upraised arms and prayed, 'Lord, accept our offerings, answer our prayers. Dido begged land from me to build a city on; now she rejects me for a beggar, a Trojan princeling. Punish her!'

As soon as Jupiter heard these words he sent for Mercury, the gods' winged messenger. 'Go to Carthage,' he said. 'Tell Aeneas that this was not why the gods twice saved his life in the Trojan war.* This was not his destiny. He is to conquer Italy, re-establish the Trojan race and rule the world. Tell him to leave Carthage; tell him to sail at once.'

Mercury fastened on the winged sandals which carry him soaring over land and sea, and glided down through the swelling clouds. Soon, as he flew, he could see the head and shoulders of the giant Atlas, who supports the sky.* A pine-forest cloaks Atlas' head and shoulders. Rainstorms lash him; rivers run ceaselessly from his age-old chin; ice crackles in his beard. Mercury hovered briefly beside him, then plunged on along the shore, swooping like a cormorant above the shallows where the quiet fish doze. When he reached the reed-huts of Libya and came to Carthage, he found Aeneas supervising workmen on the walls. 'Fool!' said Mercury. 'Why are you wasting time on someone else's city? Forget Carthage: Rome and the whole world are your inheritance!'

So saying he vanished, leaving his words burning in Aeneas' mind. Aeneas called to Mnestheus, his second-in-command, and told him to gather the Trojans and load the ships. Meanwhile, he said, he would go to Dido and break the news. Mnestheus hurried away; preparations began. But who can deceive a lover? Rumour whispered to Dido that the Trojans were loading their ships and planning to sail away. She raged through the palace, wild as a Bacchant, and screamed at Aeneas, 'Traitor! Did you really think you could sneak away? Does our love, our marriage, mean nothing to you? Because of you, every tribe in Libya has turned against me; my own Tyrians detest me. Who will protect me when you are gone? Must I wait for my brother Pygmalion to sack Carthage, or for Iarbas to snatch me into slavery? I shall have nothing, not even a baby Aeneas playing in the sun, to remind me of his father and ease my misery.'

Aeneas longed to comfort her. But the gods hardened his heart, and the answer he gave was theirs, not his. 'I never planned to sneak away,' he said, 'and I never pretended that what we did was marriage. If the Fates had let me live my life as I chose, Troy would have been my first thought. I would have rebuilt Priam's city, honoured the heroes who died for it, and made it a power in the world again. But the gods are calling me to rule Italy. There my heart must be, there must be my native land. Today Mercury came to me himself, the winged messenger. Like it or not, I must sail for Italy.'

The gods blocked all argument. Dido's raging and pleading had no more power to change Aeneas' mind than stormwinds fighting to uproot an oak. In the end he left her sobbing in her servants' arms and hurried to the harbour. The Trojans had freshly tarred the keels of their ships and were now refloating them, along the whole length of the beach. They were so eager to sail that they were cutting oars from branches with the leaves still on them, unseasoned timber straight from the forest. They bustled out of the city, purposeful as ants plundering a grain-heap. A black column threads across the plain, carrying the spoils. Some heave against corn-grains bigger than themselves; others drive the column along and gather the stragglers; the whole path seethes. That was how the Trojans looked to Dido, as she gazed out from her watchtower high in the citadel. Hiding what she planned under a mask of smiles, she said to her sister, 'Anna, congratulate me! I know a way to be rid of his love forever. In Ethiopia once, where Atlas supports the sky, I found a priestess whose magic can fill mortal minds with suffering or set them free. She can help me now. Build a pyre in the courtyard, and heap on it all the armour he left behind, his presents, and the marriage-bed that broke my heart. If nothing is left to remind me of him, the priestess says, I may blot him from my heart at last.'

So she spoke, and Anna (who thought this sorrow no greater than when Dido's first husband, Sichaeus, died) gave orders for a pyre of pine and oak in the palace yard. Dido herself garlanded it with cypress-leaves, while servants set altars in a circle and the witch-priestess assembled the foul ingredients of her ritual: water she claimed was from the river Styx, herbs sappy with poison, the afterbirth of a newborn foal. While the witch gathered these offerings on the altars, her hair straggling and her lips mumbling spells, Dido prayed to the gods who protect lovers whose love is not returned.

It was night. All over the world tired bodies were relaxed in sleep. The woods and waters were at rest; the stars were gliding in their middle courses; the fields were silent; cattle and the birds that swoop over sullen lakes or roost in desert thorn-bushes slept, their cares forgotten and their labours laid aside. Aeneas, too, with everything now ready and departure fixed for dawn, was dozing on the high stern of his ship, beside the steering-oar. Suddenly Mercury appeared again, and cried, 'How can you sleep, Aeneas? The wind has changed, the gods are calling you to sea! Madness is ebbing and flowing in Dido's heart. Set sail at once!' Aeneas snatched himself awake and shouted to his companions to take to the oars. Then, with a prayer for safety in his heart, he cut the mooring-ropes. The oarsmen whipped the waves to foam, burying their blades in the water, and the fleet set sail.

By now day was breaking. Dido, standing on her watchtower, saw the shore deserted and the ships hull-down on the horizon, and cried to the gods, 'Is he to laugh and leave unpunished? I could have torn him to pieces and scattered him on the sea. I could have killed his followers and butchered Iulus to make his own father's feast. I could have set fire to their fleet, and when I had destroyed father, son and the whole crew of them, I could have stabbed myself dead on top of them. O sun, moon, stars; O Juno, Hecate, avenging Furies and the gods of death, if Jupiter decrees that that criminal must reach safe anchorage, let that be all! Butcher his people before his eyes. Make him a beggar, torn from Iulus' side and weeping for his son. Kill him before his time, and leave him to rot on some barren beach! And may my dead ashes give birth one day to an avenger, a Carthaginian hero who will beat this Trojan' descendants to their knees and teach them the punishment for oath-breaking. This is my dying curse on Aeneas, his children and his children's children: war!'*

Now she began looking for the quickest way to end the life she hated. She ran to the courtyard, set the pyre ablaze, climbed it with a madwoman's speed and seized Aeneas' forgotten sword. Her terrified maids saw her fall forward on the blade and blood well out over the wound, hissing in the flames. Wailing rose to the palace roof, and Rumour ran gleeful errands through the streets. The noise of lament reached Anna, and she ran past the servants and screamed at her dying sister, 'So this was what you were planning! This was the reason for the pyre and the holy altars! Why did you not let me share your death? Am I not even to wash your wounds and catch your dying breath, your last gift to your unhappy sister?'

So she spoke, and it took all the servants' strength to stop her climbing the pyre and dying with her sister in her arms. Three times Dido tried to lift herself; the wound in her breast gasped each time as the air was forced from it, and she fell back helpless. At last Juno sent Iris from Olympus to end her suffering. Like a dragonfly, dew-winged in the sun, Iris hovered by Dido's head. 'In obedience to Juno I now end your life; I send you to the gods below and free you from your torment.' So saying, she cut a lock of Dido's hair, and at the same moment the Fates snipped the thread of Dido's life. Warmth left the body of the unhappy queen, and her spirit slipped away on the sighing of the wind.

Sicily

By now the Trojans were well out to sea. The fleet slid easily through waves whipped up by a southerly breeze, and as Aeneas looked back he could see nothing of Carthage but the glow of Dido's funeral pyre. He had no idea what could have caused the flames; but he feared the worst. Even so, the gods kept him on course, allowed no turning back. The land receded till nothing could be seen but sea and sky. And soon rain-clouds darkened overhead; a storm blew up and waves began roaring for the death of Aeneas' ships. All the Trojans could do was run before the storm – and once again Juno held them back from Italy and turned them instead to Sicily. They landed in the district ruled by Acestes,* on the lonely beach at the feet of Mount Eryx where they had buried Aeneas' father Anchises a year before. Aeneas gathered his followers round Anchises' funeral mound and said, 'Trojans, if I'd been lost in the deserts of Libya, or been a beggar or a slave in Greece, I'd have remembered the day of Anchises' death, and spent it in prayers and mourning. As it is, the gods have brought us to his own graveside, and we can honour him with royal funeral Games. There will be a ship-race, a foot-race and contests of boxing, archery and javelin-throwing. Garland your heads; begin the sacrifice.'

The priests made offerings to Anchises' spirit: bowls of unmixed wine, fresh milk and blood. A pair of sheep were slaughtered, with two bristly hogs and two black bulls, and Aeneas' followers built fires along the beach and began roasting meat on spits. For eight days they feasted and made offerings to the gods of the Underworld, and at dawn on the ninth day the shore began to fill with visitors, drawn to watch the Games or to take part in them. There were palm-branches and laurel-crowns for the winners, and prizes were laid on the sand beside them: gold tripods, embroidered robes, swords with jewelled hilts and inlaid blades, the pick of the treasure which had enriched generations of the kings of Troy.

Misenus sounded his trumpet and the Games began. The first event was a sea-race, for the four fastest ships in the fleet, round a rock far out at sea, a favourite perch for seagulls, and back to shore. There followed a foot-race, the runners clustering close as swarming bees, a boxing-match, and contests of wrestling, javelin-throwing and archery.* When the men's Games were done, it was time for the boys to show their skill. They formed three columns on horseback, under Iulus' command. Each boy's head was garlanded; each boy carried two cornel-wood spears with iron tips; each wore a deerskin quiver and an armlet of twisted gold. The leader of the first column was Priam, Polites' son, named after his royal grandfather; Atys led the second column, and Iulus himself led the third, on a Carthaginian pony from Dido's royal stables. The three columns rode at each other in a pretend charge. They wove and interwove in mock battle, making patterns as intricate as dance-steps, and finally lifted their spears in the air and rode in a single line while their parents' cheers echoed round the bay.*

In this way, by contests and displays, the Trojans honoured Aeneas' royal father in Sicily. And while all their attention was on the Games, Juno sent Iris to a group of discontented old women beside the ships. Glittering in her comet-tail of a thousand colours, the rainbow-goddess swooped to land and disguised herself as Beroe, the oldest and sharpest-tongued of all Aeneas' followers. 'Is there to be no end to it?' she grumbled. 'Must we drag ourselves through every sea and struggle over every land on earth? Each time we reach out to Italy, it slips away. Now we've come to a safe place at last, ruled by our own kinsman Acestes. Why can't we settle here? Look at the ships, standing in line like altars. All they need is fire!' She snatched a burning branch and hurled it into the nearest ship. The Trojan women looked at each other with horrified eyes. They were torn between their longing to stay on dry land and their terror at what they had to do. Iris settled their doubts for them. Casting off the disguise of Beroe, she spread glittering wings and soared above their heads, trailing her rainbow-tail across the sky. Frenzy seized the Trojan women. They began snatching branches from the altar-fires and hurling them into the ships. Flames licked along the rowing-benches, the hulls, the oars, the masts. By the time Aeneas and the others ran to put out the fire, even the caulking between the timbers was smouldering, pouring out black fumes. Nothing the men could do, not even the rivers of water they poured over the ships, would douse the flames.

Aeneas tore his clothes, lifted his hands to the sky and cried, 'Almighty Jupiter, have you no pity at all for us? Must every Trojan be blotted from the world? I beg you, put out these flames, or send a thunderbolt and destroy me beside my ships.'

At once the sky turned black. Grass, trees and rocks shuddered as thunder crashed overhead. Rain curtained the beach. The water danced on the ship's hulls, seeking out every tongue of fire; black smoke plumed in the sodden air. Then the sky cleared as suddenly as it had darkened. Light returned, not bright sunlight but an unnatural glow like reflected torchlight, and in it Aeneas saw a vision of his father. Anchises' ghost hovered above the funeral-mound and said, 'Aeneas, Jupiter has answered your prayers. Repair your ships; leave everyone who wants to stay in Sicily, and sail with the others to Italy. You will have wars to fight and proud peoples to conquer before you can settle there in peace. But first you must go down to the Underworld, to the Fields of the Blessed, and hear your people's destiny. Take the holy priestess as your guide, the Sibyl of Cumae; sacrifice black cattle for a safe return.'

Even as the ghost spoke, it merged with the wind and vanished. Aeneas wasted no time. He divided his companions into those who preferred quiet lives in Sicily and those who chose glory with him in Italy. The settlers began measuring out fields and homes on the slopes of Mount Eryx, and the others set about repairing the ships, replacing charred timbers, recaulking seams and cutting new oars – a small band, but hungry for conquest. As soon as the ships were ready, Aeneas took his place in the bows, an olive-crown round his temples, and made offerings to the spirits of the sea. Jupiter gathered the fleet in his immortal hand and sent it skimming over the sea to Italy.

6

THE · UNDERWORLD

The Sibyl of Cumae

The Trojans sailed on the wind's wings to Cumae in Italy. They leapt to land, dragged the ships up the beach and moored them. Hunting-parties began quartering the woods for game, while others fetched firewood and kindled cooking-fires. Shouts and laughter rang in the still air: they had reached Italy at last, and were eager to explore their destiny.

Aeneas, who had darker matters on his mind, went with Achates through the forest up the hill, along a gully choked with bracken and damp with mist. He had no idea what he was looking for or where to find it. But the gods led his steps to a cleft high above the tree-line, a wedge-shaped chasm as if some giant had ripped the rock apart bare-handed. Inside was a dark, dank cavern. There was no sound but the drip of water from the roof; Aeneas and Achates were surrounded by watchful stillness, as if the mountain were a living thing, listening, holding its breath to see what they would do. Centuries before, when Daedalus built wings and escaped from Crete,* Apollo guided him to this empty place, and in gratitude for safe landing Daedalus made a shrine of it, carving the story of his adventures along the walls. Aeneas and Achates read the stone with their finger-tips, tracing the outlines deeper and deeper into the darkness. Then, without warning, the rock sloped down underfoot, and they slithered off-balance and ended on their backs in a pool of icy water, bruised and terrified.

For a moment, as they lay there, they were surrounded by the skitter of stones dislodged in their fall. Then there were echoes, rolling to the roof-vault high above. Then the stillness returned – and in it a voice began, a relentless whisper that billowed and grew till it beat on their ears like waves against the shore. 'Aeneas! This place is Apollo's shrine. There are a hundred entrances, a hundred mouths. Speak! Ask your questions, and open them!'

Aeneas' throat was so dry that he could make no sound. But he opened his heart to the god and prayed in thoughts, not words. 'Apollo, you saw our suffering at Troy. You saw our wanderings; you saw us fight sea-monsters, plague and fire. You saw our loved ones snatched from us one by one, as we reached out for Italy. Now we have set foot at last on the land the gods promised us. What more is there? Have we reached the end, or must there be still more suffering?'

At first, as before, there was silence. Then, from an enormous distance in the rock below them, they heard a gathering sigh, quiet as corpse-breath. It moved gradually up towards them, and as it moved it multiplied, till the cavern was filled with the roaring and buffeting of a furious windstorm, hurricanes and tornadoes howling round the Trojans' ears. Aeneas and Achates scrabbled for handholds on the floor to save themselves from being sucked up and hurled against the walls. But for all the racket round them, there was no movement. The storm was in their minds; the air was as still as on a breezeless summer day. They huddled on the floor, and as the gale roared round them they heard the same voice as before, this time not whispering but shouting in ecstasy. 'Earth's mouths are open! Apollo speaks! Trojans, you will fight a second war. A second Achilles will plunder you. Juno's whip will bite. I see the Tiber red with blood. War! Death! Only Greeks will save you now!'

The words rolled round the cave, echoing and re-echoing till it was as if a hundred mouths were screaming 'War!' Aeneas and Achates hurled themselves up the slope and out of the cave like animals racing from a flood. They blundered against the walls; they tripped and slid; they tore their fingers raw scrabbling for Daedalus' age-old carvings. At last they were in the open air, and found to their astonishment that it was pitch-dark outside. What had seemed minutes in the cave had lasted hours: it was midnight, and the air was heavy with dew. They turned to hurry down the hill, and almost tripped over an old woman waiting in the entrance. She crouched like a toad in front of them, her hair blowing in the wind and her clothes tossing like autumn leaves. She put her fingers to her lips, spreading her hand like the points of a star, and spoke in the same whispering, cackling voice they had heard inside the cave. 'Aeneas! I am Deiphobe,* Sibyl of Cumae. Ask, and I shall answer.'

'Lady,' said Aeneas, in a low voice as if he were afraid that the god

67

in the cave was listening, 'one request only. They say that this is the gateway to the Underworld, a bottomless lake filled by the river Acheron. The gods have called me here, to visit my father Anchises in the Elysian Fields and hear my people's destiny. Help me, lady. Show me the way.'

The Sibyl answered, 'Aeneas, the path to the Underworld is easy; the doors of Hell gape open day and night. If for Anchises' sake you will pass the pools of Cocytus, cross the swollen Styx and gaze into the jaws of Hell, this is what you must do. Deep in the valley, in the Grove of Hecate, goddess of shadows, grows a branch with twigs and leaves of gold. Proserpina, queen of hell,* has decreed that without it no one may descend to her silent kingdom. Find it! If your fate is to make the journey, the branch will break off easily; if not, it will blunt the sharpest sword. Fetch it if you can!'

Aeneas loosened his sword in its sheath, and looked quickly at Achates. When he turned back the Sibyl had vanished as if she had never been; he and Achates were alone on the mountainside. Aeneas knew that Achates could never follow him to the Underworld, a journey allowed only to gods' or goddesses' sons. He told him to go back to the beach and reassure the others.* Aeneas himself stood where he was, wondering which way to turn in the darkness, where on the mountain the Grove of the Golden Branch might lie. As he stood there, a pair of white doves flew down and settled at his feet. They were messengers from his mother Venus, and his heart soared to see them. They fluttered into the air and flew ahead of him, staying easily in sight, down the hill into the thick woodland, through dripping undergrowth to the banks of a sulphurous, stagnant pool. There they flew up and perched on an oak-bough, a branch of yellow gold glinting through dark green leaves. Like mistletoe, which bubbles into berries in the depths of winter, crowning its host-tree, so the golden branch glowed in the darkness, and its leaves tinkled in the breeze. Aeneas broke it off and carried it triumphantly back up the hill, where the Sibyl was waiting beside her cave.

The path to Hell

The Sibyl led Aeneas into the cave, past Daedalus' wall-carvings and down the slope to the hall of the hundred mouths. The golden branch glowed like a torch to light their steps, but even its god-sent rays were too feeble to penetrate far into the gloom. There was no sound now, and no sense of the god's presence: the cave was as damp as a grave, as still as death. They came to the shore of an immense, dark lake, and the stench of death hung over it. Huddled in wickerwork pens beside it was a handful of animals: black lambs, hogs and a bull with unblemished, soot-black hide. The Sibyl kept them stabled there, ready for sacrifice, and they gazed at her with white, wide eyes, too terrified even to rear or low. Aeneas held the golden branch to light her as she cut the animals' throats, muttering spells, and gathered their blood in bowls. He shuddered, and prayed in his heart to the gods of the Underworld to grant him safe journey and safe return.

The Sibyl lit fires, which smoked and sputtered in the rancid air, and piled meat from the carcases on top for offering. Then, shrieking to Aeneas to keep step with her, she scuttled into the darkness beyond the shore. They walked all night, picking their way across a boulder-strewn plain while their footsteps echoed from the shadows on every side. They heard no other sound, and saw nothing but the pebbles underfoot and occasional gaunt ruins looming as they passed, the bones of palaces. They were like travellers in a forest at night, when clouds muffle the moon and the darkness makes every shadow seem more solid than life itself. At last they came to a wall of rock, and the Sibyl spread herself flat against it and began shuffling sideways like a spider, beckoning Aeneas to do the same. As he moved after her, clutching for handholds in the blank rock face, he suddenly sensed no more solid ground behind him but a chasm, a hole gaping to unfathomed depths. He was edging along a shelf narrower than his own feet, with his toes stubbing rock in front and his heels overhanging space behind; his muscles bunched with cramp and foul air rasped his lungs; he could hear nothing but his own tortured breathing and the Sibyl's gasps as she inched ahead of him. Then, without warning, the wall vanished and he fell forward into a cleft in the rock, a gash like an enormous, gaping mouth. By the dim light of the golden branch he saw the Sibyl scuttling ahead into the darkness, and he picked himself up and hurried after her.

Now they were entering the very jaws of Hell, the threshold of the Underworld. Light glowed and grew – a feeble phosphorescence, mirroring true daylight as sickness mirrors health, decay mirrors growth – and in it Aeneas thought he saw shapes stirring in the shadows: Old Age, Poverty, Disease, Sleep the sister of Death, and the evil Lusts that torment the mind. On the other side the Furies slept in rock-crevices, with War and Argument beside them, their viper-hair hissing and writhing as they dozed. Centaurs whinnied in iron-bound stables; the Harpies roosted; Aegeon tossed in his rocky cell, his hundred arms lolling like monstrous spider's legs. In the centre was an aged elm-tree, its branches rearing overhead, and under each leaf hung a caterpillar Dream.

Aeneas shook with horror, sudden and uncontrollable as nausea. If the Sibyl had not passed her hand through the monsters and showed him that they were spirits, insubstantial as thought, he would have drawn his sword and hacked them where they lay, made war on emptiness. The monsters stirred and whined, and the Sibyl beckoned him on while it was still safe to pass. They walked down a track that broadened at last into a marshy plain. On one side, where the floor fell away to Tartarus far below, a river bubbled up in whirlpools and cataracts, spewing mud from the depths and spreading in coils and pools across the plain. Ahead of them, where the current was sluggish and the water flowed wide and deep, an aged ferryman was mooring a leaky boat. His clothes were rags, his hair was matted and his cloak hung knotted from his shoulders. A crowd of ghosts jostled about him on the river-bank, fighting for ferry-places. Mothers clutching their children, heroes with their life's achievements done, boys and unmarried girls, babies dead before their time, all crowded round him, numberless as autumn leaves. Like a flock of migrating birds gathering on the shore of a wide, still lake before they set off to fly south, the ghosts hovered on the river-bank, stretching out their hands and begging to be first to make the journey. The ferryman moved among them, accepting some but not others, driving them angrily back from the water's edge.

Aeneas, amazed at the sight, whispered to the Sibyl, 'Lady, who are they? Why are they so eager to cross? How does the boatman choose the ones to take and the ones to leave?'

'Aeneas,' she answered. 'This is Styx, the Black River whose name forces even gods to keep their oaths.* The boatman is Charon, Ferrier of Souls, and he will still be here, working his steering-oar and trimming his sails, when generations still to be born have died and been long forgotten. The souls he carries across the river have been reverently entombed; on this side, forbidden to cross, are unburied spirits. Unless their bones are given proper burial, the ghosts are doomed to wander here for a hundred years, flitting like bats about the shore. Only when their penance is complete will Charon clear space in his boat for them and take them to the other side.'

Even as she spoke, Aeneas checked his steps in horror. He had just recognised companions of his own among the ghosts: Leucaspis and Orontes, who had drowned on the way from Troy. The wind had snatched them overboard and the sea had dragged their corpses out of reach of burial. Palinurus, Aeneas' own helmsman, was there too, weeping and wringing his hands. He had been swept overboard as they sailed from Sicily, and murdered by savages when he swam to land; now he stood there with spear-wounds gaping in his sodden flesh, a ghost doomed to torment for a hundred years.

Aeneas longed to speak to his dead companions, to give them what comfort and hope he could. But as he and the Sibyl approached the shore, Charon shouted angrily, 'Who are you, walking armed to my river with the blood of life warm in you? Why have you come here? This is a place of shadows; it is forbidden to carry living beings across the Styx.'

'Be calm,' answered the Sibyl. 'This is no Hercules, come to steal Cerberus, no Theseus, come to kidnap Queen Prosperina.* This is Aeneas of Troy; the gods have ordered him to the Underworld to speak to his father Anchises and hear his people's destiny. Look, in his hands, the Golden Branch: Venus herself protects him.' She showed Charon the golden branch, bright in Aeneas' hand. At once Charon's anger evaporated and he drew his boat further into shore and cleared the long benches of the wraiths who were sitting there. Aeneas stepped into the boat. The hull groaned under the weight of a living man, and water ran in through the seams. But Charon poled the boat carefully into the river, spread the sail and carried Aeneas and the Sibyl safely to the far bank, where he set them down on a mud-flat tufted with grey marsh-grass.

Torments

Just beyond the shore-line, where mud gave way to rock, the stones were foul with dog-droppings and yellow aconites, poison-flowers clinging like lichen to the barren surface. This was the guard-post of Cerberus, watchdog of the Underworld, and the aconites were the fruit of his spittle, that fell from his jaws each time he snapped at ghosts. He sprawled across the entrance, his three heads snuffling as he dozed. But as soon as he sensed Aeneas' and the Sibyl's footsteps – for his ears were attuned even to the whisper of ghosts' feet, no louder

71

than rustling leaves – he reared up, high as a hill, and Aeneas saw snakes like hackles on his neck, and heard his three heads growl as he bared his fangs. Aeneas drew back, clutching his sword-hilt; but the Sibyl stepped forward and tossed Cerberus three lumps of flesh from her sacrifice before the journey began. She had sprinkled them with poppy-seeds, muttered a sleep-spell over them and carried them, sticky with blood, throughout the journey. Cerberus snapped at them greedily before they touched the ground, and gulped them down. At once the sleep-spell did its work, he slumped across the entrance, and the Sibyl and Aeneas picked their way past his enormous limbs and twitching tail, into the heart of Hell.

The air was filled with the wailing of dead children, stillborn or suffocated in their nurses' arms. Next to them were those whose deaths had been the result of false accusations and lying witnesses. Here, in the halls of Hell, their cases were tried again. Minos, judge of the dead,* listened to the charges and the evidence, then put a pebble in an urn for each ghost's future and shook it, while the wraiths watched in a silent, slack-eyed throng. For some the lot fell for innocence, and they moved out of Minos' court to happiness; for others it fell for guilt, and Furies drove them with iron-spiked whips to punishment. Beyond Minos' court were the Plains of Sorrow and Groves of Grief, the home of those who had taken their own lives in the world above, who had so hated the daylight that they had hurled their own souls down to the darkness of the Underworld. What price would they not have paid, now, to live once more in the upper air, even as beggars, slaves or cripples! But that road was barred forever by the waters of the dark, encircling Styx.

Among them, wandering among those who died for love, Aeneas suddenly saw Dido with the death-wound hanging in her breast. He glimpsed her through the trees of a forest, dimly, like the moon glimmering through clouds at the beginning of the month. He ran forward, horror pricking him. He meant to take her in his arms, pour out his grief and love, and tell her once more that the gods had ripped him from Carthage, ripped him from her side, against his will. But she was no more moved than flint or marble. She gazed at him for a moment, her eyes blazing; then she hurried away among the trees to where her first love, Sichaeus, was waiting to comfort her.

Aeneas was sick with grief. But he followed the Sibyl up the path, up from the plain into hilly countryside, crags and gullies covered with spindly undergrowth. The paths were thronged with ghosts, an

army of shadows, and to his amazement Aeneas recognised them as
all the fighting-men, Greeks and Trojans alike, who had been killed
at Troy. They jostled there in full armour, their flesh still caked with
mud and blood. Old enemies, they now walked in a common herd
like cattle, gazing at each other with dull, unrecognising eyes.
Parthenopaeus, Tydeus, Adrastus; Glaucus, Medon, Thersilochus;
Antenor's sons, Idaeus, Polyphoetes – Aeneas knew every one of
them by name. Deiphobus was there too, Priam's son. He had taken
Helen hostage at the end of the siege of Troy, hoping to use her to buy
his own life, and Helen's husband Menelaus had hacked him to death
and mutilated him. Even now he was hardly recognisable, handless,
faceless, the bone of his skull gleaming white where ears and hair had
been ripped away. Aeneas would have run to talk to him, pity his
plight and promise him burial in the world above. But when the ghosts
felt his movement in the still air they scattered, terrified by the bulk of
living flesh. Some shrieked like bats; others opened their jaws in a
voiceless, powerless grimace.

The Sibyl touched Aeneas' arm. 'Hurry,' she said. 'Just ahead of
us, the path divides. Our way leads to Pluto's palace, to Elysium, the
Fields of the Blessed. The other way – that way – leads to Tartarus, the
Pit of Punishment.' She pointed to a line of cliffs on the left, rock-
ramparts rising to a wall of smooth, squared stone. On a tall iron tower
in the centre perched Tisiphone, daughter of Night; her servants
Terror, Grief and Madness fluttered round her head like huge, pale
bats. Round the foot of the rock foamed Phlegethon, the River of fire,
and boulders caught in its current roared and crashed as they tumbled
into Tartarus. Groans and screams filled the air, and the sound of
whips. In the centre of the wall, below the tower, was a gate bolted
and barred with iron, and the Sibyl said. 'No honest ghosts ever pass
inside; no good people enter the Kingdom of the Damned. Rhadamanthus* rules: he hears the sinners' crimes and announces their punishments. Then Tisiphone puts on her cloak of blood, picks up her whip
and drives the sinners to the Pit of Punishment. Tartarus yawns
downwards twice as far as Olympus soars above the earth. The Giants
sprawl in its lowest depths, Mother Earth's children who challenged
the gods: Jupiter hurled them there, to writhe in agony forever.
Tityus* their half-brother lies beside them, pegged across the floor as
far as the eye can see. Snakes wriggle over his belly, cropping his
entrails, and Tityus' innards are miraculously renewed each time, so
that his torment never ends. Ixion's fire-wheel rolls across the plain,

and Sisyphus forever heaves a boulder to the brink of Tartarus, only to see it rumble down again. Tantalus sits on a golden couch at a never-ending feast. Food and drink are set before him in royal profusion. But each time he reaches out to the food, the Fury who sits on guard flaps up and beats him back with a fiery torch.* In Tartarus, too, lie those who hated their brothers and sisters in the upper world, who struck their parents or cheated friends; misers; traitors; adulterers. They wait eternally for their suffering to begin, never knowing whether they are to be crushed by boulders, stretched on wheels or torn on racks. Anticipation is their punishment. A hundred mouths could not tell every crime that has brought people here, or the punishments decreed for them. Hurry past: we have little time. Ahead of us are the entrances built by Cyclopes long ago, the archway and the gate which leads to the Elysian Fields.'

The Elysian Fields

The Sibyl led Aeneas along the shadowy path towards the Gate, and he sprinkled himself with holy water and hung the Golden Branch in the archway as an offering. At once the gate swung back, and the way lay open to the Elysian Fields where the Blessed Spirits lived. The air was gentler there, and the Fields were bathed in golden light: the Blessed had their own sun and their own stars. Some were exercising on yellow sand; others were dancing to the music of Orpheus, who accompanied them on his lyre, plucking it with a plectrum of polished ivory.

Aeneas looked round in wonder. He was surrounded by the ancestors of his own race. Princes and princesses who had been no more to him than names in myth stood in quiet groups or walked together, deep in conversation, down shady paths. Chariots stood unharnessed on the plain's edge, with horses feeding beside them. Further off, he could see people feasting by a sweet-smelling laurel-grove, where the river Eridanus* rolls quietly to the world above. These were heroes who had died for their homeland, priests, poets, counsellors, inventors, men and women who had used their skills to benefit, not harm, the human race.

Then, in a green valley far across the plain, Aeneas suddenly saw Anchises. He was sitting on a grassy mound, and before him passed the procession of souls who were to leave their imprisonment and climb to the upper world. He was reviewing his descendants in order, pondering their appearance, their character and the deeds they would one day do. As soon as he saw Aeneas he ran to greet him, tears streaming down his cheeks. Aeneas, too, was in tears. Three times he tried to throw his arms round Anchises and hug him. But the laws of the Underworld are implacable. The ghost slipped from his grasp each time, fluttering into emptiness like the passing of a dream.

In a grove at the end of the valley, where the roots of the rustling trees were bathed by the waters of a wide river, clustered a host of spirits, the ghosts of many nations and peoples. They were like bees in a summer meadow, settling on flowers of every kind while the lilies carpeting the ground are filled with their drowsy buzzing. Intrigued, Aeneas asked his father to tell him the river's name and who the people were who filled its banks. Anchises answered, 'The river is Lethe,* and those are souls granted a second existence in the world above. They drink Lethe-water here, and it washes from their minds everything they have seen or known in the world below. Follow me, and see the future.' He led Aeneas and the Sibyl through the throng to the hill beside the river; from it they could see every passing soul, and Anchises picked them out one by one and described their destiny. There was Silvius, Aeneas' own son who would be born one day to a woman Aeneas had so far not met. There was Romulus, who would build the city of Rome itself. Tarquin the Proud was there, the tyrant-king, and Brutus who would drive him out of Rome. Scipio was there, who would fight Hannibal the Carthaginian in Africa, and nearby was Fabius who would defeat him in the hills of Italy. Gathered in a single group was the whole line of Iulus' descendants, Aeneas' own dynasty, which would stretch down the centuries as far as Julius Caesar's nephew, the emperor Augustus himself. Caesar was there, in gleaming armour, and by his side was Pompey. They were at peace now, and so long as Night was upon them they would never quarrel. But in the Light Above they would hurry from the west and the east to fight each other, and their wars would shake the world.

In this way Anchises pointed out each ghost and told its destiny, and Aeneas stood amazed at the names and achievements of generations yet unborn. He was hearing about Rome, the second Troy, the glittering new city he had sailed so far to find. Other nations would mould bronze into more breathing likenesses, or carve more lifelike features from dead marble; others would plead more eloquently in the courts, or more accurately plot the planets' wanderings or the rising of the constellations. Rome's art would be government, and its destiny was to pacify the world, to spare the conquered and to overthrow the proud. This was Anchises' prophecy, the words Aeneas had come to the Underworld to hear. For a long time father and son talked together, wandering over the whole valley, exploring the Elysian Fields in the golden light only the Blessed know. But the hours were passing, and Aeneas' thoughts kept returning to his followers, waiting anxiously on the beach at Cumae in the world above. He longed to drink Lethe-water, to forget the cares of life and stay forever by his dear father's side. But the laws of the gods denied living people existence in the Underworld, and Jupiter would not let him forget that his destiny was with his people, that his task was to set their feet on the path of the future, the path of Rome.

At the edge of the Underworld were two gates, guarded by Sleep. One was made of horn, and allowed true souls an easy journey to the world above. The other gleamed with ivory, dazzling as snow; but the Spirits here sent false dreams, nightmare-visions, to the upper air. Anchises led Aeneas and the Sibyl to these gates, and there left them. They passed into the upper world like people waking from sleep. Everything they had seen and heard in the Underworld seemed suddenly no more real than dreams. They were in the hills above Cumae. Aeneas left the Sibyl and hurried down to the shore, to the inlet where his followers were waiting.

7
WAR · COMES
TO · ITALY

Latium

The gods gave the Trojan ships fair winds from Cumae, driving them north-west along the Italian coast. At sunset the crews furled the sails and made ready to land on a low-lying island beside the shore. But from the distance, beyond the alders that fringed the beach, they suddenly heard wild animals calling: wolves, bears, lion and boar. Above them was the sound of a woman's voice, a thread of song so beautiful that it filled the men with eagerness to leap into the shallows, splash ashore and find the singer, whoever and wherever she was. But Aeneas wrenched his steering-oar round and shouted, 'Row! Row for your lives! This is Circe's island. Her singing will turn us into animals and cage us without escape!'*

The Trojans struggled to block the magic singing from their ears. They rowed frantically out to sea, till the sounds from Circe's island faded in the darkness behind them. Then they hoisted their sails, left volunteers on watch, and huddled down to sleep while the gods' following winds filled the sails and moonlight sparkled on the sea. When dawn came they breakfasted on the food-scraps and sour water which were all they had on board, and then crowded to the ships' sides to gaze at the shore of Italy and keep a lookout for the river Tiber and the safe landfall the gods had promised. The coastline was wooded, and here and there beaches gave way to high, gaunt cliffs. At about mid-day they came to a long stretch of marshland, with dunes and reeds growing right to the edge of the sea. Gradually these in turn gave way to the wide estuary of the river Tiber. It was yellow from the mud it carried to the sea, and rapids rippled the turbid waters. Its banks were covered with wading-birds, which flapped into the air in confusion at the Trojans' shouts. The trees were few and straggly;

there was nothing else but sand-bars, marshes, and the river swirling to the sea.

Aeneas shouted an order, and the ships turned inland and made for the further shore. As soon as they came into the estuary they could feel the current dragging them back to sea. They bent their oars like saplings, heaving the water aside, and Neptune himself helped them, tossing their ships over the muddy surface as a child skims stones. They anchored in a small inlet on the far bank, and ran eagerly ashore. There were tears in their eyes, and they danced up and down as though they'd never seen land before. Surely this quiet place was the end of their wanderings at last, the new homeland the gods had promised them. They gathered handfuls of earth and flung them into the air in their joy; grown men and women scampered through the trees, whooping like children.

That night they camped beside the river, under the stars, clutching the soil of Italy like lovers. Next morning, the women and children began unloading the ships and carrying their belongings up to the fields, where Sergestus and Ilioneus gave each family space to make a temporary home. Achates led a gang of men into the woods with axes and wedges; others formed a line to drag the trees to the site as soon as they were felled and trimmed. Another group began digging a wide ditch all the way round the camp, and planting in it pointed stakes facing outwards. With the earth from the ditch they built a high mound as a base for the walls, and on top of the mound they set a line of solid timbers as tall as two grown men, with a watch-tower at each corner. They covered the logs of the walls with hides, and placed barrels of water and sandpiles every twenty paces in case an enemy attacked the camp with fire.

All these precautions seemed unnecessary. For the three days it took the Trojans to build the camp, they saw no one. But Aeneas remembered the Sibyl's prophecies, deep underground at Cumae, that there would be a war to fight and that the Tiber would run red with blood. He insisted that the wall should come before all other building-work, and as soon as it was finished posted guards on it day and night. He sent Ilioneus and Sergestus upstream in the lightest of the ships, with a dozen picked men. Their job was to look for inhabitants, to persuade the local people that the Trojans were peaceful settlers, and to propose alliance. In the meantime, Aeneas and the rest of his followers provisioned their camp for war, not peace.

The place the Trojans had landed in was Latium, and its people were farmers and foresters, ruled by King Latinus. He was the son of a mortal woman, Marica, and the wood-spirit Faunus,* and throughout his long life the gods of the countryside had given his people prosperity and sheltered their farms and fields from war. Long ago, at the start of Latinus' reign, he had built a temple to Janus, the two-way-facing god who was the first-ever ruler of Italy. The temple gates were hammered from double sheets of bronze, and were bolted shut. The gods had decreed that so long as the gates stayed locked, war would never come to Italy; but as soon as they were opened fighting would pour across the land. In the seventy years of Latinus' reign the gates had remained closed. Their iron hinges were heavy with rust and their massive bronze panels were tarnished and cobwebby.

King Latinus and his queen Amata had only ever had two children, a son who died in infancy when his mother was no more than fifteen years old, and a daughter, Lavinia, born thirty years later at the end of Amata's child-bearing life and when Latinus himself was over sixty. Latium was surrounded by tribes of all kinds, hill-farmers, shepherds, river-fishers, and so long as Latinus was alive their friendship was assured. But what would happen when the old king died? Would the gates of Janus' temple be thrown open at last? Would enemies fight for Latium as dogs snarl over bones? Latinus' only hope was to marry his daughter to a strong prince, a powerful man who would have the respect of all his neighbours and would guarantee Latium's safety when the old king died. All the time Lavinia was growing up her parents had sacrificed night and day to the gods to look after her. Now that she was of an age to marry, they welcomed suitors from every tribe in Italy, and none more than Turnus, prince of the Rutulians, whom Queen Amata favoured above all others.

The wedding would have gone ahead, if it had not been for two fearful omens. In the courtyard of Latinus' palace grew a sacred laurel-tree. The people had revered it for four hundred years, believing that as long as it flourished Latium would never fall. This tree was suddenly invaded by a bee-swarm. The bees hovered above it in a dense, humming cloud, and the royal soothsayers announced that they were a sign from the gods. A swarm of strangers was coming to Latium, to take over its most sacred places and rule the land. The people were still trembling at this prophecy when a second omen, even more terrifying, took place before their eyes. Latinus was sacrificing at Jupiter's altar, and his daughter Lavinia was standing beside him. All at once flames engulfed the girl from head to toe. Her

79

hair and clothes blazed till there was nothing left but ash, and when the flames died she stood untouched, her flesh healthy as a baby's, but stark naked and bald as a stone. The soothsayers declared that this portent meant war. Lavinia would marry a stranger and would escape destruction, but her country and people would be devastated round her till nothing was left.

Alarmed by these omens, Latinus hurried to the shrine of his father, the forest-spirit Faunus. The shrine was a grove of trees with an altar at its heart and a spring of icy water bubbling from the Underworld far below. A ceaseless murmur filled the air, the water-ripple mingled with the stirring of leaves in the breeze; wisps of sulphur rose from the ground as if the earth were breathing. Latinus' people stood outside the grove in a respectful, frightened ring, while Latinus went to the heart of the shrine, beside the altar. He watched while priests butchered a hundred sheep in his father's honour and piled their fleeces in a bloodstained heap. Then he climbed the pile, spreadeagled himself on top and prayed, 'Father, Faunus, send us an oracle. Explain the omens of bees and fire.' It was a barbaric ritual, not undertaken since primitive times. But it worked. The ground heaved, the trees shook, and Faunus' answer echoed through the grove. 'Latinus, Lavinia will never marry Turnus. Her husband will be a foreigner, a stranger. He will carry the fame of our nation to the stars; our descendants will rule every land on earth.'

No sooner was this oracle spoken than Ilioneus' and Sergestus' ship appeared, rowing round a bend in the Tiber. The people ran to the shore, and the Trojans uneasily drew their swords and gripped their spears. But Latinus held out his hands to welcome the strangers, drew them one by one to shore and led them to his palace. He listened to their names and adventures and told them that their leader, Aeneas, must be the man described in Faunus' oracle, the man destined to marry Lavinia and bring new glory to the Latin race. He feasted them, and then sent them back, loaded with gifts, to fetch Aeneas upstream to Latium.

Allecto

While all this was happening in the world below, Juno, queen of heaven, had been visiting her mortal worshippers in Argos. Now she was returning, swooping like a swallow among the clouds, when suddenly from Pachynus in Sicily she caught sight of Aeneas and his Trojans. They were bustling like ants beside the Tiber, loading their ships with presents, fitting the oars and taking their places on the benches ready to row upstream. Juno's anger overflowed. The gods on distant Olympus heard her shouting with rage as she stormed across the sky; to mortals, cowering underneath, it was as if all heaven had become a giants' battleground, with the clouds stacked like boulders and spears of rage hurtling from horizon to horizon. 'Is there no way to blot out this accursed race?' she cried. 'They escaped the flames of Troy; they escaped Scylla, Charybdis and the Quicksands; now they think themselves safe on Italian soil, with friends, secure from the sea. Aeneas thinks he's outwitted me. But if my own power is too slight to hurt them, I can still call on others. If Heaven fails me, I'll find help in Hell!'

So saying she plummeted from the sky like a fireball, and the people of Sicily grovelled and hid their eyes. She hurtled through the Underworld, brushing the ghosts aside, and stood by the iron nest of Allecto, eldest of the Furies.* 'Wake up!' she shouted. 'Maker of Misery, Begetter of Grief, wake up! Mortals are mocking us; the powers of the gods are scorned. Trojans and Latins are planning an alliance, against my will. Fly up! Sow seeds of evil! Scatter them!'

At once Allecto spread her wings and flew to Latium. The tormented souls in Tartarus sensed that her evil was gone, and breathed a moment of freedom before her sisters Tisiphone and Megaera fell on them with shrieks of glee. Allecto hovered over Latinus' palace, darkening the sky, and then settled by the door of Queen Amata, Lavinia's mother, who was already troubled by the omens about Aeneas and the breaking of the marriage-promise made to Turnus. Allecto plucked a viper from her hair and flung it at the queen. Silently, sinuously, it wrapped itself round Amata's neck and body and wove itself into her hair; unseen, it flowered in her flesh as mould blossoms on a peach. Its poison seeped into her heart and filled her bones. Distracted by agony, she snatched Lavinia and ran with her, raving, to the wild hills, where she crammed her in a rock-cleft to keep her from Aeneas and prevent the marriage.

Allecto next spread her wings and flew to the palace of Turnus, the proud Rutulian prince whose place Aeneas had usurped. Changing her appearance, she took the faded skin of an old woman, ploughed her face with wrinkles and sowed her head with white. Looking like Calybe, Juno's aged priestess, she hobbled before the young prince

and said, 'My lord, why do you sit here doing nothing? Why should
Aeneas snatch the throne that is yours by right? Latinus has
abandoned you as son-in-law; he prefers a foreigner. Gather an army!
Fight for what's yours!' So saying she threw off the old woman's
disguise and revealed herself to Turnus in all her horror. Sweat poured
over Turnus' body. Insane blood-lust, the war-madness of the proud,
seethed within him. When twigs are heaped round the ribs of a
cauldron on a cooking-fire, the flames crackle and the water leaps and
boils, exulting in the heat, till steam bubbles up from the depths and
the water pours over the cauldron's edge, hissing in the steam-filled
air. This was how Turnus raged as he gave orders to his soldiers.
Envoys galloped to Latinus to demand Lavinia; smiths prepared arms
to kill the Trojans or drive them from Italy forever.

Leaving Turnus shouting orders, Allecto flew back to Latium and
the Trojans. This time she had a different plan. In the water-meadows
beside the Tiber Iulus, Aeneas' young son, was hunting, chasing
whatever quarry strayed across his path. The Fury filled his dogs'
nostrils with a false scent, so that they rushed into the woods and
cornered a huge, tawny-hided stag. This event began the war and
caused all the misery that followed. For the stag was no ordinary
animal. It was a pet of Tyrrhus' children, whose father was Latinus'
royal gamekeeper. It had been taken from its mother before it was
weaned, and was tame and gentle. Although it was allowed to wander
at will through the forest, it always went home to Tyrrhus' stable at
nightfall, returning gladly to its familiar resting-place.

This was the stag that Iulus' hunting-dogs now cornered. Knowing
nothing of its tameness, and eager for the honour of killing such a
magnificent beast, Iulus set arrow to bow and wounded the stag in the
belly. Bleeding, and uttering plaintive moans as if it were asking for
revenge, the beast staggered home to its familiar stable. As soon as she
saw it lying there in a pool of its own blood, Silvia, Tyrrhus' daughter,
cried out that an enemy had come to the forest. At once the farmers
and foresters (encouraged by Allecto, who was lurking in the woods)
ran to help with whatever weapons came to hand: charred logs from
last night's fire, gnarled tree branches, anything they could snatch up
in their hurry. Tyrrhus himself had been splitting an oak-stump with
axes and wedges, deep in the wood; now, calling his men to help, he
came running axe in hand.

Suddenly Allecto soared into the sky from the gable-end of
Tyrrhus' barn, shrieking and flapping her wings, blanketing the sun.

Mothers covered their children's ears with trembling hands, and the country folk, slow to anger, were stirred to fighting-frenzy as surely as a blacksmith's bellows stir embers on a forge. On their side the Trojans, seeing Iulus' danger, poured out of their camp to help him. Their weapons were not logs or branches, but sharp two-edged swords and flashing spears. Aeneas and his crew, rowing hard up the Tiber, wondered at the sound of battle in the distance. But by the time they landed and ran to see what was happening, it was too late to prevent disaster. Almo, Tyrrhus' eldest son, had fallen with a Trojan arrow in his throat, as had Galaesus, Latinus' aged counsellor who had stepped between the two armies to try to make peace. He was the most respected of all Latinus' lords, and the richest too – five flocks he had, and five herds of cattle; it took a hundred ploughs to turn his land.

Seeing that her work was done and that war was inevitable, Allecto glided back down into the Underworld. There was no more need of her. The herdsmen ran from their battle to Latinus' palace, carrying Almo's body and Galaesus with his death-wounds gaping. They called on the gods for vengeance, and shouted to Latinus to take action. But he stood firm. Like a rock that resists the sea, battered by storms but remaining unshaken while the waves yap and seaweed is washed up endlessly, only to fall back again into the restless sea – so stood Latinus, refusing to accept catastrophe, lashed by his people's rage. They shook their fists and shouted; they fell on their knees and cried; they called him to open the bronze gates of Janus' temple and send battle flooding across the fields. But the old king could not bring himself to do it. He turned away, flinching from destiny, and hurried inside the palace. Then Juno herself, furious at the delay, swooped from the sky and smashed the gates apart. The bolts splintered, the hinges collapsed in showers of dust, the gates crashed back against the pillars, and war-madness poured over the countryside as flood-waters engulf a plain. People reached from the rafters swords and spears not used since their great-grandparents' time; they harnessed their horses and galloped headlong across the plain; they shook the dust from battle-standards and blew trumpet-calls not heard for a hundred years.

These are the names of the kings and queens who prepared for war. Mezentius the Proud, tyrant of Etruria, and his son Lausus. Prince Aventinus, Hercules' son, riding his father's chariot across the plain with the victor's garland in his hair and on his shield his father's emblem, Hydra with her crown of a hundred snakes. Messapus, Neptune's son, Tamer of Horses; Halaesus, a Greek who had fought at Troy; Ufens of Nersae; Camilla, princess of the Volscians, a warrior-maiden who could outrun the winds. They gathered, with their followers, before Latinus' palace, and Turnus moved through the throng greeting each one as they arrived. His helmet had a triple plume, and a fire-breathing dragon was painted on his shield. A cloud of foot-soldiers followed him: Argives, Auruncans, Sicanians, Labicans with their painted shields, and his own Rutulians, goatherds from the hills. So the chieftains gathered. As their soldiers jostled on the plain, and the clatter of weapons rose to Olympus, Juno smiled to think of the war to come.

Evander

Aeneas was in despair. The Trojans were safe inside their walled camp, but they could plainly hear distant hoof-beats, shouts and trumpet-calls as their enemies massed for war. He spent hours discussing the future with Ilioneus, Sergestus and the others, and praying to the gods for guidance. At last, exhausted, he lay down by the wall nearest to the river-bank and tried to sleep.

It was night: Sleep had conquered the world. Farm animals and forest birds were asleep, and human beings forgot their cares in the luxury of rest. As Aeneas dozed, Father Tiber, god of the river that bore his name, appeared before him, rising from the waters through the poplars that lined the bank. His robes were grey, and he wore a crown of dark green reeds. 'Aeneas,' he said, 'this place is your promised home. The tribes of Latium have been waiting for you to come and rule them. As soon as the gods' anger is appeased, you will settle here. The proof is this: downriver, in an oak-grove by a line of hills, you will find a sow with a new-born litter of thirty piglets. They are all pure-white, and the place where they are lying is the site for your city. Your son Iulus will found it thirty years from now, and its name will be Alba, the White. This is the future. For the present, this is what you must do. Not far from here is a town of Greeks, ruled by King Evander. They are recent settlers, and their town is called Pallanteum. They are at war with the Latins, and will be glad to make an alliance with you. Greeks and Trojans will unite at last, to fight joint enemies. Sacrifice to Juno, to end her anger against you. Then sail upriver to Pallanteum.'

The god sank into the water and disappeared. Aeneas ran down the bank, filled his cupped hands with river-water and prayed, 'Lord Tiber, you have told the future. Go with me; help me to bring it true.' He went back into camp and shook Sergestus, Achates and a dozen other men awake. They picked the lightest of the Trojan ships, and sailed downriver to the place where Tiber had foretold the omen. There they found the line of hills, and the white sow and her thirty piglets on the river-bank, exactly as the god had said. Aeneas sacrificed the pigs to Juno, queen of heaven – to Juno alone of all the gods, for it was her anger he was eager to appease. Then he and his men rowed upriver in the moonlight, slipping past the Trojan camp, past the sleeping army outside Latinus' palace, deep into the country-side beyond. The sun was high in the sky when they rounded the last bend and saw the watch-towers and roofs of Pallanteum, Evander's settlement. They moored their ship and walked into the town, holding their hands palms outwards as a sign of peace.

As it happened, there was no need for this precaution. Pallanteum was deserted. Evander, his young son Pallas and all his people had gone to a sacred grove nearby, to sacrifice to Hercules, their patron god. Long ago, when Hercules still wandered the world in mortal form, he had rid the place of a monster, Cacus, and made it safe for human habitation.* Now Evander, his son Pallas and all the towns-people had gathered at Hercules' altar to burn incense and make sacrifice in gratitude. The air was heavy with pine-smoke and the smell of blood. As soon as the Pallanteans saw the Trojans walking towards them, Prince Pallas ran, spear in hand, to meet them. 'Strangers,' he said, 'what brings you here? Are you Greeks, Latins or people from some other tribe?'

'Sir,' answered Aeneas, 'we are Trojans, enemies of Latium. We asked the Latins for shelter, and they refused. Take Evander this message: tell him Aeneas of Troy offers armed alliance.'

As soon as Evander heard Aeneas' name, he ran to welcome him. The priests finished their sacrifice, and while servants carved the carcases for roasting, Evander ordered thrones and rugs to be brought for his visitors, and a feast of welcome to be prepared. The princes sat on a grassy mound near the altar, and servants brought dishes of roast meat, bread in wicker baskets and skins filled with wine. While they ate Evander told them the story of Hercules and Cacus, and when they had finished he led them back to Pallanteum, and showed them its landmarks, the seven hills which ringed it, the cattle-market by the riverside and the island in the bend of the Tiber which slowed the river down and made it easy to cross for trading or defence.* Then, when darkness fell, he took them into the town and gave them lodging for the night. They lay down, eager for morning when the treaty would be made; Sleep enfolded them in his velvet wings.

On Olympus, meanwhile, the gods were not asleep. Venus, Aeneas' divine mother, had spent the day looking down at the gathering of Turnus' forces, and the sight had filled her with alarm. Now she was lying with her husband Vulcan, blacksmith of the gods, in the golden bedroom he had built for her. She turned to him and said, 'My lord, help me! All the time the Greeks were besieging Troy, I asked no favours from you, even though it was clear that the city was doomed, and my heart was torn with the thought of the misery my son Aeneas was to undergo. But now Jupiter has given clear orders. The Trojans have landed in Latium, and must fight to stay there. So now I do come to you, humbly, a mother begging for her son. Will you make weapons to help him, weapons of the gods? Dearest Vulcan, will you arm my son?'

So saying, she threw her arms round Vulcan and kissed him, hiding her distaste – for she preferred the lusty wargod Mars, her lover, and only ever embraced Vulcan when she wanted favours from him. Vulcan sat up and cried, 'Darling, anything you ask is yours. Whatever my skill can make, whatever iron and fire can produce, you have only to name it and it is done.' He leapt out of bed and flew down to his forge, in rock-galleries deep under Mount Etna in Sicily. Here his servants the Cyclopes* were hard at work. They were beating out chariot-panels for Mars, god of war, and putting the finishing touches to a thunderbolt for Jupiter. But Vulcan shouted to them to put those tasks aside. They had weapons to make for a mortal, the finest their skill and strength could produce, and they were to finish them by morning. The Cyclopes stoked up the furnaces, and began pouring molten bronze, silver and gold into the moulds. One Cyclops worked the bellows; the others shaped and tempered the hissing metal. The cavern rang with hammer-blows. Swiftly the arms took shape: sword, helmet, greaves and a massive, seven-layered shield. Aeneas would soon be armed with weapons no mortal could withstand.

While this work went ahead in the caverns under Etna, dawn was caressing the world outside. As soon as it was light Evander went to the house where Aeneas and his Trojans had spent the night. While servants prepared breakfast, the princes sat at their ease in the sunny courtyard. Evander began the conversation. 'My lord Aeneas,' he said, 'like you we are threatened by enemies, and like you we have been told by the gods that help will come from the direction we least expected, from men we once fought at Troy. We are poor settlers, and can spare few fighting-men of our own. None the less I promise you an army, fully-equipped, countless as bees in summer and ready for war.'

'How can that be, my lord?'

'Fortune favours us,' Evander answered. 'Not far from here is the country of the Etruscans, a long-established, warrior people. Recently one of their kings, Mezentius, set up a tyranny and oppressed the people. No need to describe his crimes, the murder and torture he revelled in – the gods will punish him. In the end his people revolted, slaughtered his guards, burnt his palace and tried to find him to kill him too. But he fled to Turnus and the Rutulians – and now all Etruria is threatening Turnus with war unless he hands Mezentius back. The Etruscan army is camped in the fields upriver, waiting only the word to fight. Pallanteum can offer nothing to equal them; but I will send my son Pallas with four hundred horsemen to help you.'

He had hardly finished when out of a cloudless sky Venus sent her son an omen. Darkness covered them, as abruptly as water douses flame, and trumpet-fanfares blared. Then the daylight returned as suddenly as it had disappeared. The treaty was made and the gods had blessed it. Aeneas sent his men to the ship, to sail downriver and tell the Trojans what had happened. In the meantime Evander gave him a stallion, covered by a lion-skin with gold-tipped claws. He rode out of Pallanteum towards the Etruscan camp with Pallas and his four hundred horsemen, and the forest echoed to their hoof-beats as though a thundercloud was passing.

Half a day's ride away, not far from the river, a grove of trees lay in a cup of land fringed by hills. Towering pines made it a sombre, eerie place, and the country people thought it the haunt of evil spirits, and kept away from it. On one of the hills overlooking this grove Tarchon, the Etruscan leader, and his army, numerous as autumn leaves, had made their camp. Pallas and his horsemen galloped to join them; but Aeneas, struck by the silence in the grove, rode down into it to pray. And there, in the stillness, his mother Venus appeared before him, veiling her radiance in mortal flesh to keep from dazzling him. 'Look, Aeneas,' she said. 'Here are weapons, made for you by the gods' craftsmen. With them you will beat every enemy in Latium.'

She handed him the weapons, and Aeneas turned them over and over in his hands. There was a helmet, its crest blazing like a forest-fire; a sword like a lightning-flash; a bronze-studded baldrick supporting a blood-red sheath, gleaming like a sunbeam striking through clouds in the autumn sky. There were greaves made from alloy whose secret only the gods' craftsmen knew, and a shield inlaid with designs no mortal smith could ever have devised. Vulcan himself had covered it with endless, intertwining lines of pictures and magic signs. The whole future history of Rome was there. Generals, emperors and senators jostled for position with the hundreds of conquered peoples ruled by Rome. Aeneas knew nothing of the meaning of the pictures, but was filled with wonder at the workmanship. Venus smiled at his amazement, then soared away to her home on Olympus.

Aeneas tested the weapons for weight, and found that for all their magnificence they weighed no heavier on his limbs than a summer breeze. Then he strode up the hill to join Tarchon, the Etruscan leader, and take command.

8
THE · SIEGE · OF
THE · TROJAN · CAMP

The siege begins

From her throne high on Olympus, Juno watched the meeting of Aeneas and Tarchon, the Etruscan commander, with growing anger. Her rage against Aeneas had been partly soothed by his sacrifice of the white sow and thirty piglets. But now, seeing Aeneas gleaming in Vulcan's armour and with the god's sword glittering in his hand, she burst out furiously to Iris, 'Still Venus helps her son! Go to Turnus. Tell him to attack the camp now, while the Trojans are leaderless. This is the moment of fate: let him snatch it while he can!'

Iris soared down to deliver the message, hanging a rainbow in the sky to mark her path. As soon as Turnus heard the news, he called his chiefs together and gave his orders. The Latin army advanced across the plain, dense as a dust-cloud, until it was no more than a bowshot from the gates of the Trojan camp. Messapus and Mezentius led the cavalry; Catillus and Corus commanded the archers; Turnus himself rode in the centre on a huge black warhorse. Inside the camp, the Trojans swarmed to defend their walls. Aeneas had advised them, before he left, not to be tempted out into battle on the open plain, but to stay in camp, safe behind their earthworks and the deep, spiked ditch. They had withstood siege before, he said, ten years of it at Troy. However large the attacking enemy, they could easily hold out until help arrived. Remembering these words, the Trojan commanders made no attempt now to open the gates or to ride out of camp, but lined the walls with men and prepared to defend themselves.

Turnus shouted an order and the army came to a halt. He rode forward with the other Latin leaders, and began trotting up and down the line of the walls, looking for a vantage-point. The Trojans watched in silence. They knew they were safe. Behind them was the river, with its steep, muddy banks inaccessible to armed men; on the other three sides they were protected by ditch, mound and wall. Nothing but a second Wooden Horse could dislodge them, and this time they were alert for trickery. They stood in lines on the battlements, watching Turnus as he padded up and down like a wolf outside a sheepfold, trying to think of some way to lure them to death on the plain outside the gates.

At last Iris told him what to do. The watching Trojans saw him ride back to his officers, rein in his horse and give orders to Mezentius. A group of Latin cavalry left the main body and rode off into the forest. The rest of the army waited, silently. The setting sun glinted on their armour, and there was an occasional clink of weapons or the snorting of a horse. But the Latins made no move. Like the Trojans in the camp, they stood waiting impassively to see what would happen next.

Nothing happened for ten minutes. Then, without warning, the cavalrymen galloped out of the trees in the gathering gloom, shouting and hallooing. Each carried a blazing pine-torch, and the Trojan firefighters nervously checked their water-butts and dug their shovels deeper into the sand-piles. But the Latins wheeled their horses round the corner of the camp, out of sight, and disappeared. Ilioneus suddenly realised what was happening. 'The ships!' he shouted. 'They're burning the ships!' He led a rush of men to the rear of the camp, where the ships were moored at the foot of Tiber's steep banks below the wall. Mezentius' cavalrymen were there, hurling their torches into the ships and tossing down branches to feed the fire. Black smoke filled the air; the tarry timbers were well alight.

Once again, however, a god intervened. Above the ships the sky filled with dancing light, a dazzle of sunbeams, and the voice of Tiber himself, the river-god, sent the Latins scurrying as surely as a shower of spears. 'Back, Mezentius! You could as easily set the sea on fire. Go, my ships: you are set free at last. Go home!' At once the ships broke their moorings and plunged into the river in line, like dolphins. As the ships vanished into the swirling water the awe-struck soldiers saw a vision of river-nymphs gambolling beside Father Tiber, their saviour; when the water grew calm again, no trace was left of the Trojan fleet.

At first this seemed a setback for the Latins. Their horses had reared, snorting with panic, and galloped back to the plain in frenzy while their riders fought to control them. The watching soldiers, too, had heard the god's voice and were cowering in terror. But Turnus kept his head. 'This is the Trojans' defeat, not ours,' he shouted. 'Their ships are gone – the gods have destroyed them for us. The Trojans have nothing to rely on but walls and ditches. And what use to them were the walls of Troy? Make camp, and rest. Tomorrow the gods will help us to kill them all.'

The Latins hurried to obey. The main force lit fires for the evening meal, and the men on guard-duty took out dice and jacks and made themselves comfortable for a long, sleepless night. The Trojans, too, were wide awake. They went anxiously round their camp, setting double guards, strengthening the earthworks and checking the defences. The women and children huddled in the centre of camp; the men nervously patrolled the battlements or hunched down where they were and tried to rest.

Nisus and Euryalus

One of the gates was guarded by a huntsman from Mount Ida, Nisus, a seasoned fighter and one of Aeneas' bravest followers. With him was his comrade Euryalus, a boy whose beardless cheeks revealed his youth. Nisus and Euryalus were close friends, and always stood side by side in battle. It was only natural that they should have drawn the same guard-post on this occasion. In the quietness of the night Discord, goddess of quarrels,* suddenly filled Nisus' mind with eagerness for glory. 'This waiting is useless,' he whispered to Euryalus. 'Look how careless the Latins have grown. While it was light their guards were keen and careful. But now they've eaten and drunk too much; there's hardly a man awake. Our leaders are saying that Aeneas should be warned, that a messenger should find him and tell him about the siege. If you and I cut our way through the Latins to that hill across the plain, we could easily get to him.'

Euryalus laughed with excitement, and eagerly agreed. The friends woke other sentries to guard their gate, and then slipped through the camp to find the Trojan leaders. It was midnight. Everywhere else in the world men and women were asleep, easing the day's cares in rest. But the Trojan leaders had gathered for a council of war, and were desperately discussing how to get word to Aeneas and lift the siege. Suddenly Nisus and Euryalus burst in, shouting with excitement, and told them their plan. The leaders laughed to hear it. 'Gods of Troy,' exclaimed Aletes, the oldest man there, who had been a grandfather before the Greeks set sail for Troy, 'how can Trojan glory ever fade

91

from the world, while we have spirited young men like these? Nisus, Euryalus, how can we ever repay such bravery?'

'If we come safely back,' answered Nisus, 'I ask no reward but Turnus' warhorse, and his golden helmet and scarlet plumes. Let me kill him and take them from him with my own hands.'

'As for me,' Euryalus said more soberly, 'I ask one favour only. My mother came with me from Troy, and has followed me to Italy despite her great age and the miseries of the journey. My lords, if by some chance I don't come back, look after her. Cherish her as I would have done if the gods had let me live.'

The leaders gladly agreed, and there were tears in their eyes at Nisus' bravery and Euryalus' filial devotion. The two young men let themselves down the wall on ropes and crept in the darkness into the Latin camp. All round them men were snoring in drunken sleep. Chariots lay upturned, with their drivers lying beside them in a litter of weapons and empty wineskins. Once again the goddess Discord set blood-lust blazing in Nisus' mind. 'Euryalus,' he whispered, 'keep watch, while I cut a path for us.' He drew his sword and went up to Rhamnes, a proud prince who was snoring on a bed covered with a silken eiderdown. Rhamnes was a prophet and one of Turnus' most trusted advisers, but neither his prophetic skills nor his trustworthiness saved him from death. Nisus next killed his servants, who were asleep on the ground beside their master. Then he killed Lamyrus, Lamus and the handsome Serranus. The smell of blood rose into the dark sky, and Discord savoured it and chuckled with delight.

Euryalus' fury was no less than Nisus'. Fadus, Herbesus and Abaris died without ever waking up. Rhoetes was sitting on the ground, clutching a wineskin. He staggered drunkenly to his feet, and Euryalus plunged his sword through the wineskin into Rhoetes' belly. Blood and wine poured out in a mingled stream, and Rhoetes' eyes glazed as he fell dead. But Nisus now realised that in their eagerness for slaughter he and Euryalus had moved away from their path towards Messapus' cavalry. In an urgent whisper he warned Euryalus, and they hurried back – but on the way the boy picked up Rhamnes' weapons, and stole Messapus' golden helmet, with its commander's plumes, from its sleeping owner and put them on.

They had been so blinded by Discord, so intent on killing, that they had failed to notice a group of men moving quietly through the camp in the darkness. This was a recruiting force Turnus had sent round the villages of Latium, and now they were coming back to camp, leading their horses through the sleeping men. Their commander's name was Volcens. As Nisus and Euryalus hurried to find their way in the darkness, the stolen helmet betrayed Euryalus. Discord let a shaft of moonlight play on it; it gleamed like a beacon and Volcens shouted, 'Stay where you are! Where are armed men going in a sleeping camp? Stand still and answer!'

Nisus and Euryalus took to their heels, hoping that the darkness would protect them. But Euryalus was weighed down by the weapons he had stolen – his boy's strength was not up to the weight of a grown man's armour. He struggled on, not realising that he was running the wrong way. Nisus, on the other hand, with a huntsman's skill at keeping hidden, slipped easily through the enemy, clear of danger. He stopped and looked round for Euryalus, but there was no sign of him. The mists of Discord cleared at once from Nisus' mind, and he made his way, cold with panic, back the way he had come, tracking his own footsteps across the camp. He heard horses' hooves and the sound of a chase; shouts reached his ears and soon he saw Euryalus struggling wildly as the Latins overwhelmed him.

What could Nisus do? He was one man, and Euryalus was surrounded by a dozen. He drew back his arm and threw his spear, full into Sulmo's back. Gasping and coughing blood, the Latin fell from his horse and choked out his life. Volcens was furious. Because he could see no enemy in the darkness, he poured out his rage on Euryalus. 'You caused Sulmo's death, and your own will pay for it. Blood for blood!' He drew his sword and lunged at the boy.

Nisus lost his head with horror. He ran forward shouting, 'No! I killed him! Leave the boy alone, and punish me!' But he was too late. Volcens' sword pierced Euryalus' ribs, and the boy fell gasping to the ground. He was like a flower cut by the plough, or a poppy drooping in a shower of rain. Nisus ran wildly at the enemy, heedless of danger, interested only in killing Volcens and avenging his friend. Even as the whole band swarmed round him, he hurled his sword full in Volcens' face, and took the Latin's life at the same moment as he lost his own.

So died Nisus and Euryalus, before they could bring word to Aeneas. The Latins gathered up their dead comrades and carried them through the camp, which was now wide awake, full of lamentation for Rhamnes and the other slaughtered princes. High overhead, Discord soared back to her lair in the sky-vault, glutted for a time on death.

Turnus in the Trojan camp

It was nearly dawn. Turnus' commanders armed themselves and began organising their men for attack. They hacked off Nisus' and Euryalus' heads, spiked them on spears and carried them like battle-standards in front of the army. Inside their camp the Trojans, lining up on the battlements, wept bitterly when they recognised their companions' bloodstained faces.

Euryalus' mother was sitting spinning when they took her news of her son's death. Rigid with grief, she dropped the spindle: it clattered on the ground and the wool unravelled. She ran to the wall like a madwoman, heedless of the soldiers, heedless of the danger, and filled the sky with weeping. 'Euryalus, my darling, my treasure, is this all that is left of you? You were my comfort, my lasting joy – and they have snatched you away. Did I follow you from Troy for this? Here I am, Latins: kill me next. Aim your spears at me. What better favour can I ask than to share my dear son's death?'

Her words tore the heart from the whole Trojan army. It was not until Idaeus and Actor, on Aletes' orders, helped her to her feet and led her away that the soldiers could turn their thoughts once more to war. And they were just in time. Trumpets sounded and the Latin attack began. The cavalry galloped up to the wall, and behind them the foot-soldiers locked shields and marched inexorably forwards to fill in the trenches and pull down the earthworks. On the Trojan side, the soldiers manned the walls in a single, well-disciplined line, careful not to show their heads over the stockade except for the few moments needed to fire arrows or hurl spears at the advancing enemy. The Latins were baffled by the ditch with its pointed stakes. Some of the cavalry tried to jump their horses over it, but were driven back by a rain of weapons from the walls. The foot-soldiers found it impossible to scale the wall of smooth tree-trunks, and were picked off one by one as they scrambled for cover. Again and again they attacked, and each time they were driven off, leaving the plain covered with bodies.

At last, seeing that direct attack was useless, Turnus called his men back out of range. The Trojans were jubilant. No one inside the camp had been killed; few were so much as scratched. But the Latins quickly re-formed for another attack. The cavalry rode back to the edge of the plain and the foot-soldiers moved forwards, carrying spears and short stabbing-swords. In front of them lumbered an ox-cart piled with stones and earth to fill in the ditch, and at the edge of the wood Ufens' highlanders began trimming a pine-trunk to make a battering-ram.

Protected by foot-soldiers, the ox-cart advanced to a corner of the wall under the wooden tower commanded by Noemon and Prytias. Behind it were archers with fire-arrows and men with ladders, poles and ropes. As soon as they came in range the Trojans showered them with spears and arrows, and with logs and rocks from the main defences. But for every Latin that fell ten more came forward; with a shout of triumph they overturned the cart and filled in the ditch. They laid ladders and scaling-poles against the wall, and the soldiers crowded forward, greedy to be first over the stockade into the camp. The Trojans drew as many men as they dared from the gates, and concentrated on defending this one weak spot. Fire-arrows hissed into the camp above their heads, and several huts were soon ablaze.

It was the tower that interested the Latins most. It was a wooden scaffolding two storeys high, with wicker walls hung with goats'-hide to protect them from fire. It held a hundred men, and they rained stones and arrows down on the Latins, or fought them off with spears as they planted ladders against the walls. Messapus was first up the ladder, carrying a blazing pine-torch. Grinning in triumph, he hurled it into the tower. It landed inside, well clear of the protective hides. At once the dry wicker caught fire, and a sheet of flame rose up to the Trojans on the first storey. They tried desperately to put out the fire with water from barrels, but it was impossible to fight the flames and defend the tower at the same time. More and more Latins swarmed up the ladders; soon battle was raging in the tower itself. The flames had a firm hold, and the smouldering hides surrounded the struggling men in dense black smoke.

But the flames which swallowed the tower also saved the camp. The tower's supporting struts were blazing, and all at once there was a crack of splitting timber, and the tower lurched out over the earth-works, engulfed in flames. Screaming with terror, the men inside tried to jump for safety. Some lost their balance and pitched to death on the plain below; others died howling in the flames. The tower tilted further and further outwards, and collapsed with a crumbling roar on to the ox-cart and ladders below, crushing defenders and attackers alike. The Latin archers drew back hastily from the wreckage.

The Trojans gave a cheer of triumph – but it was followed almost immediately by cries of alarm from Pandarus and Bitias, the gate-guards. Messapus' attack on the tower had been a diversion, to draw defenders from the gates while Ufens' highlanders finished their battering-ram and carried it into place. Throughout the attack on the tower, throughout the fire and the tower's collapse, they had been remorselessly pounding the gates, and now there was a splintering crash as the wooden bolts split apart. A dozen Latins, led by Turnus, tried to force their way inside, and the Trojans rushed to drive them back. A fierce struggle began in the gateway itself, while Pandarus and Bitias put their shoulders to the gates, straining to close them. At first they made no progress against the surge of Latins pressing inwards. But then some of the Trojans saw what they were trying to do and ran to help. They forced the gates back against the struggling enemy, and at last·crashed them closed and laid two tree-trunks in place of the splintered bolts.

But the closing of the gates trapped Turnus and his dozen Latins inside the camp. He raged along the battlements, killing any Trojans who dared to face him. Antiphates and Meropes fell, then Erymas, Aphidnus and Bitias. Vainly the Trojans showered Turnus with weapons. His armour was too well-made, and their spears and arrows clattered harmlessly against it. He jumped down from the wall and began advancing on the main body of defenders. They cowered before him like cattle flinching from a lion. He pulled his helmet back from his face and shouted, 'What are you – children? Look: my face is bare. Aim at that!'

These words filled Pandarus with fury. He aimed his spear and hurled it at Turnus. But the cast was too high: the blade did no more than flutter a few feathers from Turnus' helmet-plume. Turnus laughed. 'The gods have abandoned you!' he shouted, and began advancing on Pandarus while the soldiers fell back in fear, leaving a clear space for the duel. Pandarus drew his sword to defend himself. But Turnus was too quick for him. Standing on tiptoe he raised his own sword in both hands and brought it crashing down on Pandarus' head, splitting it from brow to chin. Pandarus fell like a pole-axed bull, and his blood drained into the dust. Quickly Turnus snatched up a spear. He walked towards the ring of cowering men, and still no one dared to face him. Phalaris fell, then Gyges, whose knee he severed from behind; then he killed Phlegeus, Prytanis, Clytius and Cretheus. When the Trojan commanders Mnestheus and Serestus came running up, they found him surrounded by dead bodies, and the survivors watching, as if spellbound, to see who his next victim was to be.

Mnestheus tried to rally his men. 'Trojans, aren't you ashamed? Is one single man to kill everyone in camp? Have you forgotten that

96

Aeneas is your leader, that you are Trojans?' His words jerked the Trojans out of their panic. They closed ranks and began advancing in a solid line, spears and shields held out in front of them. Soon Turnus was surrounded on three sides, like a stag cornered by dogs. He looked for the companions who had burst through the gate with him. But they were long ago dead, cut down in the first onslaught of the fighting. He pulled his helmet down and began backing across the camp, away from the gates. At last he came hard up against the far wall, beside the river, and could go no further. He scrambled up on the wall and stood there at bay, while a rain of spears and arrows rattled on his armour. There was no sound but the ripple of the Tiber, the distant shouts of battle from the plain, and Turnus' harsh panting as he dodged to and fro looking for a way to escape.

At last some men leapt up on the wall to finish him. This was a mistake: Noemon and Critias fell, and he severed Gorgas' head with a single blow. After that no one dared to go near him, and the Trojans stood at the foot of the wall hurling stones and spears. Turnus' armour was dented and blood-stained, and his helmet was battered out of shape by a stone which crashed against it and sent him lurching against the parapet. At last, sweating and exhausted, he turned his back on his enemies and leapt from the battlements out of range. He crashed to the ground, rolled down the bank into the Tiber and was swept away. The Trojans ran to the wall and fired showers of arrows at his head, bobbing in the yellow water. But his death-day had not yet dawned: the Fates protected him. The Trojans watched in helpless fury as the current carried him downstream and he splashed ashore at last, safe behind his own lines.

Aeneas returns

While all this was happening Aeneas and Tarchon, the Etruscan leader, had met and made a firm alliance. Tarchon led his army by the land-route to Latium, and Aeneas embarked to row downriver back to his people. It was midnight, the time when Nisus and Euryalus, in the Trojan camp, were just explaining their plans to Aletes and the other leaders in council. High upriver, Aeneas' men slipped their mooring-ropes and began rowing, determined to reach the Trojan camp by morning. Aeneas himself sat in the bows with Pallas, Evander's young son. The boy was wearing a gift his father had given him, a leather sword-belt decorated with pictures and magic signs.* It was an heirloom, handed down for generations from king to king, and so far its magic had protected its wearers' lives even in the thick of battle. Now Pallas wore it proudly as he sat in the ship with Aeneas, asking him eager questions about his adventures, the method of navigation by the stars and the battle they were going to wage against Turnus.

The journey took all night. All the time Mezentius and his soldiers were trying to burn the ships; all the time Nisus and Euryalus were buying glory in the Latin camp with their deaths; all the time Euryalus' mother was mourning her son and the Trojans were massing to attack the camp, Aeneas and his men rowed quietly down the Tiber, hearing nothing and seeing no one. After a while Aeneas took the steering-oar himself. And even as he and his helmsman were changing places, the lookout gave a shout of surprise: there were strange creatures ahead. They were the river-nymphs into which Tiber had changed the Trojan ships when he saved them from Mezentius' fire. Leaping and diving like dolphins, they swam alongside the fleet, and Aeneas gazed with awe at their faces and breasts above the water. Their leader Cymodoce spoke to him. 'Hurry, Aeneas. Spread your sails. Your people need you. We are your own fleet, made long ago from the pines of Mount Ida. Tiber himself turned us into nymphs and sent us to warn you. Iulus and all your people are besieged in their camp; even now the watch-tower is collapsing and Turnus is raging through the camp. Hurry to help them; prepare for war!'

As soon as she had spoken the nymphs disappeared, and Father Tiber hurled Aeneas' ship downriver, so that it skimmed the water faster than an arrow racing the wind. Soon from the high helmsman's post Aeneas could see the Trojan camp, Turnus jumping from the battlements and the despairing Trojans firing arrows as he swam downstream. Aeneas lifted high overhead the shield Vulcan had made for him, and the sun's rays caught it and sent a beacon of hope flashing to the Trojans. They surged out of camp to greet their returning leader, and the Latins fell back bewildered by their sudden change of heart. It was only when they saw Aeneas' ship gliding to its moorings that they understood.

9
THE · BATTLE · ON
THE · PLAIN

The gods in council

Jupiter looked down from Olympus at the mortals below, as a mortal might gaze at ants. He saw Turnus splash ashore, coughing and gasping. He saw Vulcan's shield flash in Aeneas' hand, and the Trojans' jubilation at their leader's return. He saw Tarchon's army advancing through Latium, unstoppable as fire. And most of all, he saw the two armies locked in battle outside the Trojan camp. When two crabs fight for the same small square of beach, there is no noise, no battle-tumult: they lock claws in a determined wrestling-match, scuttling now this way now that, struggling to win every step of ground. So the armies of Troy and Latium wrestled for Italy: from above, out of earshot of the clash of weapons and the groans of the injured, it looked more like a dance than a battle.

As Jupiter watched, the gods assembled in council before him. Venus and Juno were both angry: rage streamed from them like spears. Venus said, 'Father, what crime has my son Aeneas committed, that he and his Trojans should be harried like this over land and sea? All they ask is a little stretch of Italy to call their own – and Turnus and his Latins have been roused against them, as once Scylla, Charybdis and the Cyclops were sent to blot them from the earth. If this is your will, father, if you declare that the Trojan race should be wiped from human memory, at least spare Iulus' life. I have homes in Paphus, Amathus, Cythera and Idalium – let me take my grandson there and bring him to manhood safe from war, safe from the disaster that engulfs his race.'

Juno said angrily, 'Jupiter, what crime has Aeneas not committed? Wherever his people go, they carry death. They stole Helen of Sparta and fought a bloody ten-year war to keep her; in Carthage they caused

99

Dido's suicide and turned her people from peace to war. Now **Aeneas** has landed in Italy and has set Etruscans and Latins at each other's throats. Am I to stand idly by, while this Trojan adventurer overruns all Italy?'

So Venus and Juno spoke. The gods, standing in assembly, murmured agreement with one side or the other. Their voices were like the wind in trees, or breezes gathering on the surface of the sea: a portent of storms. Jupiter lifted his sceptre, and all sound stopped. The stars halted in their courses; the universe stood still; the gods held their breath to hear their king's command. 'There is no right or wrong in this,' he said. 'Both sides are equal. My orders are these. No god is to interfere, on either side. The Trojans and the Latins must fight it out unaided. I make no distinction between them: let the Fates decide.'

He stood up, and crashed his sceptre on the floor. The whole universe, from the vaults of heaven to the lowest depths of Tartarus, shook in acceptance of his word. His decision was made, and none dared question it.

Pallas' death

Down below, Evander's son Pallas, Aeneas' ally, and his four hundred horsemen had galloped ahead of the advancing Etruscan army and reached the edge of the plain. They were in a waterlogged area, where a stream had burst its banks and covered the ground with rocks and torn-up bushes. Mud hampered the horses, and as the men struggled a group of Latins ran forward to attack them. Pallas' countrymen panicked and tried to wheel their horses out of danger. Pallas rallied them, his boy's voice cracking with rage. 'Cowards!' he shouted. 'Run into the Tiber if you like; I shall stand and fight, even if I stand alone.'

Without a backward glance, he ran straight where the enemy were thickest. His first victim was Lagus, who was bending to pick up a boulder when Pallas' spear drank his blood. Lagus' friend Hisbo ran up, shouting with fury. But Pallas' sword-point pierced his lungs and sent his anger, and his life, hissing from the wound. Two brothers next attacked Pallas, the twins Larides and Thymber. They were so alike that their own mother could hardly tell them apart. But Pallas made them cruelly different. With one blow he struck off Thymber's head, and with another Larides' right hand, still clutching Larides' sword while its owner screamed in agony.

100

Pallas' courage at last rallied his followers, and they ran to support him. But on the Latin side the mighty Halaesus had been attracted by the sound of death, and now advanced against them. Ladon, Pheres and Demodocus were his first victims, and he avenged Larides' hand by slicing off Strymonius' arm as he raised it to protect his throat. He then hurled a stone at Thoas, and crushed his skull. Pallas was horrified. He vowed to dedicate Halaesus' weapons to the gods, in return for Halaesus' death, and threw his spear, striking him full in the chest as he dropped his guard to protect Imaon. The Latins fell back in alarm. Only Lausus, Mezentius' son, a boy no older than Pallas, kept his head. He chose the largest of Pallas' followers, Abas, and cut him down. Now each side had lost its champion, and they were equal. The soldiers at the back pushed hard on the ranks in front, and in the confusion many Latins and Etruscans died without advantage: it was death for death's own sake. Pallas and Lausus ached to meet one another in single combat. But Jupiter kept them apart, for he knew that each was destined to die at the hands of a greater enemy.

Suddenly, to a shout of triumph from the Latins, Turnus walked across the plain with a knot of followers. He was bare-headed, and his face and armour were crusted with blood. His mouth was set, and he carried a war-shield emblazoned with a fire-breathing dragon. He lifted his spear, and laughed as the Etruscans cringed back, timid as rabbits. 'Leave Pallas to me!' he shouted. 'I only wish his father were here to watch him die.' Pallas shouted back, 'My father is interested only in my winning honour – either by dying nobly, or by taking home the arms of a noble enemy. Stand and fight.'

The men pressed out of the way. Pallas stood alone, waiting for Turnus, and Turnus walked slowly towards him, like a mountain-lion stalking a calf. Pallas was trembling with nervousness. He must have hoped to make up for his inexperience by striking first, for as soon as Turnus came in range he hurled his spear as hard as he could. It bit through Turnus' shield and hit him in the shoulder. But it was deflected by Turnus' armour and did no more than graze the skin. Turnus now made his own cast. The spear smashed through Pallas' shield, for all its layers of bronze, leather and iron. It cut through his breastplate and buried itself in his chest. Gasping with shock, Pallas pulled it out. His life flowed after it in a stream of dark blood, and he fell headlong, biting the blood-stained ground. Turnus bent over him and snatched the heirloom belt from his waist. The Etruscans murmured angrily and surged forward to kill him. But Mezentius galloped up in his chariot and pulled him clear just in time. Brandishing the belt in triumph, Turnus was carried back to his own lines. His soldiers cheered and ran forward to attack; soon the battle was as fierce as if Pallas had never existed.

The ghost

So fell Pallas, the young prince of Arcadia, in his first battle. When Aeneas heard of his death, he began cutting a path of blood through the Latins, looking for Turnus. He sacrificed eight young Latins to Pallas's ghost: Sulmo's four sons and four other youths brought to their first battle by their tutor Ufens. All were rash enough to challenge Aeneas, and all paid with their lives. Antaeus and Luca, front-line warriors in Turnus' army, fell; Numa and Camers, son of Volcens, the richest man in Latium, died before they could lift a shield. The monster Aegeon* is said to have had a hundred arms and a hundred hands, to have breathed fire from fifty mouths and defiantly shaken fifty swords in Jupiter's face; Aeneas was like Aegeon as he stormed over the plain, carrying death and destruction as he hunted Turnus down.

Above the battle the gods were watching. They saw Turnus kill Pallas; they saw Aeneas raging across the battlefield; they saw the Latins fall back before him, until with shouts of triumph the Trojans burst out from the camp behind them and broke the siege. 'My lady,' said Jupiter to Juno, 'if you like, just this once you can save Turnus' life. The Fates have decreed that he must die in this war, and we cannot change their decision. But if you want to rescue him now, to snatch him from this one battle, I'll not prevent you. Remember, though, that the most you can give him is a respite from death. Until he lies in the Underworld, the Trojans can never be masters of Latium.'

Juno said nothing, but her heart was heavy. Riding on the wings of the storm-winds, she flew down to the Trojan lines, where Turnus was surrounded by Pallas' angry followers, eager to avenge their prince's death. The goddess took a wisp of cloud, and moulded it miraculously into the shape of Aeneas. She armed it with Trojan arms and gave it weapons like those Vulcan had forged for Aeneas. It walked like Aeneas and spoke in his voice; but it was a ghost, a shadow like the dream-figures sent to trouble mortal sleep. It strode

102

arrogantly up and down the front line, infuriating Turnus by brandishing its spear and challenging him to fight. Thinking it the real Aeneas, he hurled his spear at it with all his strength. The ghost turned and fled, and Turnus shouted after it. 'So you're afraid after all, Aeneas! Don't try to run! You wanted a piece of Italian soil to call your own – stay and face me, and I'll give you one.'

He drew his sword and ran through the armies after the flitting ghost. They came to the banks of the Tiber, where Aeneas' ship was moored with a gangway in position. The ghost darted into the ship to hide, and Turnus followed it. As soon as he was on board, Juno swept the ship down the estuary and far out to sea.

When they were well out of sight of land, the ghost came out of hiding. It soared mockingly up, and melted into air before Turnus' eyes. He held out his hands to heaven and shouted despairingly, 'Jupiter, is this to be my fate? My people are leaderless, surrounded by enemies. Why have the gods let me live to see this day?' He began looking wildly round, wondering whether to impale himself on his sword or to throw himself straight into the boiling sea. But Juno calmed him, guided the drifting boat back to land and carried Turnus safely to Latinus' city, far from the battleline.

Mezentius

Turnus' disappearance threw his Rutulians into panic. They could not decide whether to turn and run, or to throw themselves on the spears of their enemies and so gain a quick and honourable death. It was Mezentius who rallied them: Mezentius the Proud whom the Etruscans had banished, and who was now fighting for their enemies against them. With his young son Lausus at his side, he gathered the bravest of the Rutulians and attacked the whole Etruscan army. The Etruscans, his former people, swarmed round him, greedy for his death. He was like a promontory, battered by waves and winds, standing firm against all the violence of the weather. First he killed Hebrus, Dolichaon's son; Latagus was next, and next the swift runner Palmus, whom he hamstrung and left writhing on the ground. He crushed Evanthes with a boulder, and cut down Minas who had been the friend of Prince Paris of Troy. In his anger he was like a boar which has long lain undisturbed in the marshes of Laurentum, but which is now flushed out and surrounded by yapping dogs. Like such a boar, he stood there roaring defiance, and none dared attack him.

None, that is, except Aeneas. He saw the commotion from a distance, and at once gave up his search for Turnus and ran to deal with this new challenge. Mezentius waited till he was in range, then threw his spear. It was deflected by Aeneas' god-built shield and instead killed Antores, who was standing beside him. Then Aeneas hurled his own spear. It pierced Mezentius' shield and wounded him in the groin. Mezentius fell back, hampered by the spear-shaft, and Aeneas drew his sword and advanced on him.

Now came the moment for which Jupiter had kept Lausus from fighting with Pallas. The boy ran eagerly in front of Mezentius his father and faced Aeneas, holding him at bay while Mezentius limped to safety. Aeneas was furious. 'You fool!' he shouted. 'Get out of the way! Your loyalty to your father will kill you!' He gestured with his sword, and to his horror wounded Lausus in the belly. The boy was wearing no armour: merely a linen tunic embroidered by his mother and a light leather jerkin. Blood poured out, carrying his life; he died bravely, defending his father against an enemy he should never have dared to challenge.

Mezentius was on the river-bank, bathing his wound, when they ran to him with news of Lausus' death. He raised clenched fists to heaven and cried, 'Is this my punishment? I oppressed my people, and the gods have killed my son. Lausus, what use is my life, now you are dead? Let me die too, avenging you!'

He climbed painfully on to his horse and picked up a sheaf of throwing-spears. Then he shook the horse's reins and galloped back to Aeneas. Riding in a circle round him, he showered spears till Aeneas' shield bristled like a pine-copse. Aeneas hesitated for a moment, then hurled his own spear not at Mezentius himself but at his horse. The animal reared, threw Mezentius and fell dead on top of him. Aeneas drew his sword, and Mezentius looked up at him and said, 'One favour only, Aeneas. The Etruscans hate me, and will mutilate my corpse. I beg you, keep me from them: bury me beside my son.'

With these words he lifted himself up and deliberately spiked himself on Aeneas' sword. Blood spouted from the wound, and his soul fled to the Underworld to meet his son's, and to atone there for all his crimes in the world above.

Truce

At dawn the next morning the Latins sent ambassadors to the Trojan camp. They came with olive-branches to ask for a truce so that the dead could be buried. Trojans and Latins laid their arms aside and together began the sad tasks of identifying the dead and preparing funeral pyres and burial mounds. The forests rang with the sound of axes on tall ash-trees, pines, cedars and rowans with their tufted leaves. The warriors built funeral-pyres along the banks of the Tiber, placed the bodies on them and heaped them with offerings: helmets, swords, bridles, chariot-wheels and the shields and spears which had been no help to the dead. They sacrificed black bulls to the gods of the Underworld, and left the fires burning for twelve days and nights, till the plain was covered by a pall of oily smoke.

In Latinus' city weeping and lamentation were everywhere. The people cursed the unnecessary war and Turnus' ambition. They cried that since he wanted to win the throne of Latium, it was up to him to kill Aeneas in single combat and so bring the fighting to an end. Drances, a powerful, bitter-tongued orator, put their feelings into words. 'Aeneas has not challenged us all to fight: it is only Turnus who stands between him and the throne. We are being crushed between two ambitious men – let them fight it out themselves and leave the rest of us in peace!' Turnus' supporters were equally outspoken; discussion raged for days in the stricken city.

Then came the final blow. King Latinus had sent messengers to the Greek settlement ruled by Diomedes,* who had once fought so bitterly against the Trojans at Troy. They had taken gold and silver, and begged Diomedes for help against the invaders. But Diomedes refused to listen. His quarrel with the Trojans was over, he said; the Latins should look for allies somewhere else. Latinus realised that the gods were against him and that resistance was futile. He called his people together and said, 'The gods have brought us to the brink of destruction. I can think of only one solution. There is a stretch of land beside the Tiber, protected on one side by the sea, and on the other by a range of hills covered with pine-forests. I propose that we make a peace-treaty with the Trojans, and give them this land to settle on. And I propose that we do it today. If a hundred ambassadors from our noblest families went out at once, with rich gifts, they could make an alliance with Aeneas before sunset.'

At once Drances burst out. 'Your majesty, how can anyone agree to such a plan while *he* is here? Everyone's terrified. But if no one else will speak, I at least will risk his fury. I support your plan – and I propose giving Aeneas a second gift, your own daughter Lavinia. A royal marriage will confirm the alliance; it will guarantee peace forever.'

Turnus was white with fury. He jumped up and snapped at Drances, 'You must be the biggest fool in Latium! Always first to arrive for the council; always eager to get up and air your views!' He turned to Latinus, and spoke more calmly. 'My lord, if we were truly as near defeat as you say, if the Trojans were truly on the brink of destroying us, I'd agree at once. But even without Diomedes there are a thousand princes in Italy eager to drive Aeneas out. In our own army we still have Messapus, Camilla and all their men. This is no time to yield. If the Fates decree that Aeneas and I must fight singlehanded, so be it. But if not, let him prepare for war!'

He was interrupted by messengers, hurrying in with news. The truce was over; Aeneas had marshalled his men and was advancing on the city. Without another word, Turnus strode out of the council to gather his commanders and give orders for the battle.

Camilla

By now the Trojans had almost reached the city. Their horses pranced across the plain, and the spears of their infantry were like an iron-tipped forest. Messapus and Camilla led the Latin cavalry to meet them. The two armies advanced until they were separated only by a spear-cast. Then, with a sudden shout, they charged. Spears filled the air; each man marked his victim out and hurled death at him. Groans and shouts rose to the sky, and the ground grew slippery with blood.

In the middle of the fighting, like a Fury released from the Underworld, Camilla rode dealing death. Euneus, Clytius' son, was the first to fall: she shattered his breastplate and his ribs with a single blow. Next she killed Liris and Pagasus. Liris' horse had stumbled and thrown him, and Pagasus had run up to help him; Camilla killed them both with the same spear-thrust. Then she struck down Amastrus, Tereus, Harpalycus, Demophoön and Chromis. She was like a mountain lioness fighting for her cubs: everything quails before her, but blood-lust rules and she kills for the joy of death. The Trojans fell back in dismay, and Tarchon, the Etruscan leader, tried to rally them. Spurring his horse into the thickest part of the fighting, he shouted, 'Cowards! Where are you running to? Is one woman to rout an army? Draw your swords; throw your spears; attack!'

His words rallied the soldiers, and they fell on Camilla's men like wolves. Arruns, one of Tarchon's cavalrymen, began stalking Camilla across the field. Wherever Camilla's fury led her, he followed. When she attacked, he reined in his horse and waited; when she fell back, he retreated to give her room. He knew that when the moment came to kill her, he would be there.

After a while Chloreus, priest of Cybele, galloped across Camilla's path. He was wearing golden armour, and his horse was armed with bronze plates inlaid with gold. Eager for this glittering prize, Camilla pursued him through the battlelines, and in her eagerness she let slip her guard. Arruns' moment had come. Taking careful aim he threw his spear, and everyone in the army watched as it hissed through the air: they knew what the result would be. Only Camilla knew nothing of the danger. She realised what was happening only when the spear buried itself in her chest and drank her blood. She fell gasping, and her followers ran to support her. But they were too late. Her eyes glazed, and her soul fled sobbing to the Underworld.

Camilla's death unnerved the Latins, and gave new heart to the Trojans. They massed together and with a great shout charged the Latin ranks. The entire Latin army turned tail and ran. Their one thought was to reach the safety of the city. The plain shook under their running feet, and red dust covered pursuers and pursued alike. On the city walls the Latin women stood weeping, holding their hands to the sky in piteous prayer.

The gates were opened, and the fugitives streamed in. But the front ranks of the enemy were so close on their heels that they, too, were let into the city. Death followed, laughing as the Latins were cut down in the safety of their own battlements. A group of defenders at last slammed the gates; by doing so they left many of their own people facing certain death outside, but they also shut out the advancing Trojans. Some of the Latins huddled against the wall for protection; others battered vainly against the gates, begging their friends to open them. The women on the walls pelted the enemy with logs and stones.

But it was all in vain. Below the battlements the butchery continued. The Latins were finally and irrevocably routed; the Trojans had won.

Peace

Now at last Turnus saw that the end had come.* The strength of
Latium was broken; it was for him, now, to keep his promise and meet
Aeneas in single combat. He said to Latinus, 'Fetch your priests, my
lord, make your peace. Aeneas and I will fight. Either I shall send him
gasping down to Hell, or he will kill me and have everything: your
country, your people and your daughter's hand in marriage.'

He hurried into the palace and shouted for his armour. He was snorting with eagerness, like a bull pawing the ground before it attacks its
enemies. For his part, Aeneas was filled with relief that the end of the
fighting was at last in sight. He sent word to Latinus that the Trojans
were ready to make the truce and began to buckle on the armour Vulcan
had made for him. He spoke reassuringly to Iulus and his followers,
telling them that the future was in the hands of the gods.

While the princes armed, soldiers from each side began to prepare
the ground for the duel. They marked out a flat stretch of plain, and
cleared it of grass-tufts, stones, fallen weapons and anything else that
might trip the fighters and settle the fight by accident instead of skill.
Priests fetched an altar and the animals for sacrifice, and while the
armies gathered on the plain to watch the duel, the women and
children of Latium took their places on the battlements. As soon as everything was ready and Aeneas was armed, the Latin leaders came out to
join him. There were only three of them: Latinus, Ufens and a prince
from one of the smaller towns who had led the Latin infantry. They were
blood-stained and weary, and the crowd murmured in sympathy
to see them. But the sounds changed to a hiss of hate as Turnus took
his place by the altar. He was wearing new armour, painted dull black;
nothing caught the sun but the gold inlay of Pallas' sword-belt, and his
helmet with its scarlet commander's plumes. Two of his men followed
him, leading the snow-white mares that drew his chariot.

Turnus signalled for the sacrifice to begin, and the priests led the
victims forward: a pair of young lambs and a two-year-old ram.
Aeneas and Latinus threw handfuls of corn on the altar, and the
priests sacrificed the victims and made offerings to the gods. Turnus
had been standing aloof, taking no part; but now Latinus made him
come forward and shake Aeneas' hand. The two men approached
each other warily and touched hands before going back to their own
lines. Latinus said, 'The treaty is made, and its terms are clear. Turnus
and Aeneas will fight for Latium; for the rest of us, the war is over.'

He stepped back, and Turnus and Aeneas went to their chariots and drove to opposite sides of the duelling-space. Each was armed with a shield, a spear and a short stabbing-sword. There was no more ceremony, no more formality: the hour of destiny was upon them, and the Fates* held the threads of their lives in their hands, one thread for spinning to grant a long old age, the other for cutting and sending a soul to judgement in the Underworld. The watchers on the plain pressed forward round the edges of the battle-area, and there was no sound but their intent breathing as they craned to see the fight.

Suddenly Turnus gave a hoarse shout and set his horses galloping towards Aeneas. Aeneas shook the reins and went to meet him. Their chariots came closer and closer, and both men hurled their spears at the same moment. Both missed. Turnus' spear flew on for twenty paces and stuck in the ground; Aeneas' jarred into an olive-tree at the edge of the plain.

They jumped from their chariots and rushed at each other, meeting shield to shield in a shuddering crash. Then the fight began in earnest. For a long time they thrust and parried, and neither could break the other's guard or make headway against the huge war-shields. Sweat ran from them as they battered vainly at each other's armour; red dust rose up all round them.

All at once Turnus saw an opening in Aeneas' guard. He stood on tiptoe and struck down with all his strength. A shout of horror went up from the Trojans, and the Latins, too, cried out in excitement. But Aeneas' shield had been made by Vulcan, and Turnus' sword was of merely mortal craftsmanship. The blade shattered; for a moment he gazed stupidly at the broken hilt, then suddenly realised that he was unarmed and made a dash for the open plain. Exultantly the Trojan army hemmed him in, blocking his escape. They were roaring to Aeneas to finish him. Turnus backed away like a wrestler afraid after a fall. Then he ran to the edge of the wood and snatched a spear and a sword from the nearest soldier.* Aeneas' spear had stuck in the trunk of an olive-tree, in the grove sacred to Latinus' father Faunus; now he wrenched it free and the two men faced each other again, fully armed and ready to renew the fight.

On Olympus, throned in cloud, Jupiter and Juno were watching the progress of the duel. 'My lady,' Jupiter said, 'surely it's time, now, to admit defeat and bring this war to an end. You must know that nothing you can do will prevent Aeneas from fulfilling his destiny and ruling Latium. Your storms and battle have delayed him long enough. Give up your hatred; leave Turnus to his fate.'

'My lord,' answered Juno, 'am I not sitting here with you, taking no part in the battle, as you commanded? I ask only one thing. Let the Trojans be absorbed into Latium, let them take the name of Latins, so that the accursed name of Troy is blotted from the world. If that is granted, I admit defeat. They can sign their treaty; my anger is at an end.'

As soon as Juno had spoken, she hurried away: she had no wish to see her champion killed. But Jupiter acted to end the duel as quickly as possible. There was a Fury crouched beside his throne: daughter of darkness, servant of his rage. He sent her down to the battlefield, swift as an arrow. Disguising herself as an owl, the bird which sits on tombstones and in dark forest glades and sends its unearthly cry echoing through the shadows, the Fury flew suddenly into Turnus' face, flapping her wings and pecking at his eyes.

Turnus was terrified. He had picked up a boulder, a boundary-stone left by some farmer long ago, that would have crushed Aeneas instantly if Turnus had ever got near enough to hurl it at him. But now he dropped it, snatched up his shield and cowered back from the Fury, trying to protect his eyes. The Fury soared into the sky for another attack. Again and again she swooped on Turnus, as he staggered about the plain holding his shield over his head to fend her off.

This was Aeneas' chance. He took careful aim and hurled his spear. Turnus whirled his shield down to protect himself. But the spear smashed into the painted dragon's mouth, tore its way through the bronze and the seven layers of bull's-hide, and wounded him in the thigh. He fell on one knee, and the watching soldiers gave a shout which echoed from the hills. The Fury soared into the sky and disappeared.

Aeneas stood still. Even now he could not bring himself to lift his sword and murder his helpless opponent. But then, buckled round Turnus's waist, he saw the gold-inlaid belt of Prince Pallas, whom Turnus had killed and despoiled earlier in the battle. It was this belt that caused Turnus' death. When Aeneas saw it his heart filled with bitter anger and he shouted, 'Do you dare to face me wearing spoils from a murdered boy? It is Pallas I am avenging; Pallas now guides my hand.'

With these words he buried his sword in Turnus' chest, and at once the Fates snipped the thread of Turnus' life. Death came exultantly to claim the Rutulian prince, and his soul fled weeping to the Underworld. The war was over; the Trojans' new home in Italy was theirs at last.

110

STORIES · OF · ROME

10
THE · BIRTH
OF · ROME

Lavinium and Alba Longa

Turnus' death took all the fighting-spirit from his men. They threw down their weapons and held their hands palms upwards as a sign of surrender. One by one Trojans, Latins and Rutulians filed past Aeneas, bowing their heads in homage. Then, for the second time in that unnecessary war, they set about burying the dead. For ten days the gods curtained the sky with clouds in honour of the dead. Only a few Rutulians, Turnus' bodyguard, refused to accept Aeneas' victory. They picked their way home to Ardea, and when they reached their city they were filled with sudden madness. Rather than endure the shame of surrendering themselves and their families to Latin rule, they ran into Ardea and set fire to it. The roar of flames and the screams of dying people filled the air. Jupiter took pity on their innocent suffering, and hurled a thunderbolt not to quench but to speed the flames. Ardea and its inhabitants were charred to ash in an instant, and a long-winged bird flapped from the smoke and dust and disappeared low across the Tiber. It was a heron, the first ever seen on earth, and herons have kept ever since the gauntness, the greyness and the mournful cries learned from that first ancestor, a stricken town changed into a bird.*

As soon as the last funeral-pyres were ash, Aeneas married Lavinia and changed the people's mourning to shouts of joy. The two races, Trojans and Latins, united under the single name of Latins: so Juno's wishes were carried out, and the name of Trojans at last vanished from the world. In the months that followed Aeneas left as many of his followers as wanted to make their homes in Latinus' city, and he and the others built a new settlement, naming it Lavinium after Queen Lavinia. The people marked out fields, built streets and houses, and began looking forward to weddings, birthdays and the other celebrations of family life they had hardly known since the Greeks set siege to Troy. From Olympus, the gods smiled down in satisfaction. Here at last, they thought, was the beginning of the new race of mortals, the people whose honesty and justice would triumph over all the evil of the world. Venus was especially delighted. Now that Aeneas' people were safe at last, it was time for her to be reunited with her own dear son, to call Aeneas to Olympus to take his place with the immortal gods. She went round the gods, throwing her arms round them one by one and begging them to agree to Aeneas' immortality. His veins, after all, were filled not only with mortal blood, but with her own immortal ichor; he had already tramped through the Underworld and sailed across the Styx, as it was mortals' doom to do; his glory and honesty were no less than those of Minos, Rhadamanthus or Hercules, three other heroes granted immortality. One by one, the gods agreed; even Juno smiled. Venus rode in her white dove-chariot from heaven to earth, hovered above the river Tiber, and called on the river-god to help her. Tiber surged from his underwater palace, his heart pulsing with love for her, and agreed to do all she asked. That same day, seeing Aeneas riding beside the river, Tiber conjured river-mists into the wraiths of men, and dressed them as a raiding-party from Etruria. Aeneas galloped after them, slicing them with his sword, and although the blade slid harmlessly through the empty air, the effort left him sweaty and uncomfortable. He dived into the Tiber in full armour to cool himself, and the river took him in its arms as a nursemaid cradles a child, and carried him gently out to sea. The waves washed his mortality from him as dirt is scoured from clothes, and Venus gathered his soul and carried it to Olympus. She gave him ambrosia to eat and nectar to drink; every last vestige of his humanity was pared away, and he took his place as an equal in the councils of the gods.

At first, when Aeneas disappeared from earth, his people were bewildered. Lavinia sent search-parties along the coast and up and down the Tiber, calling his name. But that night Aeneas himself appeared to her in a dream, in the full glory of an immortal god. He held her in his arms, comforted her and told her the destiny of his people, the whole future of the Roman race. At dawn he disappeared, and she called for her priests and ordered them to crown Iulus king in his father's place. Then, because she was pregnant with Aeneas' child, and the baby was kicking its eagerness to be born, she went to a grove of trees sacred to the wood-nymph Silvia, and when the child appeared gave him into Silvia's care, begging the wood-nymph to bring him up as her own son. Silvia named the child Aeneas Silvius, and brought him up both as a forester and a royal prince.* Meanwhile, when Iulus grew to manhood, he decided to leave Lavinia to rule in Lavinium, and to build a new town of his own. He chose the place on the edge of the valley where Aeneas had long ago seen the omen of the white sow and thirty piglets, and made it the new town's heart. He called the place Alba Longa, Alba ('white') after the sow and Longa ('long') because its streets ran along a ridge of hills. He ruled there until he died, when his half-brother Silvius succeeded him. After Silvius there were thirteen more kings, and under them Alba Longa flourished for three hundred mortal years.

Wolf-twins

The thirteenth and fourteenth rulers of Alba Longa, Numitor and Amulius, were brothers. Rather than divide the kingdom between them, or favour one brother above the other, their father had made them joint kings. Amulius was the war-leader, and commanded the city's army against enemies far and wide. Numitor stayed in Alba, governing the people and controlling affairs of state. As the years passed, Amulius' jealousy of his brother began to grow. Because Amulius spent his time in army camps or in battlefields, he had never married and had no children; Numitor, by contrast, had a daughter, Rhea, and as she grew up she was courted by young princes from the whole surrounding area. Amulius was afraid that if Rhea married, Numitor would give his (Amulius') half of the kingship to her children; before this could happen he marched his army into Alba, threw Numitor into prison and declared himself sole king. To prevent Rhea ever marrying, he made her a priestess of Vesta: her duties were to live forever veiled from the sight of men, to tend the undying flame, and to remain a virgin.

For a time it looked as if Numitor's wickedness would prevent the Roman state before it was even born. Once more the gods took a hand. One of Rhea's duties was to walk to the sacred spring each morning and fetch water to wash the holy vessels. She went alone, veiled, and looked neither to right nor left in case she saw a man. Usually the morning air was cold and heavy, and mist shrouded the sacred grove.

114

But one morning the Sun rose early, swept the mist from the trees and blazed down with the full glare of noon. Under her thick woollen cloak, and carrying the heavy water-pot, Rhea was soon stifling from the heat. She sat down in the shade of a willow-tree, threw off her veil and shook out her hair in the cooling breeze. At once Venus poured a sleep-spell over her, her eyes closed and she lay back on the ground and dozed. Juno filled the grove with unearthly radiance, so that no mortals, birds or animals dared approach, and Mars flew down from Olympus, made love to Rhea where she lay and left her pregnant. He soared back to heaven, Venus lifted the sleep-spell,* and Rhea filled her pitcher and hurried back to the temple. She put the heaviness in her limbs and body down to her sudden drowsiness – how could she know, yet, that she was pregnant, and that one of the gods had made her so?

As the months passed, however, Rhea's pregnancy grew more and more obvious, and in the end she gave birth not to one child but to twins: Romulus the first-born and Remus who followed moments afterwards. Like all gods' children they were advanced for their age, able to sit up and support their heads the instant they were born. When Amulius' courtiers told him that Rhea had desecrated Vesta's temple by giving birth, that she had broken her oath of sacred virginity, and that there was not just one newborn child but two, he ordered immediate, savage punishment. His soldiers dug a pit in Vesta's sanctuary, beside the undying flame, flung Rhea into it and buried her alive. Then two servants carried Romulus and Remus in a basket to the Tiber to drown them. As they went, the servants looked at the twin babies, gurgling and waving their hands, and pity filled their hearts. Instead of tipping them out of the basket and drowning them, they set the basket upright in the water and let the current float it out of sight downstream. 'If the gods want them dead,' they said, 'they can drown them themselves. Let the guilt be theirs, not ours.'

As soon as the river-god Tiber felt the weight of the basket on his surface, he carried it gently to a mudbank beside a grove of trees. Romulus and Remus were safe. But they were also cold and soaking wet; as all babies do, they howled. By chance, or by the guidance of the gods, their thin crying reached the ears of a she-wolf, wandering among the trees. She had recently given birth to stillborn cubs, and was heavy with milk. She took Romulus and Remus for her own lost offspring, and began nuzzling them, patting them with her paws and licking them. The twins' crying stopped immediately; they sat up, unafraid, and began suckling from the wolf's teats. When they had drunk as much as they wanted of the rich wolf's-milk they fell contentedly asleep, and the mother left them to hunt for prey. So it was for several days, and the twins thrived. Then the gods sent a human that way: Faustulus, a shepherd of the royal household. He was looking for stray lambs in the wood, when he found the babies sleeping at the foot of a fig-tree on the river-bank. He took them home to his wife Larentia, and she, because she was childless, fed them in the only way she knew, like newborn lambs, dipping twists of cloth in boiled milk and putting them to the babies' lips to suck.

As the twins grew, Faustulus and Larentia brought them up as their own children, so that Romulus and Remus had no idea that they were anything but shepherd-boys. They spent their days guarding the flocks against wolves, their own foster-mother's relatives, and as they grew older they helped with the autumn shearing and with lambing in spring. Their friends were farmers' and huntsmen's sons, and with them they practised the skills of riding, shooting and tracking game. Gradually, led by Romulus and Remus, the gang of boys grew more and more adventurous, until they even began lying in wait for robbers and robbing them. In the end a group of bandits, ex-soldiers of Amulius, kidnapped Remus and took him to their former master, demanding that he be executed as a terrorist and a cattle-thief. But before Amulius could say a word, Romulus swaggered into the palace at the head of his gang of farmer's sons, cut Amulius' throat and freed both Remus and his grandfather Numitor, the old imprisoned king. As soon as Numitor saw Romulus and Remus, he guessed that they were his long-lost grandsons. He showed them to the people, and told the story of Amulius' treachery and the twins' miraculous birth. Jupiter confirmed the truth of it by sending lightning in a clear sky, and the people acclaimed Numitor once more as king.*

So Romulus and Remus avenged the death of their mother Rhea, and restored just rule to Alba Longa. They lived for a while as courtiers of their grandfather; but they were used to action, not courtly ceremony, and soon grew bored. The gods put it into their minds to build a new town of their own, on the floodplain of the Tiber where they had once been left to drown. They collected as many of their followers as chose to join them, young men eager for adventure, and left Alba with spades, pickaxes and surveying-lines. The site for the new city was a mixture of flat land, ideal for farming, and the stony slopes of seven low hills. Romulus and his men began planning fields and roads, digging ditches and building low earth walls to mark the new town's boundaries. Remus, whose taste was more for adventure than for building-work, spent his time hunting in the woods along the Tiber. One evening he came back, loaded with game, and found Romulus proudly standing by one of his knee-high walls. 'You're wasting your time, brother,' he joked. 'What enemy will ever be afraid of these?' He dropped the carcases he was carrying and jumped easily over the wall – and the gods filled Romulus with sudden rage, so that he stabbed his own brother dead and shouted, 'So die anyone else who scorns these walls!'*

Women

It was as if the new settlement had been nourished by Remus' blood. The walls were soon finished, solid earth ramparts too high to climb. Inside them was a grid of fields, separated by irrigation-ditches and cart-tracks. In the centre was the cattle-market with its wooden byres and its stone-built shrines to the gods. Each man had his own patch of land, ready for cultivation; they were so busy with ploughing and sowing that they built no houses, but slept rough in their furrows or in lean-to shelters along the walls. If there was to be harvest in the autumn there had to be planting now: the need was for work, not comfort.

The young men called their settlement Rome, after Romulus its founder. It was soon a match in size and strength for any of its neighbours. But its power seemed unlikely to last more than a single generation – and the reason was that all the new citizens were men. There were no women and no children. As the months passed, Romulus sent messenger after messenger to the people of nearby towns, the Caeninans, Crustuminans, Antemnans and above all the Sabines, begging them to let their daughters marry Romans and move to Rome. Everywhere the messengers went, they were laughed to scorn. Their neighbours regarded the young Romans as gipsies and vagabonds, and their settlement as little better than a thieves' hideout. They would tolerate the Romans as enemies, they said, or even as neighbours, but never as sons-in-law. As the year wore on and the lonely months of winter loomed, Romulus decided on a desperate plan. He decreed Games in honour of Neptune, god of horses,* and sent word to all Rome's neighbours inviting them to attend, bringing

117

their wives, sons and daughters to enjoy the show. The Sabines and the other local people had heard of Neptune god of the sea, but never of his power over horses. They were also curious to see inside the new Roman settlement, and thought that the presence of their wives and children, and the sacred peace of festival, would keep them safe. They dressed in holiday clothes, left their weapons at home and flocked to Rome.

As soon as each group of visitors arrived, the young Romans met them, invited them into the settlement and welcomed them with food and wine. They showed them everything: the walls, the roads, the newly-harvested fields and the barns bulging with grain. They, too, wore holiday clothes and laughed and joked with their guests as if festivals were the most natural thing in Rome. Then, when everyone was gathered and it was time for the Games, they led their visitors to a wide, flat stretch of ground beside the Tiber. The crowd stood five deep on the edges of the field, craning for the first glimpse of horses or racing-chariots when the Games began. A hush fell as Romulus rode out, wearing purple and gold and surrounded by a royal bodyguard of twelve armed men. He lifted his arm to the trumpeters. But when the fanfare sounded, it was a signal not for Games but for attack. The young Romans, as soon as their visitors were settled, had crept back to their byres and huts and armed themselves. Now they streamed from the seven hills with spears and swords, snatched the young women of the visitors from under their parents' noses and dragged them away. The girls screamed and struggled, and their parents searched frantically for weapons. But there was nothing to hand except sticks and stones; the visitors were also outnumbered and hampered by their own elderly relatives and small children, clinging and whimpering. They called on their gods to witness the wickedness done to them; then they hurried to their own towns, muttering threats.

It was one thing to vow vengeance, but quite another to exact it. Rome was well-fortified, and unlike the nearby settlements it had its fields and barns inside its walls, not outside on the open plain. Roman raiding-parties, if they chose, could steal their enemies' cattle, destroy their fields, and then snap their fingers in perfect safety behind their own battlements. None of the tribes whose daughters had been snatched, not even the Sabines, were strong enough to make war on Rome alone, and they were too disorganised, too distrustful of one another, to join together and overwhelm the new settlement by force of arms. They fumed and plotted for seven useless years, and the

118

Romans spent the time blithely sowing and harvesting, cattle-breeding and raising families with their new wives. As time passed, the girls' rage at their kidnappers softened into love, and they soon worked happily beside their husbands, while the sound of playing children filled the streets.

The Caeninans were the first of Rome's enemies to lose patience. They began raiding Roman farms outside the city walls, and kidnapping fishermen on the Tiber. Romulus led three hundred men against them, sacked their town and hung their leader's armour and weapons on Jupiter's sacred oak on the Capitoline Hill in Rome. The whole Roman people gathered to watch this ceremony – and the Antemnans and Crustumians, whose daughters the Romans had also stolen, seized their chance to invade unguarded Roman farms. They uprooted crops, burned barns and killed cattle, but were quickly overwhelmed by the returning Romans and killed. The Romans sent settlers to their villages, and gave land in Rome to any who wanted to join their daughters there.

In this way the Romans made peace with their smaller neighbours, and extended their own territory, with little bloodshed. Things were different with the Sabines, the largest of the tribes whose daughters they had snatched. Instead of attacking Rome openly, the Sabine king Tatius bribed his way in by treachery. The Roman commander Tarpeius had a six-year-old daughter called Tarpeia. One day she went outside the town walls to fetch water, and found herself surrounded by tall, armed strangers. Instead of hurting the little girl they played with her, bouncing her on their knees, giving her piggyback rides and whittling sticks to make her toys. They said they wanted to come into Rome to visit her father, as soon as it was dark that night, and asked her what presents would make her borrow her father's keys, open the gates and let them in. Tarpeia, dazzled by the attention she was getting, pointed to the warriors' gold bracelets and said, 'Give me the things you're wearing on your left arms.' But that night, when she crept out of bed, stole her father's keys and opened the gates, the invaders crushed her to death with their shields – which they also wore on their left arms. This one act of treachery would have won them the town, if the gods had not been watching. The Sabines were spreading out stealthily along every street, across every square, when Janus suddenly opened the sluice-gates of every irrigation-canal in Rome. Water poured out, flooding the walkways, and Janus tossed lighted sulphur into it, so that the sleeping Romans were awakened by

119

a sudden lurid glow and by the shouts of the terrified Sabines, scattering to avoid the fire.*

The Sabines quickly recovered themselves, and by the time the Romans had armed and run to the attack, their enemies were drawn up on the Capitoline Hill, the highest point in Rome, so that any Roman attack would be uphill and doomed. Romulus gathered his soldiers on the Palatine Hill opposite and on the land between. The Sabines stayed where they were till dawn, then streamed to the attack. Their war-leader was Mettius Curtius, on a spirited warhorse. He galloped down the hill into the thick of the Roman foot-soldiers, swinging his sword and riding down all who stood in his way. For some time a Roman champion of equal bravery, Hostius Hostilius,* kept him at bay; but Hostius fell at last with a spear through his neck, and Curtius spurred his horse even deeper into the Roman ranks. 'Follow me!' he shouted to the Sabines. 'They're good at stealing girls – let's see how they stand up to men!' He pulled back the reins and his horse reared proudly, pawing the air and snorting foam. The Roman foot-soldiers fell back in alarm. But Romulus himself shouldered his way through the crowd, with his twelve-man bodyguard, shouting his warcry and whirling his sword. Curtius' horse panicked, took the bit in its teeth and galloped out of control away from the Forum and into a marshy field. Its hooves floundered in the mud and stuck, and when Mettius jumped furiously down and tried to run back to the fighting, he too sank thigh-deep and was forced to throw down his weapons and wade ignominiously to dry land, where his enemies were waiting.*

Both sides had now lost their champions, and were ready to begin massed battle on the flat ground between the Palatine and Capitoline hills. But before another drop of blood was spilled, the gods brought the fighting to a miraculous end. The Sabine women, daughters of one of the fighting armies and wives of the other, had gathered with their children for safety in the temple of Juno goddess of marriages. Their leader was Romulus' own Sabine wife, Hersilia. The gods inspired her with sudden courage, and she wrapped her cloak firmly round her head, took her baby son in her arms and strode out of the temple and down the hill. The other wives picked up their children and followed. A stream of women walked down into the Forum, into the midst of the fighting men, and the soldiers lowered their sword-points and drew back in amazement to let them pass. Silence fell, broken only by the women's sobs and the cries of children holding out their arms and called 'Daddy!' or 'Grandad!' to soldiers on this side or that. The gods snatched away the will to fight from Romans and Sabines alike. Both armies threw down their weapons; the Romans ran to hug their wives and the Sabines, tears streaming down their cheeks, picked up grandchildren they had never expected to see alive. In the confusion of sobs and smiles, Romulus and Tatius shook hands. The war was over, and the two peoples lived in friendly alliance from that day on.

The end of Romulus' reign

Rome's pact with the Sabines filled other local peoples with alarm. The Romans were growing too powerful too quickly. The first of their neighbours to rebel were the people of Lavinium, the town founded long ago by Aeneas and named after his wife Lavinia. Claiming that Tatius, the Sabine king, had insulted them, they staged a riot when he next visited their town, murdered him, and then sat in ambush for the Roman invading-force they felt sure would come. But instead of leading an army to Lavinium, Romulus rode into the town alone, unarmed, and astounded the townsfolk by begging pardon for Tatius' insults rather than demanding vengeance for his death. Impressed, the people signed a hundred-year truce with Rome.

With two other towns, Fidenae and Veii, Romulus wasted no time on such diplomacy. The people of Fidenae were harrassing the Romans as dogs torment a bear. They ran out of hiding in twos or threes, burnt a Roman farmhouse or killed a Roman traveller and then scurried to safety behind their battlements. Romulus gathered the Roman army and marched on Fidenae – and as soon as the defenders began throwing spears and shooting arrows from the battlements they were astonished to see the Roman army break ranks and run. Congratulating themselves on their own evident ferocity, they poured out of the town in pursuit – only to be ambushed by the Romans in the nearby woods. With Veii, an Etruscan settlement on the very edge of Rome, Romulus' tactics were even simpler. Instead of parleying or setting siege, he ordered his soldiers to burn the corn in the Veientines' fields and kill their animals. The blow so impoverished Veii that its people were forced to beg for peace, and with them, as with Lavinium earlier, Romulus made truce for a hundred years.

The more territory Rome captured, the larger it grew. Once Romulus had known every citizen by name, and the whole people could gather in a single spot to vote on state affairs. But now the town had spread far beyond his original walls (the ones Remus had so contemptuously jumped): there were three generations of Roman citizens, far too many people to have a say in law-making or debate. Accordingly Romulus appointed a council of one hundred men, fathers of leading families. He called them senators; their council was the senate, and it guided Rome's affairs ever afterwards.

To the gods on Olympus, mortal time was meaningless. Their immortality made them heedless of hours, days and years, and what would seem a lifetime to mortals was to them no more than a nod of the head or the blink of an eye. One moment they were looking down on a settlement of rowdy young men, stealing women from their neighbours; the next, Rome was a prosperous, dignified town, the centre of power along the Tiber, and Romulus had moved from youth to grey-haired age. Mars, his divine father, said to Jupiter, 'My lord, they have no more heed of him. Let Rome manage its own affairs; let me welcome my son to Olympus as one of the immortal gods.' Jupiter gladly agreed, and Mars vaulted into his chariot, supporting himself on his war-spear, took the driver's rail in one hand and his whip in the other and urged his horses on. Snorting with eagerness, they strained at the yoke-pole and drew the bloodstained chariot arrow-fast from heaven to earth. Romulus was sitting enthroned on the slope of the Palatine Hill, while his soldiers marched past him in formation; harness jingled and trumpets sounded. Without warning, Jupiter curtained the sky overhead with storms. Thunder rolled, lightning sliced the air and a thick cloud covered Romulus where he sat, so that no one there could see him. The storm passed as suddenly as it had come, the cloud lifted, and Romulus was nowhere to be seen. At first the crowd was dumb with terror. Then, one by one, people began whispering, 'The gods have taken him,' until they all raised their hands to heaven and worshipped Romulus as an immortal god.

Even then, there were a few Romans who disagreed. They said that jealous senators must have torn him to pieces under cover of the cloud and hidden the fragments under their clothes. For days Rumour ran through the streets, gleefully spreading doubt and fear. Then Julius Proculus, a senator, spoke out. He said that he had come back to Rome that morning from Alba Longa. He was riding along in the moonlight when Romulus appeared before him, a gigantic figure in silver robes whose dazzle outshone the stars. 'Tell my people to be calm,' the vision said. 'On earth I was Romulus; among the gods I am

122

Quirinus, son of Mars. My people must build me a temple on Quirinal Hill, and pay me immortal honours. I shall guide and protect them forever, and their power will grow till they rule the world. Tell them to learn, and to teach each new generation, that no power on earth will ever rival Rome.' Proculus' words sent Rumour whimpering from the town, and the Romans, senators and people alike, gratefully set about building a temple on the Quirinal to their founder and newest god.*

11
STORIES · OF
THE · KINGS

Numa and Egeria

At first after Romulus' disappearance, the senators tried to govern by committee: they divided themselves into ten groups of ten, and ruled Rome in rotation. But after a year of it they decided to elect a single king instead, and since there were no suitable men in Rome they went to the Sabine village of Cures and asked Numa Pompilius to take the throne. He was the most learned man in Italy: people said that he spoke every known language, had visited every country on earth and had discovered many strange facts on his journeys, including that the universe is made of numbers and that no mortal ever truly dies, but instead we are reborn as princesses, bears, owls, ants or other creatures according to our goodness or wickedness in our mortal lives. He had once been married to Tatia, the daughter of the Sabine king Tatius; it was after her death that he began his travels, and he finally settled in Cures, on the river Fabaris east of Rome.

The truth was that Numa was neither a scholar nor a traveller, but a prophet. The gods had given him second sight (the ability to see the past and the future as well as the present) and second hearing (understanding of the language of every creature in the world). He loved Egeria, one of the nymphs of the hunting-goddess Diana, and often visited her in the woods of Mount Albanus, less than a day's ride from Rome, near the town of Aricia.* When he became king of Rome, he used to question Egeria about the gods' wishes, write her answers on wax tablets, slivers of wood or stones and carry them in his saddlebags to Rome, where he kept them in a wooden chest. In this way, with the gods' help, he ruled Rome for over forty years, and when he died the people buried his body on Janiculum Hill, and announced that he had been carried to Olympus to live with the gods.

As for Egeria, she suffered the fate of all immortals who fall in love with humans. As the years passed, she was forced to watch her lover withering before her eyes, while she herself stayed ever young. When Numa died she begged Diana to take her, too, into Olympus and let her live forever with her beloved. But Diana was furious that one of her servants, sworn to chastity, had been enjoying a secret love-affair. She told Egeria that a nymph's place was on earth and that Olympus was barred to her. Day and night, Egeria's sobbing filled the groves of Mount Albanus, and in the end she turned entirely into tears: she became a stream of water, cascading down the hillside and throwing herself, time after time, into the Alban Lake.

The Horatii and the Curiatii

Ever since Romulus took settlers from Alba Longa and founded Rome, the two towns had lived in peace. But war flared suddenly in the time of Tullus, the third king of Rome, and before either city realised what was happening their armies were drawn up and snarling, waiting only the signal to leap at each other's throats. Both Tullus and the Alban leader Mettius Fufetius were filled with alarm. Their towns were small, and nearly every able-bodied man had snatched up weapons and rushed to fight. If it came to a pitched battle, how many men would be left alive, victors or vanquished, to gather that summer's harvest? The two leaders met in anxious conference, and the gods suggested a solution. It happened that in each town there was a group of triplets, the Horatius brothers (Horatii) from Rome and the Curiatius brothers (Curiatii) on the Alban side. The six young men were friends, and the sister of the Horatii had been promised in marriage to one of the Curiatii. But now both families laid friendship aside for the sake of their towns and sent their sons to fight. Tullus and Mettius agreed peace-terms: the Roman and Alban armies would lay down their arms, the three Horatii and three Curiatii would fight before them all, and whichever brothers won, their town would rule the other.

Centuries before, when Turnus fought Aeneas, the outcome of history had been settled by just such a duel, and the six young men were fired by such a noble example and eagerly armed themselves. Priests prayed, the commanders sacrificed, and the three Horatii and three Curiatii walked into the space between the armies like actors stepping out onstage. The women and children of Rome watched from the battlements – among them the young girl Horatia, her heart torn between anxiety for her brothers and her beloved Curiatius.

The trumpet sounded, and the Horatii and Curiatii lowered their spears and charged. Weapons crashed; spears glittered; the watchers held their breaths, waiting to see which side the Fates would favour. The young men threw down their spears and fought hand to hand with swords. Nothing could be seen but struggling bodies, the glint of sword-blades and the flash of blood. When the dust cleared two Horatii lay dying and all three Curiatii had been wounded. The Alban army shouted in triumph, and the Romans groaned to see their third champion, uninjured though he was, surrounded by all three Curiatii. To everyone's surprise, instead of fighting, the third Horatius took to his heels and ran. At first it looked like cowardice; but when he was halfway across the plain he stopped and turned to face his enemies. His plan was to deal with them one at a time, rather than be overwhelmed by all three of them. Accordingly, while they spread out across the plain and panted after him as fast as their wounds allowed, he ran at the nearest and sent him flying. The Albans shouted to the other Curiatii to help their brother, but it was too late: Horatius had already killed him and was stalking his second victim. The Romans' groans changed to cheers as Horatius killed the second Curiatius and ran to fight the third.

The duel was now even-handed, one to one. But Horatius was uninjured, and his double victory had honed his fighting-zeal; Curiatius was slowed down both by his wounds and his grief at seeing his brothers slaughtered before his eyes. It was no contest. Horatius said savagely, 'Two Albans have gone to the Underworld to avenge my brothers' deaths. The third now follows, to buy Rome victory.' He stabbed downwards with his sword. Curiatius was struggling to lift his shield when the blade sliced into his neck and he fell dead. Horatius stripped him of his weapons, and the Roman soldiers clustered round, shouting all the more exultantly because they had been so near despair. Both sides set about burying their dead, the Romans with victorious high spirits, the Albans with the gloom of the conquered.

Even now, the Roman triumph all but turned to disaster. The soldiers carried Horatius shoulder-high, and the women and children surged out of the town gate to greet him. In the midst of them Horatius suddenly caught sight of his sister. Everyone else was

126

laughing and cheering, but her cheeks were wet with tears; even as he watched she murmured the name of Curiatius, her dead beloved, and drew her cloak across her face. Horatius jumped furiously down, and stabbed her with his sword still wet with her lover's blood. 'Traitor!' he shouted. 'You care more for your lover than your brothers or your city. Go down to the Underworld and join him there!'

What was to be done? The penalty for murder was to be hanged outside the walls of Rome on a barren tree, and for the body to be taken down and flayed with whips. But Horatius had just brought his entire people victory. His father added to the confusion by falling on his knees before King Tullus and begging not to be stripped of all four children on a single day. The gods told Tullus what to do. 'Horatius is guilty,' he said, 'and the punishment is clear. But all guilty men have the right to appeal to the people for mercy. Romans, answer! Do you want him hanged on a barren tree, here amid the spoils of his enemies, or set free as the saviour of Rome?'

'Free him! Free him!' the people shouted, and Horatius walked into Rome unhindered. But although human justice was satisfied, the gods were not. They let Horatius' crime hang over the city for days, oppressive as plague. The victory-celebrations died on people's lips; everyone crept about his or her business, as if waiting for Jupiter to send thunderbolts and splinter Rome. At last Tullus proclaimed that as the Horatius family had brought fear to Rome, only they could lift it. He ordered that a stone tomb should be built for Horatius' sister beside the gate, that Horatius' father should offer sacrifices in every temple in the town, and that Horatius himself should suffer a symbolic punishment. A wooden beam was set up across the road on which Horatius had killed his sister, and the young man bowed his head and passed under it, as if enslaving himself to the authority of Roman law. This custom, and the sacrifices which went with it, were repeated by the Horatius family every year afterwards, as long as the Roman state remained.

Rome and Alba

Peace between Rome and Alba lasted only as long as it took the Alban army to march back home. The Alban people complained about the stupidity of staking the town's future on just three men. They blamed the army commander, Mettius, and their anger led him to add treachery to weakmindedness, to try to save his reputation in Alba by breaking his word to Rome. He went secretly round local towns, encouraging them to revolt from Rome: as soon as they did, he said, the Alban army would support them openly. The peoples of Fidenae and Veii took Mettius at his word. They had made hundred-year peace-treaties with Rome; but now they tore them up, declared war, and began recruiting men. They drew up their armies where the river Anio joins the Tiber. Tullus led massed Roman troops against them, and ordered Mettius and the Alban army to deal with the Fidenates on the wing, while his men fought the Veientines in the centre.

This was Mettius' moment. Instead of fighting, he told his men to melt out of sight in the hills until the battle was nearly over, and then hurry down to join the victors. His treachery left one wing of the Roman army undefended, open to flank attack. Tullus could have regrouped his men; he could have turned and fled; instead he kept his head and shouted to his soldiers, in a voice loud enough to carry to the enemy, that everything had been done exactly to his orders. Mettius had vanished into the hills to swoop down behind the enemy and take them by surprise. These words encouraged Tullus' own men and disheartened the enemy, who hastily began regrouping to fend off a surprise attack. While they milled about in confusion Tullus ordered the advance, and the Romans drove them like sheep down the banks into the Tiber, staining the river red.

No sooner was this slaughter over than Mettius brought his soldiers out of hiding. He congratulated Tullus on his brilliant tactics and the bravery of his men, and said how disappointed the Albans were to find no enemies left to kill. Tullus' answer was to announce a victory-sacrifice next morning and to invite Mettius, as co-commander, to come early and play his part. Next day, as soon as dawn scattered the river-mists, Mettius and his men gathered at the place of sacrifice, unarmed as custom was. At once Tullus' Roman soldiers surrounded them, in full armour, with swords at their belts and spears in their hands. Tullus said, 'Men, we are here to bring unity, to punish and to sacrifice. Long ago, when Romulus took men from Alba to build the new settlement of Rome, our peoples were divided; now we shall unite the peoples again, by moving Alba bodily to Rome, giving its people citizenship and making them Romans. The treachery was Mettius', when he encouraged our allies to revolt and led his own soldiers to break their loyalty-oaths; that treachery must be punished.

128

For this purpose, for the honour of both Rome and Alba, we will now sacrifice – and the victim will be Mettius.'

Mettius looked round the ring of soldiers, licking his lips in fear. But he and his men were helpless. Tullus' centurions set two chariots back to back and spreadeagled Mettius between them, tying his shoulders to one and his ankles to the other. Grooms harnessed four horses to each chariot, and at Tullus' command their drivers whipped them to the gallop, so that pieces of Mettius' body were strewn across the plain.

While Mettius' army began the grim task of gathering his remains for burial, two detachments of Tullus' soldiers marched on Alba. The first group's orders were to organise the transfer of citizens, and the second group carried pickaxes, rams and spades to demolish the town. There was no resistance. The Romans moved silently about their work, and the Albans stood where they were or went where they were told, their minds numbed by the disaster Mettius had brought on them. Some made bundles of their belongings, or asked their neighbours' advice about what to take; others gazed like strangers into their own front doors, or wandered wide-eyed through their own familiar rooms. At last the Romans shouted the order to march, and the column began shuffling out of the gates. Even as they walked, the Albans heard the crash of masonry as demolition-work began. The line of refugees soon stretched all the way to the Tiber. They moved forward like pack-animals, dull-eyed, not looking to right or left, clutching all they owned. Behind them the Romans pounded their homes, their streets, their walls to rubble, destroying the work of four hundred years in a single hour.*

Tullus' death

The gods of Alba made no effort to rescue their people or to protect the town. They knew that like the mortals who worshipped them, they were at the mercy of superior powers. Instead, they thronged into Venus' bedroom on Olympus and demanded justice. 'Your own grandson Iulus founded Alba. For four hundred mortal years it was a symbol of the gods' peace and justice on earth – and now the brutal descendants of your lover Mars* have plundered it. Did you agree to this? If not, if it is news to you, punish them as they deserve!'

Venus put on a gown of saffron silk, dabbed perfume on her

129

temples, her wrists and between her lovely breasts, and hurried to Jupiter's throne-room with the Alban gods at her heels. Jupiter was sitting on his royal throne, and Juno, Minerva, Phoebus and the other Olympians were gathered in council before him. Only Mars was absent, sowing terror on a battlefield in some distant part of the mortal world. The Alban gods fell on their knees, hiding their eyes from Jupiter's magnificence, and Venus poured out their complaints. Jupiter said, 'Why are you so surprised? We tried to make a sinless race, but war and treachery are ingrained in mortals as dirt is ingrained in fleece. How am I to judge between them? Both the Romans and the Albans are protected by Olympian gods, and if I take sides it will bring war to heaven itself. The leaders, not the people, are to blame, and they must be punished. Mettius, the Alban war-leader, has already met his fate. But Tullus of Rome must be taught respect.'

He crashed his staff on the ground, and Olympus shook in witness of his words. Phoebus the sun-god, whose arrows of disease no mortal can withstand, offered to punish Tullus, and hurried from the throne-room, beckoning the Alban gods to follow him.

In the short time these events had taken in heaven, many mortal years had passed on earth. Tullus had closed his grip on all the surrounding peoples, welcoming those who offered peace and showing no mercy to any who refused. He had extended and fortified the walls of Rome; he had spent so many years drilling the young Romans for battle that they had come to prefer killing to planting, grown more familiar with spears than with pruning-hooks. Tullus and his nobles spent their days fighting or feasting; apart from a few old women, no Romans bothered any longer with the gods.

One morning, while Tullus and his lords were sleeping off the effects of a victory-banquet the night before, a messenger galloped to Rome with news. In the night a shower of pebbles had rained down on the rocky ridge by the Tiber where Alba Longa had once stood. The streets and fields of the ruined town were ankle-deep in stones the size of eyes; the downpour would have killed any human being or animal caught in it. Shaking sleep from their minds, Tullus and his nobles rode out to see for themselves. No sooner had they reined in on the hillside, their horses' hooves slipping and sliding in the stones, than the sky darkened overhead, the air grew heavy and voices began whispering all round them. 'These pebbles are gods' tears, our tears. We are the gods of Alba, whose people you stole. Take us to Rome, build us temples and give us the honour we deserve. Respect the

130

gods!' The sound ceased, the air cleared, and Tullus wheeled his horse and galloped home. He sent workmen to collect the pebbles, bring them to Rome and use them to build shrines to the Alban gods; as soon as the work was done he ordered a nine-day festival of prayers and hymns in the Alban language and sacrifices in every temple and every shrine.

These offerings delighted the Alban gods: they settled happily in Rome and lived there ever afterwards. But the Olympians were still not satisfied. For days Phoebus swooped low in his sun-chariot across the town, withering crops, scorching buildings and sucking moisture from the soil. Father Tiber drew into himself, so that what had once been a broad, deep stream dried to muddy ooze. Rome's merchant-ships lay stranded; the Forum stank of river-weed and rotting fish. Then Phoebus, hovering in his chariot, began firing arrows of disease. Cattle died in the fields; dead cats and dogs putrefied on the streets; one by one, human beings felt plague-sores blossoming, swelled and died.

At first Tullus refused to believe that the gods had sent these sufferings. 'The cause is overcrowding,' he said. 'Call the young men to their army units, and send them campaigning. Clean air and discipline are all they need.' But the plague continued, and one morning Tullus, riding at the head of his ragged army, felt a sudden glow of heat on his own body, and knew that Phoebus' arrow had pierced him too. He galloped back to Rome, and ordered his wise men to try every spell, rite or ceremony they could think of, to find a cure. While they pranced and muttered, he began scrabbling through a chest of papers, clay tablets and sheets of wax, the writings of his pious predecessor Numa. For thirty years Numa had daily written down messages he claimed were sent by the gods – surely, somewhere among them must be a cure for plague. One by one, Tullus read the writings and threw them impatiently down. Then, by chance, he found Numa's account of the ritual of Elicius, a magic ceremony meant to draw Jupiter down from sky to earth. The ritual was secret, forbidden to any mortal but Jupiter's own priest on the Aventine Hill; but now Tullus clutched the clay tablet in both hands and began mumbling the sacred words. In Olympus, Jupiter felt the magic tugging him from his throne. Enraged, he picked up a thunderbolt and hurled it. Tullus' palace, and the summit of the Caelian Hill on which it stood, were smashed to splinters; the rock boiled as water bubbles in a pot; Tullus, blazing like a pine-torch, was sucked into the Under-world, and neither he nor Numa's spells were seen on earth again.

131

Tarquin

Horrified at Tullus' death, the Romans took their time choosing a new king, and finally elected Ancus Martius. He was Numa's grandson, and was as knowledgeable as his grandfather had been about every kind of religious ritual or ceremony. His first acts were to order the cleaning of Rome's shrines and temples, and to sacrifice at each of them in honour of the gods. The Olympians' rage grew less against the Roman people. Phoebus drove his sun-chariot back to its normal course, high in the sky; Tiber reopened his water-springs; the plague began to lift. Ancus next set his mind to remembering every prayer or prophecy his grandfather had ever taught him, and passing them to the priests for temple use. It was a long job, painstaking and uneventful, and it gave the Romans time to recover from the plague and to relearn the delights of peace. None the less, those of their allies who thought that they had forgotten how to fight, who imagined that Ancus preferred to play the priest rather than the warrior, soon realised their mistake. At the first sign of rebellion he gathered the army, gave it spears and swords from the dusty town armouries, and showed himself as implacable in war as he was wise in peace.

Ancus had been king for several years when two strangers, Lucumo and Tanaquil, arrived in Rome. They came from Tarquinii, an Etruscan town about three days' riding to the north. Forty years before, Lucumo's father Demaratus had emigrated there from Greece, and made his fortune; when he died he left all his money to Lucumo and to Tanaquil, Lucumo's Etruscan wife. The pair had large estates in Tarquinii, a luxurious villa and hundreds of servants. But Tanaquil was still unsatisfied. 'You're an important man,' she said, 'far too big for this provincial town. Sell everything and move to Rome. It's growing: you'll find fame, and a second fortune, there.' The idea delighted Lucumo. He sold all his property, and converted it to gold bars which he loaded in a convoy of carts. These he sent under guard to Rome, and he and Tanaquil followed in a light riding-carriage. They reached Janiculum Hill, one of the seven hills of Rome, in the blazing heat of noon, and stopped to rest. While they were sitting quietly in the shade, an eagle swooped out of the sky, snatched Lucumo's hat and carried it away, then flew down again and replaced it on his head. Lucumo was terrified. But Tanaquil threw her arms round him and said joyfully, 'It's an omen! The eagle is Jupiter's royal bird; a hat is what crowns the head; the gods mean to crown you king of Rome!'

Flushed by this good luck, and with his mind full of his own future greatness, Lucumo drove on to Rome.

The first thing Lucumo did in Rome was to drop his foreign-sounding name and call himself Lucius Tarquinius Priscus, in Roman style. Lucius was a Roman name, Tarquinius came from the name of his birthplace Tarquinii, and Priscus ('the first') was a sign that he meant to found a dynasty. As soon as the treasure-carts arrived, he and Tanaquil bought estates, built a palace, and began giving parties and entertaining the most important people in Rome. They quickly made a name for themselves, and their friends included King Ancus himself. He enjoyed Tarquin's company, consulted him on every matter of state, and soon relied on him so much that he often asked him to lead armies, hear cases in the lawcourts or supervise religious ceremonies in the king's own palace. In a few years Tarquin was one of the most popular men in Rome, and King Ancus even gave him charge of the king's two sons, with orders to bring them up and teach them the skills of princes. All this time, until the princes were thirteen and fourteen, Tarquin behaved like the noble citizen everyone thought he was. He was lavish with his money, wise and humorous; he preferred to end quarrels than to make them; he did what he was asked quietly and successfully – and he told no one his secret thoughts. Then, in the spring of King Ancus' twenty-fourth year of rule, the old king caught a sudden chill and took to his bed. At once Tarquin sent for the two young princes. He told them that there was nothing to worry about: Tanaquil was nursing their father, and he was in safe hands. The risk was that they, too, might fall ill: these chills were more dangerous to young men than to old. For that reason, he said, he had ordered a carriage to take the boys to his own country estate for a hunting holiday. They should stay there until he sent for them, and leave everything in Rome to him.

The young men thanked Tarquin for his thoughtfulness, jumped into the carriage and drove away. As soon as they were gone, Tarquin sent banquet-invitations to every senator in Rome. He spent the evening praising their good sense and their concern for the people in these terrible times of the king's illness; he knew, he said, that if Ancus died they would make the best possible choice of a successor. In the days that followed he went round the Forum, the cattle-market and Rome's other public places. Wherever he went he said how sorry he was that the king, his closest friend, was so near to death. He declared his own love of Rome, a town he had chosen above his own birthplace.

He talked about the earlier kings of Rome, mentioning as if in passing how many of them had been strangers from other towns, chosen because of their outstanding abilities and their love of Rome. 'Why,' he finished jokingly, 'if King Ancus' two young sons were not both alive and well, even if they have abandoned their sick father and gone off on a hunting trip, I might have put myself forward as the ideal man to wear Ancus' crown.'

Tarquin was the first person ever to go round canvassing for votes, and he was as successful at this as at everything else he did. No sooner had Ancus breathed his last than the people elected Tarquin king, and the senators eagerly agreed. Tarquin repaid the people by holding a magnificent Games, the most glittering public celebration Rome had ever seen. He repaid the senate by adding one hundred more members, his own loyal supporters; he said that they made the senate the largest and most powerful group of men in Rome. He gave his followers land beside the Forum, built shops and covered walkways, and made plans to extend Rome's walls all round the town. The work was hard, and took young men from the fields and farms; but the people accepted it gladly, overjoyed at the way their town was being strengthened and beautified before their eyes. It soon became clear why strong defences were needed. The Sabines and Latins, who had been Rome's loyal allies since the time of Romulus, suddenly revolted, and Tarquin's young men had to drop their building-tools, snatch up spears and march to the attack. By the time the enemy was defeated, and a string of their towns – Ameriola, Cameria, Collatia, Corniculum, Ficulea, Medullia, Nomentum – had been sacked and their populations transferred to Rome, Tarquin's grip on royal power was unshakeable.* No one remembered the two royal princes, living in exile in a hunting-lodge far outside the city: Tarquin was king for life.

In the next few years Tarquin continued his building-work in Rome. He finished the walls; he made a system of pipes and water-tunnels to drain the marshland beside the Tiber; above all, he began a temple to Jupiter on the Capitoline Hill, a shrine to the king of the gods on the highest and best fortified place in Rome. And as the years passed, he began worrying more and more about his successor. All his life he had dreamed of founding a dynasty, a line of kings that would make his name and glory echo down the centuries. But he and Tanaquil were elderly, and Tanaquil was long past child-bearing age. One day the gods sent an answer. There was a little boy in the palace, Servius Tullius, the child either of a slave or of a prisoner-of-war from one of the captured towns. He was lying asleep when his hair suddenly burst into flames. The whole palace saw it; some of the servants ran for water, others to fetch the king and queen. Tanaquil told them on no account to disturb the child. 'Let him wake up naturally,' she said. Soon afterwards Servius opened his eyes, the flames went out of their own accord, and not a hair of his head was harmed. Tanaquil took Tarquin aside and said, 'My lord, another omen. We must bring this child up as our own son; he will blaze like a torch in our darkest hour.'

From that time on Tarquin and Tanaquil treated Servius as a royal prince, their adopted son. He grew up wise, brave and popular, and no one in Rome doubted that he would one day succeed to Tarquin's throne.

Far away, however, in a hunting-lodge in Etruria, two men took a very different view. They were the sons of Ancus, the former king, whom Tarquin had tricked from town and out of their father's throne. For thirty-eight years they had sat in exile, hearing reports of Tarquin's successes and brooding on revenge. Now they were men in their fifties, embittered and desperate. All through Tarquin's reign they had prayed to the gods to kill him in battle or to send some painful disease that would wipe him from the earth. But he had survived to the age of eighty, and now he had adopted a slave's son and was proposing to hand on to him the throne that was rightly theirs. The more they brooded, the more Tarquin seemed to them like Amulius, the war-leader of Alba Longa who had snatched his brother's throne and ordered his own baby nephews to be drowned in the Tiber. They saw themselves as a second Romulus and Remus, and determined, like them, to win back the throne by force. Because they were too old and too well-known to do the deed themselves, they hired two young shepherds as assassins, dressed them in sheepskins, as Romulus and Remus had been dressed, and sent them to Rome with axes in their belts. The shepherds went to the courtyard of Tarquin's palace, and began brawling like a pair of drunks. The palace guards crowded round to break up their quarrel, and the shepherds shouted that only the king could settle it. The noise reached Tarquin, dozing in his throne-room, and out of curiosity he sent for the shepherds and ordered them to speak. One of the young men began waving his arms and shouting his grievances, and while Tarquin's attention was distracted the second shepherd ran behind him and sank his axe in the old king's skull. Tarquin fell gasping, with the blade embedded in his wound, and while his servants ran to help him, the guards seized both shepherds and cut their throats before anyone could question them.

By this time the uproar had drawn a crowd. They thronged the street outside the palace, anxious for news, and Rumour filled their minds with ideas of enemy attacks, plague, civil war, each more terrifying than the last. In the confusion, the aged queen Tanaquil took command. She ordered the palace gates to be barred and guarded, and sent for doctors with herbs and potions to bathe Tarquin's wound. She took Servius aside and said, 'This is your moment! Blaze like a torch to save our dynasty: follow my lead, and you'll be king of Rome,' She flung open a window overlooking the street, and shouted to the crowd for silence. 'My lord the king was no more than stunned,' she said. 'Doctors are treating him; his life is in no danger. Soon he'll speak to you himself. In the meantime, he asks you to give your voices and your obedience to Servius, his son.' For ten days Servius ruled the city as regent, hearing lawsuits, managing senate business and sacrificing, and wherever he went he reassured people that he would give up his power as soon as Tarquin recovered. Only when Tanaquil was sure that all opposition had been removed did she dress herself in black, walk in a tearful procession to the senate-house and announce that Tarquin was dead. The senators at once proclaimed Servius king, and messengers rode secretly to the two princes in Tarquin's old hunting-lodge to tell them that their *coup* had failed and that their exile would last for life.

12
THE · LAST · KING
OF · ROME

Tarquin and Tullia

Servius had been on the throne for twenty-five years, and Tanaquil was long dead and buried, when two young men galloped into Rome on Etruscan horses and claimed to be Tarquin's long-lost sons. Their names, they said, were Lucius and Arruns; they were twins, born to a wood-nymph in Etruria not long after the aged Tarquin had passed that way on a hunting-trip.* Although they gave no proof of their identity and made no demands, it was not long before Servius' enemies in Rome began muttering that he was a usurper, a slave's son, and should give up his throne to the rightful heirs. To quell the unrest, Servius married his daughters to the two young Etruscans and declared them royal princes; then he demanded the people's approval of his right to rule, and was rewarded by a vote which gave him the throne for life.

This vote put ideas into Lucius' head. Servius may have been given the throne for life – but what was to stop that life being short? Greek myths were full of old kings whose lives were brought to a sudden end by the ambitious young princes who succeeded them. He said nothing of his plans, and instead set about making himself the most popular man in Rome. He took the name Tarquin, to remind everyone that he was his father's son, and like his father spent money lavishly on banquets for the rich and handouts for the poor. He seized every chance to make impressive speeches in the senate, to sponsor Games and festivals and to ride out in command of soldiers and show off his fighting skills.

Tarquin's brother Arruns shared none of his ambition. He was a mild-mannered man, more interested in farming than in state affairs. He spent his time growing vines on the slopes of Mount Albanus, and

137

seldom went to Rome. His wife Tullia despised this lack of ambition. The more she scorned him, the more she admired her brother-in-law Tarquin: he was her idea of a husband, her idea of a man born to rule. In the end ambition spoke to ambition, villainy called to villainy. One morning Arruns was found mysteriously dead in bed, Tarquin's wife died shortly afterwards, and Tullia and Tarquin played the sorrowing widow and widower for as long as it took to persuade Servius that their grief was real, and then married each other.

From that moment on, Servius' life was in mortal danger. At first, Tarquin was reluctant to risk a third murder. He preferred to sit it out and wait for the old king to die. But as year followed year, and Servius moved from his seventies to his eighties with no sign of failing powers, ambitious Tullia began jeering at Tarquin and trying to taunt him into violence. 'Coward!' she said. 'If you want nothing for yourself, think of me, your wife! Tanaquil, a foreigner, saw her husband and her adopted son crowned kings of Rome – am I, a princess, to be denied as much? Think of our sons. Are Sextus, Titus and Arruns to be barred from their rightful royal inheritance?' These words fanned the ambition in Tarquin's mind. He began going round the town, stirring up his supporters, and one morning he walked into the senate-house surrounded with soldiers, sat on the royal throne and ordered the senators to swear loyalty-oaths. There was uproar. His supporters jostled round him, hailing him as king; the other senators sent slaves running to fetch King Servius. When the old man's litter-bearers carried him in, he found Tarquin lounging on the throne, denouncing Servius as an ex-slave who had favoured his own kind for forty years and denied the senate its rightful power and authority.

'Get up!' shouted Servius. 'How dare you steal my throne?'

'Your throne?' answered Tarquin. 'You mean my father's throne, a king's throne. It's been too long in the power of slaves!'

These words caused a riot. Tarquin's and Servius' followers began brawling on the floor of the senate-house, and the shouts of a mob could be heard outside. Servius battered Tarquin feebly with his fists, and Tarquin picked the old man up like a sack, carried him out of the senate-house and threw him down the steps. Servius' supporters ran for their lives, and Servius picked himself up and staggered towards his palace. Before he had gone half a dozen steps a gang of men surrounded him and clubbed him to death, and as he lay there Tullia galloped into the Forum in a carriage, whipped her horses over her

138

own father's body and drove into the senate-house, her carriage-wheels wet with blood, to kneel to Tarquin and call him king at last.

Who shall take command?

Tarquin refused to let Servius' family bury the body. He said that it could rot where it lay, as a warning to any other over-ambitious slaves. The gods could take Servius into Olympus any time they chose, as they had once taken Romulus: it was up to them. He went on to order the execution of every senator he suspected of opposing him, and added their property to his own estates. He took charge of the lawcourts, made himself sole judge, and condemned people to torture, slavery or death as the fancy took him. Soon all Rome was trembling, and he extended his tyranny to the allies too. He sent word to the chiefs of every nearby town, ordering them to meet him at dawn in the Grove of Ferentia east of Rome to hear his orders. The men gathered, their eyes white in the darkness, and waited. Dawn passed and the morning began to stretch towards noon; there was still no sign of Tarquin. Turnus Herdonius, a leader from Aricia, said, 'No wonder the Romans call him Tarquin the Proud. Why did he send for us? He wants to test us, to see how ready we are to crawl beneath his heels. You can stay if you like; I'm going home.' This speech cost Turnus his life. That same night Tarquin sent soldiers to Aricia, armed and with torches. They dragged Turnus out of bed, searched the house and claimed to have found weapons hidden in the thatch. Turnus was declared a terrorist, and Tarquin ordered him to be tried by a method he'd just devised: Turnus was tied to a wickerwork shield weighted with stones and thrown into the Tiber. If he was innocent, Tarquin said, he'd float; if he was guilty he'd sink. Turnus sank and drowned.

With the people of Gabii, a small town near the river Anio, Tarquin used subtler methods. One day his son Sextus galloped into the town with his clothes torn and his arms and face wet with blood. He said that Tarquin's tyranny had spread from strangers to members of his own family. Sextus had dared to disagree with him that morning, and next minute murderers were hammering on his door. He begged the Gabians to shelter him, and said that theirs was the only town in the area strong enough to stand up to Rome. For two years, during which Sextus became a favoured citizen of Gabii and one of its richest and most powerful men, it never occurred to the Gabians to ask why

Tarquin sent no armies against them and made no effort to claim back his son. At the end of two years Sextus sent a secret messenger to Tarquin, to tell him that the plan had worked. The Gabians suspected nothing; the town was ripe to fall; what were Tarquin's orders? All the time the messenger was talking, Tarquin said nothing. He stood in his palace garden as if deep in thought, slashing a bed of poppies with a stick and scattering the ground with heads. The messenger rode back to Gabii, and told Sextus that his father had given no answer. But when he described what Tarquin had been doing, Sextus realised that the answer had been in deeds, not words. Soon afterwards, the leading citizens of Gabii began falling like poppy-heads: some were condemned to death on trumped-up charges, others fell to assassins in the night, others gathered their families and fled for their lives. Within a month Sextus was master of the town, able to deliver it and its riches into Tarquin's hands.

When his power was secure in Rome and in the nearby towns, Tarquin made peace-treaties with his most powerful neighbours, the hill-dwelling Aequi to the east and the Etruscans, his father's former people, to the north. Then he turned his attention to the gods. His plan was to finish the temple his father had begun to Jupiter on the Capitoline Hill, to make it a symbol not only of Rome's wealth and power but also of his own. He financed the work by plundering the richest of Rome's allies, Pometia, and ordered building-materials from as far away as Etruria. But the gods are not always impressed by mortal show. Jupiter showed his displeasure by sending an omen. A wooden roof-pillar in Tarquin's palace split apart, and a snake wriggled out of the crack and disappeared. The sight caused panic; even Tarquin felt a chill of fear. He decided that if the gods were questioning his right to rule, it was too important a matter to trust to local Roman soothsayers: the thing to do was to send messengers to Phoebus' shrine at Delphi, the most famous oracle in the world, and ask the priests there to explain the omen. Two of his sons, Titus and Arruns, and his nephew Brutus set out for Delphi, sailing over seas and riding through countries no Roman had ever seen before. Brutus was less the princes' companion than their jester. The whole Tarquin family regarded him as an idiot – this was why they had nicknamed him *Brutus*, 'animal' – and had poked fun at him for years. What none of them knew was that Brutus, seeing the slaughter of every noble Roman who might challenge Tarquin's rule, including his own father, Tarquin's brother-in-law Junius, had chosen quite deliberately to play

140

the fool, to make other people's mockery his armour. In the same way, he cloaked his real gift to Phoebus, a rod of pure gold, by hiding it in a hollow stick plucked from the nearest hedge. The three young men reached Delphi, and Titus and Arruns asked the oracle to explain the omen, as Tarquin had commanded. Then they asked Phoebus a second question on their own account: who would be the next king of Rome? The oracle answered with a riddle: 'Whoever kisses his mother first will take command.' Titus and Arruns decided to keep this prophecy secret, in case their brother Sextus, who was still in Italy, got to hear of it and kissed their mother Tullia before they could sail back home. But Brutus, who had heard every word (since neither Titus nor Arruns even noticed he was there), realised at once what Phoebus had really meant. He pretended to trip over his own feet, fell face down and kissed Mother Earth, the ancestor of all living things. Then he jumped up, slapped the dust from his clothes and went on playing the idiot as before.

The rape of Lucretia

After twenty-five years of tyranny, the candle of freedom was flickering low in Rome. A whole generation had grown up in Tarquin's shadow, knowing no other life but the hardship and suspicion of a tyrant's state. The dark side of human nature was triumphing; it was time for the gods to act. They chose their man: Brutus, whom the Delphic oracle had said would take command in Rome. And they chose their moment: the Roman siege of Ardea, a Rutulian town built where Turnus, who fought Aeneas, had once been king. The Ardeans had been allies of Rome for centuries, and it never occurred to them to fear attack. But they were wealthy, and their wealth caught Tarquin's eye. His building-work had bankrupted Rome, and just as he had financed the work's beginning out of the spoils from one loyal ally, Pometia, so now he decided to pay for its completion by plundering another. He led the Roman army against Ardea, and when the people slammed their gates against him he ringed the town with troops and sat down to starve them out.

The siege was long and tedious, and Tarquin's young officers (who included his son Sextus and his nephew Collatinus) soon grew bored. They spent their days hunting in the woods of Mount Albanus, terrifying Diana's nymphs, and their nights gambling and carousing.

One afternoon they were drinking in Sextus' tent, when the gods put it into their heads to talk of wives. Each man boasted that his wife was the most beautiful and most trustworthy woman in Rome. The boasting turned to argument, and finally Collatinus banged his cup down and said, 'There's a simple way to settle it. Let's ride home, this minute, and see just what each of our wives is up to.' It was no sooner said than done. The young men saddled their horses, rode out of camp and galloped in the dusk to Rome. They found their wives at a dinner-party, eating, drinking and enjoying themselves. Only Collatinus' wife Lucretia was missing, and when the officers rode to Collatia, her home village, and burst into her house they found her sitting by lamplight, placidly spinning with her maids. She jumped up to welcome them, and sent the servants for food and wine.

The young men made polite conversation, ate and drank – and as soon as they were riding back to camp, agreed ruefully that Lucretia was the most trustworthy wife, and Collatinus the luckiest man, in Tarquin's army. Collatinus' cousin Sextus rode silently behind, apart from the rest. While they had been eating and drinking in Collatinus' house, Cupid had pricked him with lust for Lucretia, and he was determined to make love to her whether she agreed or not, as soon as he could slip away from camp. Two nights later Lucretia, asleep in bed in Collatia, was startled awake by a hand on her breast and a voice whispering in her ear, 'Don't scream. It's your cousin Sextus. There's nothing to be afraid of.' She felt a man slip into bed beside her, and when she began to struggle the same cold voice said, 'If you don't make love with me, I'll cut your throat and then kill a servant and lay him beside you. What will Collatinus think of a wife caught in adultery with a slave and punished for it?'

The threat to Collatinus' honour conquered where fear would not. Lucretia let Sextus make love to her. But as soon as he had ridden back to camp, glowing with self-satisfaction, she sent letters to her father and her husband Collatinus, begging them to come at once. Her father hurried from Rome, and Collatinus galloped from Ardea with one companion: Brutus. They found Lucretia sitting alone, and asked what the matter was. Tears sprang to her eyes and she said, 'The matter is rape. Another man has defiled Collatinus' bed. Give me your hands: swear to take revenge. Prince Sextus is guilty. Promise to punish him. Let what he did lead to his death, as it leads to mine.' They tried to comfort her, to persuade her that the guilt was only Sextus', not hers, but she took a knife from her sleeve, cried, 'May all unfaithful wives

142

die as Lucretia now dies', plunged it into her heart and fell forward dead.

Lucretia's father and husband broke down and wept like children. But Brutus drew the knife from Lucretia's wound and said, 'By this girl's innocent blood I swear to hunt down Tarquin the Proud, his son Sextus, his wife and all his brood. Neither they nor anyone else will ever again be kings in Rome.' He held the knife out to the others, and one by one they touched the blood-stained hilt, staring in surprise at the change in Brutus, who had discarded his simpleton's disguise as a man throws off a cloak. At once, while anger still ruled their grief, they ordered slaves to carry Lucretia's body to Rome and display it in the Forum. By now it was morning, and a crowd soon gathered. Brutus shouted to the people that it was time to act. If they rose up now, they could sweep Tarquin's tyranny from Rome forever. Eagerness fired their hearts. They began prising up cobblestones and running to their houses for pitchforks and kitchen knives. They left armed guards in control of Rome, and marched on Ardea with Brutus and Collatinus at their head.

Long before the marchers reached Ardea, a messenger on a sweating horse brought news of the revolt. Tarquin tried to stir his soldiers to fight for him. But the fire of freedom glowed in their hearts; they mutinied as one man and declared their loyalty to Brutus. Tarquin and his sons Titus and Arruns fled to Rome, where they found the gates barred against them. Muffling themselves in their cloaks to avoid being recognised and murdered, they forded the Tiber and galloped across the border to safety in Etruria. In the royal palace in Rome, as soon as word came of the uprising, Queen Tullia's servants turned on her, beating her, tearing her clothes and praying to the Furies to rise from the Underworld and gulp her blood. She fled, an old woman with streaming hair and terror in her eyes, and was never seen again. As for Sextus, whose rape of Lucretia had caused the uprising, he galloped to Gabii, where he was sure he had loyal supporters still; but the Gabians remembered how he had betrayed them to Tarquin years before and clubbed him dead.

As soon as the tyrant and his family were swept from Rome, the senate met to decide the future. Excited talk of liberty blended with memories of the arrests, mutilations and murders that had marked Tarquin's reign, and the senate decreed that Rome should never again submit to a single king. They chose instead to appoint two commanders, neither of whom could act without the other. They called them

143

consuls, because their job was to consult and advise the senate, and said that they must lay down their power and hold elections at the end of a single year. The first two consuls were Collatinus and Brutus, the men who brought liberty to Rome.

Tarquin in retreat

Tarquin tried three times to win back his throne. He began, fittingly for a tyrant, with treachery. He sent letters to the Senate claiming back his and his family's property: it was bad enough to be exiles, he said, without being paupers too. The senate, as Tarquin guessed they would, spent days discussing the rights and wrongs of his case, and in the meantime his messengers went about their real business: finding out which Romans were still loyal to the idea of kings, and plotting with them to bring Tarquin back. There were plenty of young lords, drinking-companions of Tarquin's sons, who had no liking for democracy and would be happy to reopen Rome to tyranny; they included the two teenage sons of Brutus the Liberator himself. The young men met secretly with Tarquin's messengers, handed over letters promising support, and arranged a date and a time to betray their town. They thought that they were unobserved; but a horrified slave overheard their conversation and ran to tell the senate. The consuls threw the Roman conspirators into prison, and put Tarquin's messengers under house arrest while they decided what to do. If they killed Tarquin's messengers, it would mean war with the Etruscans. If they handed the messengers over, the furious Roman people would throw the entire Roman senate out of office, consuls and all. In the end they announced no direct decision, but instead left Tarquin's palace unguarded and let the mob swarm inside, looting all the valuables they could find and burning the rest.* In the confusion, the guards allowed Tarquin's messengers to slip clear from their house arrest; they scuttled to their master in Etruria with news of the people's rage. When the commotion died down, the Roman conspirators were dragged from their prison cells for trial. The verdict was guilty, and the sentence was death. The people of Rome gathered in the Forum, and the consuls and senators took their places on thrones to witness the execution. The prisoners were stripped, tied to wooden crosses, flogged and beheaded – and all the time Brutus sat on his consul's throne, tears running down his cheeks

144

as he put love for his country before his family and watched his own sons die.

Since treachery had failed, Tarquin turned to force. He went to the leaders of two Etruscan towns, Tarquinii and Veii, and demanded troops. In Tarquinii he said that the Romans had dishonoured not only him but his father Tarquin the First and the town from which the Tarquins took their name; unless the Tarquinians took revenge their name would be a laughing-stock forever. In Veii he reminded the people how often the Romans had defeated them in the past and plundered their land; they should seize the chance for revenge, he said, before yet another invasion and the replacement of kingship by democracy in Veii as well as in Rome. Both peoples eagerly agreed to support him, and soon their armies were marching on Rome. Tarquin commanded the infantry, and his son Arruns led the cavalry. On the Roman side Brutus spurred ahead with the cavalry, and the other consul led the main force behind on foot. When the two armies were still some way apart, Arruns recognised Brutus in the Roman lines and shouted, 'There he is! There's the man who stole our kingdom, threw us into exile and looted our property. Gods, help me to take revenge!' He lowered his spear and spurred to the attack. On his side, Brutus too galloped out of his troops with lowered spear. The two men met with such force that each drove his spear full through the other's body and pinned him to the ground; they glared at each other with glazing eyes and cursed each other with their dying breaths. On each side the infantry ran up behind them, and fierce hand-to-hand fighting began. Fury took the place of battle-plans: men sliced and stabbed blindly, slipping and staggering in one another's blood. Their commanders galloped up and down on panting horses, shouting useless orders: nothing could be heard above the shouts of triumph, the clatter of weapons and the screams of the dying. At last the gods put an end to it. Jupiter cloaked the sky in cloud and poured night over the battlefield till it was too dark to see. The armies drew back, shouting defiance at each other across their comrades' corpses. They set up camps, made fires and prepared to spend a restless night, chafing for dawn when the fighting could begin again. But in the night the forest-god Silvanus appeared to the Etruscans, who were encamped in his sacred grove, and filled their ears with a warning only they could hear. To mortals, the fighting had seemed exactly even, but in the darkness the gods had counted the corpses and the Etruscan dead outnumbered the Romans by a single man. They had lost the battle, and unless they wanted to join their companions in the Underworld, flitting unburied beside the river Styx, they should leave everything where it was and slip out of camp. Accordingly, when the Romans snatched their weapons at dawn next morning and ran to invade the Etruscan camp, they found the cooking-fires still glowing, the ground littered with weapons and personal belongings, but not a single person to be seen. They marched back to Rome, their joy at victory mixed with grief at the death of so many of their comrades, and especially of Brutus who had brought liberty to Rome.*

For his third attempt, Tarquin begged the help of one of the most powerful of all Etruscan kings, Lars Porsena of Clusium. He said that if the gods, with the Romans as their instruments, once got the taste for expelling kings, there would be no end to it: every monarch in Italy would be at risk, even Porsena himself, the most glorious of them all. Porsena gathered his army, equipped it with siege-catapults, fire-towers and battering-rams, and marched on Rome. The soldiers advanced across the countryside, plundering farms, seizing cattle, stealing grain, burning buildings and murdering anyone who opposed them. It was like unrolling a carpet of conquest: wherever Porsena's army passed, Etruscans ruled. The Romans panicked. As the enemy came ever nearer, the outlying farmers snatched their belongings and poured into Rome, camping on the Capitoline Hill* in the safety of the citadel. There was one bridge across the Tiber, a wooden structure built on piles, and day and night it echoed to the rumble of cartwheels and the scrape of feet. The gods looked down at the ant-columns of people on the bridge and the Tiber swirling below, and decided to use them for Rome's defence. They sent a man called Horatius Cocles to the senate. He pointed out that the bridge was the only crossing-point on the Tiber for a day's march in either direction, and that it was narrow and rickety. 'A handful of men could hold the enemy at bay,' he said, 'while workmen chop the bridge down behind them.' The plan was risky, but the enemy were in sight and the consuls hastily agreed. As soon as the last refugee was safe in Rome, Horatius closed the bridge and took his place at the far end with two companions, Lartius and Herminius. Porsena brought his Etruscan army to a halt in astonishment. How could three men hold off an entire invading force? Then he heard the sound of axes from the Roman end of the bridge, and the cracking of timber. Red with rage, he shouted to his men to attack. His idea was that his soldiers should overwhelm the three Romans in a single rush; but when the soldiers saw the determination in the Romans' faces and the battle-glow in their eyes, they were filled with panic and hung back, each waiting for someone else to lead the attack. Meanwhile, on the Roman side, the defenders had chopped through the supporting struts and the bridge was sagging. Porsena shouted again to his troops to move, and they made their attack at last. While the main body fired arrows and hurled spears, a few men at a time ran to tackle Horatius, Lartius and Herminius single-handed. For half an hour, while the bridge creaked and swayed behind them, the three champions dodged every missile, killed every attacker, kept a whole army at bay. Then there was a cry from behind, 'It's going!', and Horatius shouted to his companions to save themselves. Lartius and Herminius ran back across the bridge and leapt to safety while he, single-handed, thrust the Etruscans back. At the very last moment, as the bridge collapsed with a roar behind him and the way into Rome was barred, he threw his sword in the faces of his enemies, dived into the Tiber in full armour and swam to the Roman bank, where his comrades pulled him out of the water and carried him shoulder-high into Rome.

Even this success was not enough to end the war. The Etruscan army was kept from Rome, but the Romans were barred by the Etruscans from crossing the Tiber to their farms on the other side. The gods breathed courage into a second young nobleman, Caius Mucius. He waited till darkness, then swam across the Tiber with his clothes bundled on his head. He dressed in a countryman's tunic and cloak and walked into Porsena's camp with a dagger in his sleeve. The camp was full of farmers; no one challenged him as he rolled in his cloak beside a camp-fire to wait till dawn. As soon as the sun was up, Porsena's men gathered in the open space before the king's tent, and the king and his officials came out to pay their wages. There were a dozen men sitting at a long table, checking names and handing out money from sacks of coins. They were all muffled in cloaks against the morning air, and Mucius had no idea which of them was Porsena. He chose the most important-looking, moved gradually towards him through the crowd, then sprang out and stabbed him dead. The soldiers shouted in alarm, and the royal guards snatched Mucius, with the knife still bloody in his hand, and dragged him before a second man, the king. The person he'd killed had been one of the royal secretaries. The guards tried to make Mucius kneel before Porsena, but he braced his shoulders, looked the Etruscan in the eye and said, 'I am a freeborn Roman, sworn like all my people never again to kneel to kings.' Porsena took this as a threat that there was a plot to kill him, and ordered Mucius to be burnt alive unless he gave the names of all the conspirators. But while Porsena's men were fetching branches and building the pyre, Mucius stood at an altar beside the royal throne, and thrust his right hand into the sacrificial fire. Without once flinching, while the flames charred his hand to ash before their eyes, he said, 'If there is a conspiracy, Porsena, it includes every young man in Rome. For each one of us you kill, another will come forward to hunt you down. Never rest again; never trust anyone; the moment your guard slips, you will die.' These words, and Mucius' heroism in the face of unendurable agony, so impressed Porsena that he ordered the young man to be freed and sent him back to Rome with peace-terms.* The Etruscans withdrew to their own borders and promised never again to make war on Rome; the Romans agreed to hand back the territory they had won at Veii and Tarquinii, and to call off all conspiracies against Porsena. There was no discussion about restoring Tarquin's throne.

Abandoned by Porsena, Tarquin had little hope of ever ruling Rome again. For a few years he went round the Italian towns trying to raise revolt, and whenever he could persuade troops to attack the Romans, he eagerly took the field. But he was aging and his efforts were useless; in the end he settled in exile at Cumae, near the sacred cave where the Sibyl had long ago led Aeneas down to the Under-world. Day and night the Furies haunted him, panting to punish him for murdering his brother and his wife so many years before; in his ninetieth year they finally choked the mortal life from him and snatched him to unceasing agony in Tartarus.

With Tarquin dead, the gods hoped that their purpose for mortals had been fulfilled at last. The last king had gone from Rome; democracy ruled; justice had triumphed over wickedness. From that moment on, the gods hoped, Rome would lead the entire human race in honour and nobility, protecting the poor and punishing the proud. It was the fulfilment of the prophecy Aeneas' father Anchises had made in the Underworld centuries before the founding of Rome. The gods put their trust in Rome, looking to the Romans to sweep injustice from the earth and to rule with humanity, prosperity and peace till the end of time.

ADDITIONAL · STORIES
ALTERNATIVE
VERSIONS · AND · NOTES

Many of the gods and goddesses of Roman myth are nowadays known equally by Greek and Roman names. This book uses Roman names throughout. This chart lists the most important gods and goddesses, and the names of their Greek equivalents.

Roman name	Greek equivalent	Function
Bellona	—	Goddess of fighting (especially favoured by gladiators)
Ceres	Demeter	Harvest-goddess, especially of corn
Cupid	Eros	Venus' son, a small, blind boy shooting arrows of love
Diana	Artemis	Goddess of the moon, of hunting and of childbirth
Dis or Pluto	Pluton or Hades	King of the Underworld
Faunus	—	God of flocks and herds
Fortuna	—	Goddess of chance and destiny
Juno	Here	Queen of heaven, goddess of marriage and of oaths
Jupiter	Zeus	Sky-god, king of the gods
Lares / Penates	—	Guardians of the household / larder
Mars	Ares	God of war, father of Romulus and Remus, protector of the Roman state
Mercury	Hermes	God of markets and bargaining
Minerva	Athene	Goddess of wisdom
Neptune	Poseidon	King of the Sea, earthquakes and horses
	Phoebus / Apollo	God of the Sun and of prophecy
Proserpina	Persephone	Queen of the Underworld
Saturn	Kronos	God of work and of old age
Silvanus	Pan	God of fields and forests
Venus	Aphrodite	Goddess of love and beauty
Vesta	Hestia	Goddess of hearth and home, whose ever-burning flame symbolised the life of the Roman state
Vulcan	Hephaistos	Blacksmith-god who supervised the making of Jupiter's thunderbolts

TITANS (*page 2*)

There were 45 Titans, the offspring of Father Sky (Uranus) and Mother Earth (Tellus). They were enormous beings with no fixed shape: whatever they chose, winds, storms, blackness, hill-sides, they had only to think it to become it. Sky was terrified of his children, and hunted them through the gulf of space, trying to destroy them. In the end they cowered for safety in the innermost crannies of their mother Earth, and when Sky swooped down to the surface to claw them out, Saturn, the youngest and boldest Titan, snatched Sky's penis and cut it off with a diamond-edged sickle. Drops of Sky's blood fertilised Mother Earth, and she gave birth to a race of gigantic monsters; Saturn flung the severed penis out to sea, and the foam of its falling gave birth to Venus, queen of love, the first-born of the gods.

GODS AND TITANS (*page 4*)

Saturn, king of Titans, had long suspected that his children might one day make war on him as he had made war on his own father Sky (see above). Accordingly, as soon as his children were born – their names were Ceres, Juno, Neptune, Pluto and Vesta – he swallowed them alive. Saturn's wife, Rhea, saved the sixth child Jupiter by giving Saturn a stone wrapped in baby clothes to swallow instead. Jupiter grew up in hiding in the caves of Mount Ida in Crete, and as soon as he was old enough he went in disguise to Saturn's court and tricked Saturn into drinking a cup of Styx-water. The water would have chilled most other beings dead, but its only effect on Saturn was to make him vomit up his swallowed children, now full-grown gods. War at once began in heaven, the six gods and their supporters on one side, and Saturn and the Titans on the other.

JANUS (*page 5*)

In some accounts, Jupiter also punished Janus by putting him in charge of a single moment in time, endlessly repeated throughout eternity: the instant when the old year dies and the new year is born.

In other versions of the myth, Janus was the son not of Sky or of Hecate but of Phoebus the sun-god. He was a kindly, benevolent ruler, and was given the ability to see both ways not as a punishment but as a reward for his wisdom and a symbol of his prophetic powers. The people of Latium, his former kingdom in Italy, never forget him. They built a temple to him on Janiculum Hill, and it later became one of the main shrines of Rome. His place at the year's turning-point made the Romans regard him as a kind of door-keeper, or 'janitor', of the seasons, and they named the first month of the year January after him.

PROMETHEUS' MORTALS (*page 9*)

This Roman version of the myth of the making of mortals differs considerably from the one told in ancient Greece. In the Roman account, Prometheus' mortals were insignificant and sinless, no threat to the gods: it was only when Mother Earth made mortals of her own, from giants' blood, that they turned evil and the gods made plans to destroy them (see page 23). In the Greek account, Prometheus tried to give his creation godlike intelligence, by stealing the fire of knowledge. He was punished by being pegged to a rock for a thousand generations, while Jupiter's eagle pecked his liver and

151

his liver was unceasingly renewed. Fire, meanwhile, gave human beings understanding of the ways of Olympus, and they began to be jealous of the gods and to challenge them, until at last Jupiter decreed that the earth should be flooded and washed clean of them (see page 27).

POMONA AND VERTUMNUS (page 10)

In the version of this myth in Ovid's *Metamorphoses*, as well as hugging Pomona Vertumnus tried to win her sympathy by telling her a sad tale of unrequited love. 'Iphis, a poor peasant, fell in love with Princess Anaxarete. But she despised him for his humble birth, and made her heart hard as a stone towards him. In the end, filled with despair, he hanged himself, and when Anaxarete found his body the stone in her heart engulfed her whole body and turned her into a statue.' Like all Vertumnus' other efforts, this story had no success – and it was then that he threw off the old-woman disguise, showed himself to Pomona as he truly was, and finally won her heart.

PICUS (page 14)

In another legend entirely, Picus, king of Latium was the son not of Saturn but of Pilumnus, the god of baking. He was renowned for the oracles he gave his people by interpreting the tapping of a pet woodpecker on the wooden arms of his throne. Some say that this was the origin of the legend that he was himself a woodpecker; others say that the gods, impressed by his goodness, turned him into a woodpecker at the end of his reign on earth, and also, in his honour, gave all woodpeckers prophetic powers.

PSYCHE AND THE GODS (page 20)

In the version of this story by the Roman writer Apuleius, the gods refused to help Psyche at all, and she was eventually arrested as an escaped slave of Venus and taken in disgrace to Olympus, where Venus beat her and set her slave-tasks.

THE RAM WITH THE GOLDEN FLEECE (page 21)

The legendary golden ram was a gift from Neptune to Phrixus, prince of Thebes. Phrixus was heir to his father's kingdom, but heard that his step-mother Ino planned to murder him and to promote her own son to the throne. Phrixus escaped from Thebes with his sister Helle on the back of the flying, golden ram. The ram flew north towards the Black Sea, and on the way Helle fell off and was drowned in a stretch of water later called Hellespont ('Helle's Sea') after her. Phrixus flew on to Colchis on the Black Sea coast, where he sacrificed the ram to Phoebus god of the sun and hung its fleece in a temple beside the palace of King Aeëtes, son of the Sun. This golden fleece was the one Jason and the Argonauts later sailed from Greece to find.

THE TASKS (page 21)

In some versions of the story, including Apuleius' (on which the one in this book is based), Venus set Psyche four tasks. First, she had to separate the grains – and was helped by ants. Second, she had to pluck wool from the gold-fleeced, flesh-eating sheep – and was told what to do not by Pan but by a talking reed by the riverside. Third, she had to fetch a cup of water from the Styx – and was helped by Jupiter's eagle. Fourth, she had to visit the Underworld and beg a magic box from Prosperpina, queen of Hell. She was told not to open it, but disobeyed, was plunged into a magic sleep and was only rescued in the nick of time by Cupid, who flew down to the Underworld in person to bring her back.

JUPITER AND CUPID   (*page 22*)

In Apuleius' version of the story, Cupid went to Jupiter to beg him to end Venus' persecution of Psyche, and Jupiter agreed only if Cupid stopped firing arrows of desire at the Olympian gods and found him, Jupiter, a mortal girl as beautiful as Psyche to share his bed.

PSYCHE'S SISTERS   (*page 22*)

In some versions of the story, including Apuleius', Psyche herself tricked her wicked sisters into jumping by telling them, one after the other, that Cupid had fallen so much in love with them that he had divorced her (Psyche) and was waiting to make love to them.

AEGEON   (*page 22*)

Only one of Mother Earth's children was ever summoned from the Underworld and the reason was Juno's fury at Jupiter's constant love-affairs. He no sooner set eyes on a pretty nymph, wood-spirit or mortal, than he changed shape, visited her and made love with her. Juno asked Neptune and Apollo to help her punish him. They crept up on Jupiter while he lay asleep and tied him with a leather rope fastened in a hundred knots: unless they were all untied at the same moment, he could never be set free.

Jupiter lay helpless, shouting with rage, and none of the gods but Mother Earth dared act. She reached into the depths of the Underworld where the giants lay sleeping, woke Aegeon the Hundred-handed, and whispered to him what to do. He scrambled up the slopes of Mount Olympus and untied Jupiter, loosening all hundred knots at once. Then he sat at Jupiter's feet while the king of the gods punished the rebels. Jupiter enslaved Apollo and Neptune for a year to a mortal, King Laomedon of Troy (see page 155), and hung Juno by golden chains from the roof of the sky, dangling an anvil from her ankles until she begged for mercy. When the punishments were over, Aegeon hoped for his reward. But there was no place for a giant in the World of Light, and Jupiter sent Aegeon scowling and muttering back to his dungeon in the depths of Hell. See also pages 102, 171.

THE PALLADIUM   (*page 31*)

The Palladium ('Pallas-statue') was called after one of Minerva's honorary names, Pallas. She earned the name when the giants attacked Olympus (see page 23). She killed one of their leaders, Pallas, made his hide into a leather shield, and was ever afterwards given the honorific nickname Pallas.

When mortals were looking for a place to build the city that was to be called Troy, they camped on a windy plain between mountains and the sea. That night the wooden statue of a goddess, a metre high, fell from Olympus and embedded itself in the earth in front of them. They decided that it was a statue of Pallas Minerva, called it the Palladium and built the city round it. It lay in the same place for hundreds of years, and the story grew that as long as the Trojans revered it, Minerva would protect them and keep their race from extinction. In some accounts, this statue was the one Aeneas took into exile after the fall of Troy (see page 155).

EPEUS (*page 38*)

In some accounts, the man who opened the Horse and let the warriors out was not Sinon but Epeus. He was the craftsman who built the Horse, and he was a coward: he agreed to the work only on condition that he could stay with the ships and keep well away from Troy. Unfortunately, the fastenings he made for the trapdoor in the Horse's side were so ingenious that no one else could open them, and Ulysses forced him, grumbling and trembling, to join the task-force inside the Horse and be trundled into Troy.

ANCHISES (*page 38*)

A cousin of King Priam, Anchises as a youth was the handsomest young man in Troy. The love-goddess Venus spent the night with him on the slopes of Mount Ida, and in the morning realised that she was pregnant. She gave birth, in due course, to Aeneas, and told Anchises that if he ever revealed who the child's mother was, he would be struck down by a thunderbolt. For years Anchises kept the secret, but at last he told Aeneas his mother's name, and Venus borrowed a thunderbolt from her father Jupiter and hurled it at Anchises. However, either because she was unused to thunderbolts or because her aim was deflected by love for Anchises, the thunderbolt only grazed him, and instead of killing him left him a prematurely senile, crippled invalid, too feeble to take any part in the Trojan War or to lead the survivors into exile afterwards (see page 42).

COROEBUS AND CASSANDRA (*page 39*)

Coroebus was not a native Trojan, but a prince of Phrygia who came to Troy to fight as Priam's ally. He fell in love with Cassandra, and asked Priam to let him marry her when the war was won. Priam knew Cassandra's temperament, and shrugged his shoulders; for her part, Cassandra bluntly told Coroebus not only that she was Apollo's bride and would marry no mortal husband, but that if he (Coroebus) stayed in Troy the Greeks would kill him. Like everyone else who heard her prophecies, Coroebus disbelieved them, and he stayed in Troy hoping that she would change her mind. So it was that he joined Aeneas' band of warriors after the Greeks entered Troy, and so it was that he was killed.

The Greeks led Cassandra away with the other prisoners-of-war; in the division of spoils she was chosen by lot to be Agamemnon's house-slave, and sailed with him to Mycenae. She prophesied that his homecoming would be his death, and as usual was ignored. Soon after Agamemnon walked into Mycenae on the crimson carpet set out for him by his treacherous wife Clytemnestra, and was butchered in his bath, Cassandra was hacked to death at Apollo's altar like a human sacrifice – exactly the fate she had always known awaited her.

PYRRHUS (*page 40*)

There is confusion about who exactly Pyrrhus was. His father was certainly Achilles, and many writers say that his mother was Deidamia, daughter of King Lycomedes. (Achilles' own mother Thetis, not wanting Achilles to go to the Trojan war, disguised him as a woman and hid him among Lycomedes' palace

154

women, under the name Pyrrha ('blonde'); his disguise was revealed when the recruiting Greeks visited Lycomedes and blew a war-trumpet, whereupon Achilles ran forward to fight.) These accounts say that Achilles' son was called Pyrrhus until he, too, joined the Trojan war, when he changed his name to Neoptolemus ('late warrior') because he only arrived in the closing months of the war.

Other authorities say that the Neoptolemus who went to Troy (and who was Achilles' and Deidamia's son) was a boy of twelve years old, far too young to be the 'Pyrrhus the destroyer' who sacked Priam's palace. They say that this Pyrrhus was the son of Achilles and another, unknown woman, perhaps a princess of Asia Minor, and that he was one of the savagest of all Greek warriors at the fall of Troy. Soon after butchering Priam, he killed Achilles' concubine Polyxena as a blood-sacrifice on his father's grave, and threw Hector's baby son Astyanax over the city battlements to prevent the Trojan dynasty ever rising again. After the war, instead of returning to southern Greece or the islands, he went to Epirus (modern Albania) and he founded a piratical royal dynasty. His descendant Pyrrhus, centuries later, was one of the fiercest enemies of Rome, and lost so many men in battle that even though he won battles his power was totally destroyed – the origin of the phrase 'a Pyrrhic victory'.

PRIAM   (*page 40*)

Priam's birth-name was Podarces, and he was the youngest son of Laomedon, king of Troy. Two gods, Apollo and Neptune, rebelled against Jupiter, and their punishment was a year's forced service to a mortal. Their master was Laomedon, and their task was to build walls for Troy which no mortal could ever overthrow. When the walls were built the gods asked for payment, and Laomedon skipped inside his city and said, 'Get it if you can!' For answer, the gods asked Hercules (no mortal, but Jupiter's illegitimate son) to batter a hole in the walls. They killed Laomedon and made his baby son Podarces king in his place, renaming the child Priam. Priam ruled for the rest of his long life (over eighty years), but his people never had the gods' full-hearted support, and Apollo's and Neptune's dislike for Troy, added to Juno's fury after the judgement of Paris (see page 31), led to the city's eventual destruction.

One of Priam's first tasks when he became king was to rebuild the section of the wall smashed by Hercules. His workmen were mortal, and their part of the wall was weaker than any other; it was this section that the Trojans demolished to let in the Wooden Horse (see page 37).

AENEAS AND ANCHISES   (*page 43*)

Most accounts say that it was Anchises that Aeneas carried from Troy on his shoulders, and this is the scene shown in most Greek and Roman pictures of the escape. In this version, the Palladium (the statue of Minerva which guarded the life of the Trojan people: see page 153) was carried away separately, perhaps in the wooden chest with Aeneas' household gods (see page 47). But there is an alternative account, which says that Anchises made his own way out of Troy, or was helped by servants, and that Aeneas carried the Palladium on his shoulders, covering it with a lion-skin so that from a distance he and it looked like a single, running figure. This version of the myth goes on to say that Aeneas handed the Palladium on to his descendants after the Trojans settled in Italy (see page 112). When Romulus built the city of Rome (see page 117), he placed the Palladium in the temple of Vesta at the new city's heart, and it remained there ever afterwards, guaranteeing the safety of the Roman state and cared for by the Vestal Virgins who also tended Vesta's sacred fire. (see page 114).

TROJAN ROYAL HOUSE

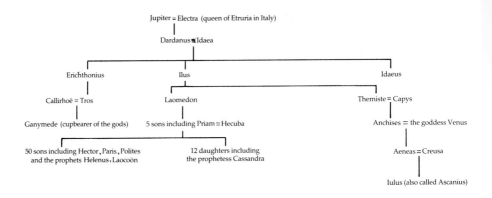

LYCURGUS (*page 44*)

When the god Bacchus was advancing from Asia into Greece, bringing the gift of wine, many people opposed him and suffered for it. One of them was Lycurgus, king of the Edonians. He was appalled at the thought of wine-crazed hooligans rioting across his peaceful land, fought Bacchus' followers with an army, and finally took an ox-goad and drove the survivors into the sea. The Bacchants were all drowned; Bacchus himself only escaped by hiding in an underwater cave.

When the goddess Rhea saw what had happened she rescued Bacchus, brought his followers back to life and punished Lycurgus by driving him mad. Lycurgus raged through the hill-villages of his country axing down vineyards wherever he found them; Rhea made him mistake his own son Dryas for a vine, and he chopped the boy down and began lopping his legs and arms as if they were branches. The Edonians were so sickened that they took Lycurgus high into the hills, attached wild horses to his legs and arms and had him torn to pieces.

156

THE MURDER OF POLYDORUS;
POLYDORUS AND HECUBA   (*page 45*)

There are many accounts of Polydorus'
death. In some he never left Troy at all,
but was a grown-up prince who fought in
the war and was killed by Achilles. In
others he was a child sent for safekeeping
to Polymnestor, king of the Edonians,
and his wife Ilione (Priam's sister or,
some say, his daughter and Polydorus'
elder sister). Throughout the war Polydorus grew up safely, but when the
fighting was over the Greeks were anxious to wipe out every one of Priam's
descendants, and paid Polymnestor a
fortune to murder Polydorus. Though
Polymnestor was reluctant to kill the son
of his old ally, he was also terrified of the
Greeks, and in the end he killed his own
son Deiphilus and told the Greeks it was
Polydorus. For this crime, an echo of his
ancestor Lycurgus' murder of *his* son
Dryas (see page 156), Polydorus later
executed him, becoming king of the Edonians in his place.

It was only in the versions of the myth
followed by Virgil (in his *Aeneid*, the
account used here), that Polydorus was
really killed and the Edonians changed
sides from Troy to Greece. Virgil's account says that Polydorus' body was
buried under the myrtle-mound, but
other versions say that it was tossed into
the sea and floated south until it was
washed ashore near Troy. After the capture of Troy, Polydorus' mother Hecuba
stumbled on his corpse rotting in the
shallows, ran to find Polymnestor, his
murderer, and gouged out his eyes with
her own bare hands. She screeched at her
maids to tear him to pieces, and Polymnestor's servants had to drive them away
with showers of stones. The gods
changed Hecuba into a she-wolf (or,
some say, a greyhound bitch), and she
fled howling into the foothills where no
Greeks dared pursue her. Visitors to the
plain of Troy from that day to this have
claimed to hear her wailing in the distance as she mourns for her dear dead
son.

DELOS AND APOLLO   (*page 46*)

Latona, the beautiful daughter of the
Titans Phoebe and Coeus (or, some say,
Saturn) was courted by Jupiter and
became pregnant with immortal twins.
Juno, queen of heaven, vowed that
Latona would have no resting-place on
earth to bear her children, and sent the
monstrous serpent Python to hunt her
down. Trembling with terror, Latona
flew from earth to Olympus, from Olympus across the heavens and back to earth,
and the only way Jupiter could devise to
save her from Python's fury was to disguise her as a quail. He begged help from
his brother Neptune, king of the sea, and
Neptune anchored the floating island of
Delos to give quail-Latona a resting-
place. Latona settled on the island,
changed back from quail to goddess, and
in due course gave birth to twins: Apollo
and Diana. One of Apollo's first acts was
to kill the monstrous Python, and he
celebrated his victory by establishing the
Pythian Games near Delphi and the
Pythian priestess to speak his oracles in
the sanctuary there. He and Diana never
forgave Juno for her treatment of their
mother. They seldom visited Olympus,
preferring to spend time in their holy
places on earth or to gallop with their
followers in hunting-parties across the
sky. Delos, Apollo's birthplace, became
the centre of his worship on earth, and
was renowned for the accuracy of the
oracles he granted there.

ANIUS   (*page 46*)

The Trojans had no need to be wary of the Delians. Like the guardians of all oracles, the Delians were sworn to impartiality, and in any case Anius, if he had taken sides between Greeks and Trojans, would have favoured Troy. The reason was his children. He had four daughters, and when they were babies he asked the gods to give them gifts. Bacchus gave them the Touch of Plenty, the power to transform anything they touched into bread, wine or olive oil. (It was like Midas' golden touch in the Greek myth, except that, unlike Midas, they could choose when, and on what, to use it.) They used the touch sparingly, to feed their father's people, and he hoped for rich marriages for them when they grew up. But the Greek fleet called at Delos on its way to Troy, and Agamemnon snatched the girls from the sanctuary and dragged them to the ships, to guarantee provisions for his soldiers throughout the war. Helpless, Anius lifted his hands and prayed for help to Bacchus, and the god transformed the daughters into doves, cooing and fluttering in the Greeks' astonished hands. So they were saved and stayed in Delos, and to this day the island is filled with cooing doves, their descendants. But their transformation broke their father's heart, and made him no friend of Greeks.

SCAMANDER   (*page 46*)

There was famine in Crete, and one third of the inhabitants, led by Prince Scamander, left the island and sailed north to find a new homeland. They landed on a wide, windy plain at the foot of a mountain which they called Ida after Mount Ida in Crete, Jupiter's birthplace. Scamander married one of the mountain-nymphs,

Idaea, and their son Teucer founded a city which later came to be known as Troy. Scamander himself died in battle, leaping into the river Xanthus which ran across the Trojan plain. (The river's name was changed to Scamander after him.) The water gave miraculous lustre to the skin of any living thing it touched, and the Trojans used it to wash their sheep's wool before shearing them. Legend says that the goddesses Juno, Minerva and Venus swam in the river before they appeared to Paris and asked him to choose the most beautiful (see page 31).

IDOMENEUS   (*page 46*)

Idomeneus left Crete to help the Greeks in the Trojan war, with ninety ships and several thousand men. Sailing home after the war with the remnants of this fleet, he was caught in a storm and promised that if Neptune spared his life he would sacrifice the first living thing he saw when he came to land. Unfortunately this turned out to be his own child (some say his son Idamantes, others an unnamed daughter), and his people were so disgusted by this murder that they banished him, whereupon he sailed to Italy, founded a city in the south (Salentum in Calabria) and lived contentedly there until the day he died.

DARDANUS   (*page 47*)

Dardanus was the second son of King Corytus and Queen Electra of Etruria, a farming settlement in central Italy. When he grew up his mother told him that he was not Corytus' son at all but Jupiter's, and that his divine ancestry gave him the right to rule. Fired by this news, Dardanus waited until Corytus' death, then murdered his own elder brother Iasius and claimed the throne. Jupiter, however, refused to let even his own bastard son win a kingdom by fratricide, and stirred Dardanus' people to banish him from Italy. Dardanus fled to Asia Minor, married the daughter of King Teucer, son of Scamander (see page 158), and in due course inherited the throne and established the royal dynasty of Troy (see family tree on page 156).

In some versions of the legend, the gods showed Dardanus their forgiveness for the murder of Iasius by dropping at his feet the Palladium – the statue of Minerva which later guarded the life of Troy.

THE HARPIES (page 48)

In the earliest age of the universe, before the era of the gods, all living things were created from the mating of Sky, Sea, Night, Air and Earth. The three Harpies were daughters of Sea and Earth, an experiment in the making of life from a blend of feathers, bronze and flesh. They were so hideous that even their parents were disgusted by them, and hid them deep in the Underworld, in the crevices of Mother Earth which were the home of misshapen monsters of every kind. Later, in the age of the gods, the sun-god sent them to torment Phineus, a prophet who revealed the whereabouts of the secret palace where the Sun went to rest each evening and was reborn each morning. Once the Harpies were released into the upper world, not even the gods could ever force them back to the Underworld, and so Calais and Zetes, sons of the North Wind, sent them hurtling to the Whirling Islands, the Strophades, for imprisonment. For most of each year the Strophades whirled like spinning tops, creating a vortex which imprisoned the Harpies as securely as a dungeon. Every so often, however, the islands came to rest, and set the Harpies free, for a time, to prey on visitors rash enough to land.

LEUCATE (page 49)

Leucate, also called Leucas and Leucadia, was a small island off the coast of Epirus, famous for its high white cliffs – hence the name Leucate, 'white' – from which unhappy lovers used to hurl themselves to death on the rocks below. It was originally not an island, but a headland jutting out from the mainland, with a temple of Apollo built on the clifftop. But its people quarrelled with the mainlanders (some say in legendary times, others in the fifth century BC, at the time of the Peloponnesian War) and dug a sea-channel to make their home an island.

HELENUS AND ANDROMACHE (page 50)

Priam's son Helenus, a prophet of Apollo, hoped to marry Helen after the death of Paris, and when she was given to Deiphobus instead he deserted to the Greeks and told them that Troy would fall as soon as the hero Philoctetes was brought back from exile with Hercules' magic bow and arrows. (Philoctetes had originally been a shepherd. But when Hercules was treacherously poisoned by the centaur Nessus, he laid himself on a funeral pyre, asked Philoctetes to light it, and gave him the bow and arrows as a reward.) After Troy fell, Philoctetes became Pyrrhus' slave, but warned him of a deadly storm and was rewarded with his freedom. Pyrrhus took him back to Epirus, gave him a kingdom (Chaonia) and married him to Andromache.

159

Andromache was originally Hector's wife, and after the fall of Troy Pyrrhus took her to Epirus and married her to Helenus. She and Helenus made their kingdom a refuge for Trojan survivors; intermarriage there between Trojans and Greeks finally ended the two peoples' long-standing enmity.

In versions of the myth which says that 'Pyrrhus' was no more than another name for Neoptolemus (see page 155), Neoptolemus took Andromache as his mistress after the fall of Troy, but deserted her to marry Menelaus' daughter Hermione. For this Orestes, who had hoped to marry Hermione himself, murdered Neoptolemus in Apollos' sanctuary at Delphi. Hermione, left in Epirus, plotted to murder her rival Andromache, but the people revolted against her and she eloped with Orestes, leaving Andromache (and Helenus, her new husband) to rule Epirus.

SCYLLA AND CHARYBDIS (page 50)

Neither Scylla nor Charybdis began their lives as monsters. In one version of the myth, Scylla was a beautiful sea-nymph, and Neptune's jealous wife Amphitrite changed her into a monster when Neptune fell in love with her. In another version, her lover was the sea-spirit Glaucus, and he asked the witch Circe to give him a spell to make Scylla love him more. Circe, however, was herself in love with Glaucus, and instead of a love-spell gave him poison, telling him to pour it into the pool where Scylla bathed each morning. If the water had not diluted the poison, Scylla would have died as soon as she set foot in it. As it was, she became a monster. Above the waist she was sea-nymph, just as before, but below the waist she was a fish and round the waist she sprouted an apron of twelve bony legs and six yapping heads on sea-snakes' necks. Her nature changed from gentleness to savagery, and she skulked ever afterwards in her clifftop lair, alert for human prey.

Charybdis was the daughter of Neptune and a mortal woman, and began her life in human form. But like all the creatures of her father's sea-kingdom, she was unceasingly, ravenously hungry, and one day she fell on Hercules' herd of sun-cattle and devoured them, hide, hair, hooves and all. Hercules' father Jupiter punished her by imprisoning her on the seabed below Scylla's lair, and changed her from a beautiful girl into a whirlpool: as befitted someone whose nature was nothing but greed, she became an insatiable, ever-gaping gullet.

ENCELADUS (page 50)

Enceladus was the leader of the giants who built a stone-pile and swarmed up it to attack Olympus and unseat the gods (see page 23). Jupiter punished him by spreadeagling him across the eastern edge of the island of Sicily and planting a mountain, Etna, on top to hold him there forever. Ever afterwards, whenever Enceladus heaved or writhed in his torment, the flanks of the mountain shook, and his fire-breath poured from vent-holes in the top and sides, melted the rock and sent it flowing as lava to the fields below.

POLYPHEMUS, ACIS AND GALATEA (page 51)

Polyphemus was not always a blood-thirsty, mindless murderer. He and his people were originally peace-loving shepherds, pasturing their sheep in the foothills of Mount Etna. At that time the area was dotted with mortal villages, and giants and humans lived in untroubled friendship. Nymphs, too, spirits of trees, springs and fields, used to gather flowers, gossip and picnic in the meadows.

One sea-nymph, Galatea, was the prettiest person on the island, and Polyphemus fell in love with her. The poor girl was terrified of being wooed by a tree-sized giant who combed his hair with a harrow, cut his beard with a scythe, played uncouth love-tunes on a set of panpipes made from a hundred reeds, and recited poems in a voice like crows cackling in the elm-tops. 'Galatea!' he said, 'Your skin is whiter than columbine, your eyes are clearer than streamwater, your lips are as red as cherries; why do your glances burn me like fire, your words roar in my ears like a river in spate? Be my wife, and you shall have strawberries, grapes and plums to eat, and bear-cubs and fawns for pets. Are you afraid of my size? Does my one eye disgust you? Think of my body as a tree, tall to protect you; think of my eye as a sun sending beams of love.'

Polyphemus thought this a truly plaintive song, fit to melt any maiden's heart. But the more he sang it, the more Galatea was afraid of him. She was also in love with a handsome mortal shepherd called Acis – and one day, when she was lying in Acis' arms, the sun was suddenly darkened overhead and Polyphemus stood over them, grinding his teeth with jealousy. The lovers fled, and Polyphemus hurled a lump of rock from the cliffside and crushed Acis dead. The gods took pity on the boy and transformed him into a rippling stream, whose sparkling waters carried Galatea out to sea, far out of Polyphemus' reach.

Losing Galatea turned Polyphemus from a gentle shepherd to a raging monster, sworn to destroy every member of the human race. He and his fellow-Cyclopes developed a taste for human flesh, and until Ulysses and his crew sailed to Sicily, no visitors to the island ever lived to tell the tale.

THE WINDS AND AEOLUS (*page 53*)

The winds were children of Dawn, grandchildren of the Titans who ruled the Universe before the gods. They had huge owls' wings, dragons' tails and raincloud cloaks, and their leader was Boreas the North Wind. Because they were older than the gods they had no fear of them, and bucketed like pirates across the universe, making mischief whenever they pleased. In the end Jupiter and Neptune made a trap for them. There were seven islands floating in the sea off Sicily, the Aeolides, lumps of volcanic stone, fissured and honeycombed with tunnels. Neptune lured the Winds into these tunnels, promising them treasure-trove inside: his own sea-mares (which the winds found irresistible as mates). But as soon as the winds were all inside, Jupiter hurled a thunderbolt and blocked the entrances, anchoring the islands forever on the seabed. Under the largest of the islands, Lipara, he built a vast underground throne-room, a meeting-place for the furious winds, and he appointed Neptune's son Aeolus as their king and gaoler, all in one.

Aeolus and his twin brother Boeotus were sons of Neptune and the mortal Arne, wife of King Desmontes. When the babies were born, Desmontes was so furious that he buried Arne in an underground dungeon and left the twins to die on a mountainside. A shepherd rescued them and brought them up, and in due course they released their mother from her dungeon and avenged her ill-treatment by killing Desmontes. Then, exactly as in the myth of Romulus and Remus (see page 117), the brothers quarrelled, and one of them, Boetus, became the sole ruler of the kingdom (renaming it Boeotia after himself). The second brother, Aeolus, roamed the world seeking his fortune, and became as swashbuckling a pirate as the winds themselves – the ideal person to rule Lipara and control the winds. Jupiter bribed him to do the job by giving him immortality and the gods' favour; but because of his piratical past he was never welcome at the banquets of Olympus, and spent eternity in his underground throne-room in the midst of his rebellious, restless subjects.

DIDO IN EXILE   (page 56)

Dido was the sister of Prince Pygmalion of Tyre. She married Sichaeus, a prophet of Apollo and the richest man in Tyre. Almost immediately, however, Sichaeus prophesied that he was about to be murdered, and advised Dido to take his treasure and sail as far away as possible. She loaded a fleet with gold and gathered a band of followers – and no sooner had she set sail than word came that Pygmalion her brother had sacked Apollo's temple, looking for the treasure, and murdered Sichaeus. Juno guided Dido and her Tyrians to Libya in north Africa, and Dido used Sichaeus' treasure there to buy land from King Iarbas and to build a magnificent city, Carthage. Some say that Iarbas gave her the land on condition that she marry him, and that it was about the breaking of this promise that Iarbas later complained to Jupiter: (see page 59).

AENEAS RESCUED BY THE GODS   (page 59)

At first Aeneas refused to fight the Greeks in the Trojan war. He felt that his father Anchises had a better claim than Priam to the throne of Troy, and had been passed over just because he was a cripple. Aeneas spent the early months of the war far from Troy, breeding cattle in secluded valleys down the coast. But Achilles, the fiercest of all the Greek heroes, began leading raiding-parties further and further from the plain of Troy, and ended by stealing Aeneas' cattle and murdering his cowherds. Aeneas himself would have been killed if Jupiter had not surrounded him with a mist of invisibility and snatched him out of the fighting. Aeneas went to Troy to join his countrymen, and became one of the Greeks' most ferocious enemies. Then, after he led a party one day across the plain as far as the Greek ships, sowing death among the Greeks, Diomedes smashed his hip with a boulder and lifted his spear to finish him. Venus, who was watching from Olympus, flew down in the nick of time to help her son, and bravely tried to deflect Diomedes' spear. The spear-blade grazed her wrist, and ichor (the pale liquid which flows in gods' veins instead of blood) oozed out. Diomedes lifted his spear for a second blow, but was prevented by Apollo, who flew down and carried Aeneas and the tearful Venus to safety on Olympus.

ATLAS   (page page 59)

Atlas was a giant, ruler of the fertile country of Atlantis in the world's far west. He was one of the giants' war-leaders against the gods (see page 23), and Neptune and Jupiter punished him. Neptune drowned his country under the Atlantic Ocean, and Jupiter forced Atlas to stand on the shore of Africa and to support the sky on his shoulders until the end of time. As the aeons passed, Atlas began more and more to take on the appearance of a mountain-range (the Atlas Mountains, straddling Morocco and Tunisia, still bear his name). But for all his granite appearance he still had the emotions of a living being, and the streams which ran down his face were tears.

DIDO'S DYING CURSE   (page 62)

Later Romans took this curse to refer to the Carthaginian Wars of the third century BC, and in particular to Hannibal, the Carthaginian general who invaded Italy and all but captured Rome.

ACESTES AND ACESTA   (page 62)

Acestes was the son of the river Crinisus and the Trojan princess Egesta. Long before, when sea-monsters, relatives of those which ate Laocoön and his sons: see page 37), were ravaging the coast near Troy, people tried to placate them by feeding them live victims, young girls offered up one. by one to save the city. Fearing this fate for Egesta, her father floated her out to sea in a barrel, and the gods carried her to Sicily. Here she caught the eye of Crinisus, a Trojan who had been banished for feeding his own daughter to the sea-monsters, and who had changed into a river; their child Acestes grew up to be prince of the region near Drepanum. Later, when Aeneas divided his people into those who wanted to stay in Sicily and those who wanted to seek glory with him in Italy (see page 64), the Sicilian settlers built a city on Mount Eryx, made Acestes its king and called it Acesta after him.

THE FUNERAL GAMES   (page 63)

Virgil's *Aeneid* gives details of several events in the funeral Games. The four ships in the ship-race were *Pristis*, commanded by Mnestheus, Gyas' *Chimaera*, Sergestus' *Centaur* and Cloanthus' *Scylla*. Gyas' ship was the largest, rowed by three banks of oars, and he was sure that he would win. But his steersman Menoetes was afraid of the sunken reefs beside the turning-rock, and steered well clear of it, leaving a large enough gap for Cloanthus to slip past on the inside. Gyas was so angry that he knocked Menoetes into the sea, and Menoetes had to splash to the rock for safety, and sit there soaking and dejected till the end of the race. Sergestus went too close to the rock as he turned, and his oars splintered and left *Centaur* floundering. Cloanthus, meanwhile, prayed for help to the spirits of the sea, and they scooped up his ship and swept it to shore to win the race, followed in order by Mnestheus, Gyas and Sergestus.

The runners in the foot race included two Trojan friends, Nisus and Euryalus, and their Sicilian rival Salius. Nisus was ahead when he slipped in a pool of blood from a sacrifice, and Salius, seeing his chance, speeded up to pass him. But Nisus reared up suddenly in front of him and tripped him, so clearing the way for Euryalus to win the race.

The main boxing-match was between Dares, a Trojan with fists like rocks, and Entellus, an elderly Sicilian who had once boxed with Hercules and who owned Hercules' enormous, iron-studded boxing-gloves. Entellus was reluctant to use his full force, but the crowd jeered at him so much that he chased Dares all over the beach, pelting him with punches till Aeneas stopped the match and awarded him the prize. Then, to show the crowd what he could have done if he

163

had used all his strength, Entellus stood four-square in front of the bull which was his prize, brought his clenched fist down and pole-axed the bull bare-handed.

THE GAME OF TROY *(page 63)*

In later years, after the foundation of Rome and right through the city's history, a mock-battle on horseback between young boys was a standard part of the *Ludi Romani* or Roman Games, held every year in honour of Jupiter, Juno and Minerva. It was called the Game of Troy, and its origin was said to be the war-game played by Iulus and his companions on the shore at Drepanum.

DAEDALUS *(page 66)*

Daedalus was the most skilful craftsman in the world, a mortal counterpart to Vulcan, craftsman of the gods. He went to Crete, and his invention of sails for ships helped the Cretans to build the fastest and largest trading-ships ever seen on earth. But Daedalus' skill also brought tragedy. Queen Pasiphae the wife of Minos, King of Crete, fell in love with Neptune's sacred bull, and asked Daedalus to invent a way of tricking it into making love to her. He built a wooden cow-framework, so lifelike that the bull mated with it, and so with Pasiphae as she spreadeagled herself inside. Pasiphae became pregnant with the Minotaur, a flesh-eating monster with a human head, a bull's body and a giant's strength. King Minos forced Daedalus to build a labyrinth, a maze of passages to hide the Minotaur from human sight, and imprisoned him in the palace to prevent him telling its secret. But Daedalus built wings of wax, wood and feathers, and he and his son Icarus flew from the royal battlements while Minos' guards shouted in helpless rage.

Daedalus flew carefully, skimming the waves like a cruising gull. But Icarus, dazzled with ambition to outfly the gods, soared higher and higher in the sky till he challenged Phoebus Apollo, god of the sun, and the heat melted the wax on his wings and plummeted him into the sea to drown. Daedalus was helpless to save him; all he could do was fly broken-heartedly on to land on the Italian shore near Cumae. Here, to placate Apollo, he built a shrine in a cavern on the hillside, a honeycomb of wind-filled passages; he decorated its walls with carvings showing every part of his adventures except the death of Icarus, and painted them with pigments ground from roots, rock and earth.

Daedalus then flew to Sicily, and lived there until he died. The shrine at Cumae, with its cavern high in the cliff and its mysterious carvings, remained one of Apollo's prophetic shrines long after the paint-pigments faded, and the god often visited it to give mortals guidance in omens and oracles.

DEIPHOBE *(page 67)*

Deiphobe was once a beautiful sea-nymph. (She was a daughter of the sea-spirit Glaucus whose love for Scylla was so disastrous: see page 160). Apollo saw her sunbathing on a beach and offered her any gifts she asked to sleep with him. Deiphobe chose all-knowledge and all-life: she asked to have understanding of past, present and future, and to be given a year of life for every grain of sand on the beach she lay on.

Apollo gave her the gifts, but each of them were flawed. Her prophetic knowledge told her everything except that her second gift, immortality, was useless without eternal youth and that she was doomed to grow older and older, one year for every sand-grain on the beach, without any hope of death to end her misery.

As the centuries passed, Deiphobe grew into a bent, discontented hag. She spent her life in the darkness of Apollo's cave, near Cumae, serving her master without ever seeing the light of the sun, his radiance. Many centuries after Aeneas and Achates saw her in the cave, she began to shrivel, until she was no bigger than a grain of sand. The people of Cumae hung her up in a bottle in the cave-wall, and when visitors unstoppered it and asked, 'Sibyl, what do you long for?' they heard a tiny whispered answer from inside, no louder than the rustle of one sand-grain against another: 'I long to die.'

PROSERPINA (page 68)

Pluto, king of the Underworld, could find no wife among the shades, and one day he surged from the ground in the meadows of Sicily and stole Proserpina, Ceres' daughter, to be his queen. No one knew where Proserpina had gone; Ceres wandered from country to country, distraught, trying to find Proserpina, and when no god or mortal helped her she held back the harvest, declaring that just as her daughter was dead to her, so should all the mortal world be dead. Winter and Starvation gleefully overran the earth, and mortals were reduced to huddled groups holding out stick-arms to the gods for help.

At length Jupiter heard the thin crying from the earth, and understood at once what the trouble was. He ordered Pluto to give Proserpina back. But Proserpina, in the Underworld, had eaten six pomegranate pips, and the laws of Hell decreed that anyone who ate food of the Underworld was condemned to stay there forever. Jupiter, Ceres and Pluto bargained, and in the end agreed that Proserpina should spend six months each year, one for each pomegranate seed, in the Underworld, while barrenness ruled in the world above. Then, each spring, she would rise to the upper world, and bring six months of growth and harvest to mortals until autumn, and her time in the Underworld, came round again.

MISENUS (page 68)

In some versions of this story, Aeneas went back to the shore with Achates. One of the Trojan crewmen had died and the Sibyl had said that unless the body was reverently buried Aeneas would be forbidden to enter the Underworld. The crewman's name was Misenus. He was a trumpeter, employed to play signals in battle and to guide the rowers' rhythm when ships put out to sea. When Aeneas' ship reached Italy at last, Misenus was so overjoyed that he ran to a headland and began blowing triumphant arpeggios and fanfares. Swimming in the bay below was a Triton, one of Neptune's servants who blow on conch-shell trumpets. He took Misenus' playing for a challenge, hurled a wave at him and swept him from the headland to death on the rocks below.

When Aeneas and Achates reached the shore, Aeneas ordered Misenus to be buried on the headland with his trumpet beside him. He piled a funeral-mound over him and made sacrifices to the spirits of the dead. The sight of his grief for his dead friend, and the thought that Misenus had died because of a misunderstanding, so moved Neptune that he hollowed the headland with tunnels and passages like the tubes of a trumpet, so that whenever the wind blew the whole place played trumpet-calls in Misenus' memory. In later Roman times the headland was called Cape Misenum after him.

STYX AND HER CHILDREN *(page 70)*

Styx was a river-goddess, the daughter of Oceanus, whose swirling water kept the earth in place, and she had four children: Force, Might, Victory and Zeal. When Jupiter, Neptune and Pluto were fighting to win kingdoms (see page 4), Styx sent her children to help them, and in gratitude Jupiter gave her power over all the other gods: it was in her name that they swore their oaths.

Styx lived in a rock-palace at the edge of the Underworld. From its highest peak gushed a river of icy water, called after her. It spread out in ten streams, Acheron, Cocytus, Phlegython and others, and held the Underworld in its icy grip as the river Oceanus gripped the upper earth. The last of the ten streams was called Oath of the Gods, and any god in Olympus who swore an oath had to drink from it (see page 5).

HERCULES AND THESEUS IN THE UNDERWORLD *(page 71)*

Only four living beings had ever entered the Underworld before Aeneas. One was Orpheus, who tried to charm the gods of Hell with his music into letting his wife Eurydice return from death. Another was Hercules. He was sent, as the last of his labours, to steal Cerberus, the three-headed watchdog of the Underworld. Charon was reluctant to ferry him across the Styx, but Hercules menaced him with his club and gave him no choice. Instead of recrossing the Styx with Cerberus, Hercules battered his way through solid rock to the upper world, and dragged Cerberus in chains, snapping and slavering at the daylight, across the world. Mortals soon became so panic-striken that the gods had to order Cerberus back to hell.

Just before Hercules' quest for Cerberus, Theseus and his friend Pirithous visited the Underworld on an even more reckless errand: they went to steal Proserpina, queen of Hell (see page 165), as a wife for Pirithous. Instead of threatening the ferry-man Charon, they flattered and persuaded him to carry them over the River Styx, and in their arrogance they thought that they would trick Pluto just as easily into parting with Proserpina. But Pluto knew exactly what they had planned, and tricked them first. He welcomed them as honoured guests, and sat them on thrones for a banquet – and the thrones grew into their flesh and began to engulf them where they sat. Pirithous was turned to stone before Theseus' eyes, and Theseus would have suffered the same fate himself if Hercules (on his way to steal Cerberus) had not appeared in the nick of time. Hercules tore Theseus from the clinging stone, leaving most of Theseus' flesh behind, and sent him stumbling and bleeding to the upper world, where he lived a twisted cripple till the day he died.

MINOS *(page 72)*

Minos, the king of Crete whose wife Pasiphae gave birth to the Minotaur (see page 164), was the son of Jupiter and the mortal princess Europa. Although parts of his reign were ruthless – for example his treatment of Deadalus (see page 164), – he was generally one of the justest of all mortal kings, and when his time on earth was done Jupiter granted him immortality and made him a judge of the Underworld. He sat on a throne in the Halls of Hell, and the lots he cast for guilt or innocence were guided by the gods themselves; his decisions were as irrevocable as they were impartial, and there was no appeal against them.

RHADAMANTHUS (page 73)

Like his elder brother Minos (see page 166), Rhadamanthus was the son of Jupiter and Europa. He ruled an island kingdom in the Cyclades, and was such an honest, impartial king that Jupiter made him a judge of the Dead, like Minos, when his time on earth was over. Souls whose cases had been heard by Minos, and who had been judged guilty, passed to him for sentence, and he declared the torments they were to suffer in Tartarus before passing them to Tisiphone for punishment.

TITYUS (page 73)

In some accounts Tityus was the same monstrous creature as Python, who was killed by Apollo and Artemis for attacking their mother Latona (see page 157). Other accounts say that he was Jupiter's own child, fathered on an earth-spirit, and that he was so enormous and so powerful that neither mortals nor gods could master him. In the end Jupiter weakened him enough with thunderbolts to topple him to the floor of Tartarus, and Pluto's servants pegged him over nine acres of the rock-floor before he could recover. It was to prevent him ever growing strong enough to attack the gods again that Jupiter sent snakes to feed on his entrails; his groans were the source of the rumblings people often claimed to hear in caves and passageways far underground.

TORMENTED SOULS (page 74)

Apart from the giants (see page 23) and for monsters like Tityus who were punished for challenging the gods, Tartarus was filled with mortal sinners. Ixion had been invited to feast with the gods in Olympus, and had repaid Jupiter's hospitality by trying to rape Juno queen of heaven; for punishment he was hurled from Olympus to Tartarus, spreadeagled on a fire-wheel which rolled through the Underworld for all eternity, burning ever deeper into his flesh. Tantalus had invited the gods to a feast, and served them stew made from his own son Pelops; then he went to Olympus and not only stole the ambrosia which renewed the gods' immortality but also raped Ganymede, their beautiful boy cupbearer. His punishments were eternal starvation at a table of plenty in Tartarus, and terror: a house-sized rock hung over his head, settling and slipping but never finally crushing him and giving him the oblivion he craved. Sisyphus' crimes were against the gods of the Underworld itself. He tricked Death and imprisoned him, so that no mortals ever died in the upper world, until the gods, jealous that human beings were sharing their immortality, sent Mars to rescue Death and to frog-march Sisyphus to Rhadamanthus, judge of the Dead, for punishment.

ERIDANUS (page 74)

The river Eridanus (nowadays called Po) flows across the upper world from the Alps to the Adriatic Sea. It is broad and deep, and because of the coldness of its water, and the fact that poplar- and cypress-trees, the trees of death, thrive on its banks, people used to believe that its course was circular: it flowed, they thought, to the Underworld through

167

secret entrances on the Adriatic seabed, across the Elysian Fields and back up to the high Alps to nourish the upper world once more.

LETHE   (*page 74*)

Lethe (Oblivion) was one of the ten branches of the river Styx (see page 166). It flowed through the Elysian Fields, not far from the place where souls granted a second mortal existence passed from the Underworld to the world above. One sip of its water produced instant forgetfulness, so that the reborn soul ran no risk of telling the secrets of the Underworld and angering the gods. In ancient times, people thought that Lethe flowed to the upper earth in many parts of the world, from Africa to northern Greece, and that drinking its waters, for mortals, either allowed them to see visions of the future or froze their blood and killed them instantly.

CIRCE   (*page 77*)

Circe was the daughter of the Sun and the sea-nymph Perseis. Like all sky-children she was incurably lustful, and longed to make love with every mortal man she met. But although she courted her mortal lovers in human shape, and sang them love-songs which drew them to her as a flame draws moths in the night, she was made of fire not flesh, and her embrace charred her lovers to cinders. At last she withdrew in despair from the mortal world, and took refuge on a floating island called Aeaea. It never visited the same place twice, and it was

impossible for mortal sailors to steer a course for it. When any landed there by accident, Circe tapped them with a magic wand before she could lose her heart to them, transformed them into wild beasts and put them in cages, where they howled and wept for the mortal natures they would never know again.

The only mortal to master Circe's magic was Ulysses, who visited her island by accident on his journey home from the Trojan War. The god Mercury gave him a herb which counteracted the spell of Circe's magic wand, and his protector Minerva made him immune, for a time, to the scorching heat of Circe's embrace. He stayed on Aeaea for what seemed to him a day and a night, but was in fact many mortal months, and he and Circe spent the day-hours turning the creatures in Circe's cages back to human form, and the night-hours making love. In some versions of the myth, they were the parents of Latinus, who later became king of Latium in Italy where the Trojans landed (see page 79).

The alder-trees, trees of mourning, which fringed Circe's island were her own half-sisters, daughters of the Sun. Their brother Phaethon stole his father's chariot and galloped with it across the sky (see page 5). But he lost control, plummeted into the sea and drowned – and the sisters wept so grievously that the gods took pity on them, turned them into alders and planted them on Aeaea as a warning to visitors that the island was a place of tears.

Some versions of the myth say that Circe's island floated forever across the sea, and that sailors on dark nights often afterwards heard the howling of unseen beasts and the high, unearthly sound of Circe's song. Others say that Neptune anchored Aeaea at the mouth of the river Po, and that it is the island people now call Lussin.

FAUNUS (*page 79*)

There are several accounts of who Faunus was, and of how he came to be a god of trees and pastures. Some versions say that he was the son of Mercury the trickster-god, and inherited his father's slyness. He pretended to welcome strangers to his kingdom, tricked them to the altar to watch a sacrifice, then butchered them in Mercury's honour. The gods punished him by giving him goat's hindquarters and horns and imprisoning him in the woods, where he and his descendants the Fauns have hidden from mortals, and tricked them, ever since. Other versions say that Faunus was the son of Mars and a mortal woman, and was such a just king that the gods honoured him by giving him immortality and making him the guardian spirit of the countryside he had once so wisely ruled. Still other accounts say that Faunus was the son of Picus, the young man turned into a woodpecker by Circe (see page 12): it was this ancestry that gave Faunus both his prophetic wisdom – woodpeckers are among the wisest of all birds – and also his love of woods and trees.

THE FURIES (*page 81*)

At the beginning of existence, long before the era of the gods, the two powers in the universe were Uranus (Sky) and Tithea (Earth). They had children, called Titans, and each time a child was born Sky grew furiously jealous and attacked it; Earth saved the children's lives only by hiding them in her most secret caves and crevices. At last the latest-born child, Saturn, lay in wait for his father Sky, cut off Sky's penis with a diamond-sickle, and freed the other Titans from captivity.

From the drops of Sky's blood which fell on the ground, Mother Earth's last

children were born. They were monsters: the Cyclopes (see page 170), the Hundred-handed Giants and the Furies. At first there were three Furies, Allecto, Tisiphone and Megaera. But over the centuries others were hatched to join them: a nameless brood with women's faces, birds' bodies, dragons' fangs and nests of snakes for hair. There was no place for them in the upper world, and they roosted sullenly on iron nests in the Underworld. Then Pluto, king of the Underworld, gave them iron-spiked whips and made them his servants, punishers of human crime on earth and torturers of the damned in Hell.

HERCULES AND CACUS (*page 85*)

Cacus' father was Vulcan, the deformed blacksmith of the gods, and his mother was the Gorgon Medusa, one glance of whose eyes turned human flesh to stone. He had a bloated, spider's body, legs and arms like spindly saplings, and three fire-breathing heads on a single scrawny neck. He could not bear the sun's rays to touch him, and lurked all day in a cave beside the Tiber. At night he went out to hunt, and preyed on anything warm-blooded which crossed his path. He snatched owls on the wing, stole cattle from the fields, wolves and lions from the woods and human beings from their beds. The floor of his cave was greasy with blood, and he fixed his victims' heads on poles outside his lair.

As one of his twelve labours, Hercules had been ordered to steal the cattle of Geryon, a gigantic herdsman who lived on an island in the river which girds the world, beyond the land-bridge connecting Europe and Africa. He drove the cattle back through Italy towards Greece, and one night stopped to let them drink from the river Tiber. Exhausted, Hercules fell into a doze, and while he slept Cacus crept out to steal the cattle. He took four bulls and four heifers, turned them round and dragged them backwards to his cave, so that when dawn came there were no tracks leading from the herd to show where the animals had gone.

Hercules began rounding up his herd, ready to leave. As they moved off, the cattle began lowing, and one of the cows in Cacus' cave heard and answered. Hercules snatched his club, with its blood-stained knobs and knots, and strode to the mouth of Cacus' lair. The monster barred the entrance by dropping in front of it a massive boulder chained above it by his father Vulcan for just such an emergency. The boulder's fall smashed the doorway, making it impassable.

Hercules stood blazing, looking for a way in. Three times he tried unsuccessfully to break through the shattered doorway, but it was too much even for him. At last he saw a way. There was a pinnacle of rock jutting from the side of the cliff, remote and sheer, fit only for vultures to perch on. Hercules took hold of it and wrenched it sideways, tearing the cliff apart. Cacus peered terrified out of the gaping hole, and Hercules showered boulders on him from above. Cacus retaliated by breathing fire, trying to scorch Hercules dead – and Hercules jumped down inside the cave and snatched him by the neck. While Cacus screamed, spouting useless flames from his mouths and noses, Hercules tied his neck in a knot and left him to choke to death, his six eyes bulging and his heart leaping like a beached fish. Hercules battered the cave-door open from inside, led out his cattle, and then dragged Cacus' carcase out feet-first. The heat of the Sun instantly withered Cacus' flesh from his bones, leaving his skeleton lying like the branches of an enormous, thunderbolt-stricken tree. Hercules went

on his way, and the country people, free to live in peace at last, decreed an annual sacrifice to him in gratitude.

EVANDER'S SETTLEMENT (page 86)

Later Roman writers adapted this legend of Evander's settlement, fitting it with geographical details to make Pallanteum seem the same place as the later Rome. The hills, they said, were the seven hills of Rome – Aventine, Caelian, Capitoline, Esquiline, Palatine, Quirinal and Viminal; the cattle-market was the place later called *Forum Boarium*, a flat area beside the Tiber; the island, in the bend of the river, was the one later connected to the bank by the wooden bridge which Horatius, in another legend (see page 146), held against attacking enemies.

CYCLOPES (page 86)

The Cyclopes, like the Furies (see page 169), were children of Sky and Earth, born from the blood-drops spattered on Mother Earth after their father Sky was mutilated by Saturn. They were giants, made of a mixture of flesh, rock and fire, and they had human form, with a single, unblinking eye in the centre of their foreheads – hence the name Cyclopes, 'Round-eyes'. They were so powerful, and so hideous, that the gods hid them underground in Sicily. Even so, a few escaped, led by Polyphemus, and terrorised the island, eating alive any mortal sailors who landed on their shores. Others, more peaceable, were allowed out at last; they settled first in Syria and then in Greece, where they built the fortress at Argos from stone blocks the size of barns. The three most powerful Cyclopes of all, Arges, Brontes and Steropes, stayed underground and worked for Vulcan, blacksmith of the gods, forging thunderbolts for Jupiter. The smoke from their forges was vented to the surface through the crater of Mount Etna in Sicily, and from time to time molten rock poured from the volcano in lava-streams which devastated the woods and fields.

DISCORD *(page 91)*

Discord was the daughter of Night; her brother was Death and her sisters were Destiny and the three Fates (see page 173). She was a creature of darkness, malevolent and malicious, and she grew fat on other people's quarrelling as a vampire thrives on blood. At first the gods gave her a home on Olympus, but she sowed so much argument among them that Jupiter finally banished her. She lurked ever afterwards in the vaults of space, and fed on every quarrel, argument or rivalry among the gods or in the mortal world. It was she who stirred up the disagreement between Juno, Venus and Minerva which caused the Trojan War (see page 31).

PALLAS' BELT *(page 98)*

In the version of this story by the Roman writer Virgil, the pictures on Pallas' belt told the myth of Danaus' daughters. Danaus and his twin brother Aegyptus each had fifty children; Aegyptus' children were sons and Danaus' were daughters. Aegyptus wanted his sons to marry Danaus' daughters and inherit the kingdom. But Danaus refused and sailed with his fifty daughters to a foreign country. Aegyptus' sons sailed after them and enforced the marriage – and on the wedding night each of Danaus' daughters slit her husband's throat. Only Hyperm-

nestra was filled with love as she gazed down at her sleeping husband Lynceus, and took no part in the murder. In punishment for their crime, Danaus' daughters were condemned to endless torment in the Underworld, with the promise of release only when they had drained a lake with sieves. Hypermnestra and Lynceus became heirs to Danaus' kingdom in the upper world, and inherited it when he died.

It was the scene of the murder of the husbands which Virgil says was incised on Pallas' belt. The belt gave protection because of the magic writing which bordered the pictures, and because the legend symbolised the downfall of any arrogant, invading army (such as Aegyptus' sons) who attacked without reason. But the gods knew, as no mortals did, that the belt also meant the end of war in Latium. Because Turnus tore it from Pallas' body after he had killed him, and wore it himself (see page 102), Aeneas would finally be moved to kill Turnus and so open the way for the settlement at last of the Trojan race in Latium (see page 110).

AEGEON *(page 102)*

Aegeon (also known as Briareus) was one of the monstrous children of Earth and Sky, born at the beginning of the universe long before the era of the gods. His shape was tree-like: a hundred arms branched from his knotted trunk, and fifty heads sprouted from twig-like necks. For all his size, he was also as brainless as a tree, and his parents were afraid that if his huge strength ever won him power in the universe, he would destroy creation in mindless tyranny. Accordingly they buried him deep in Mother Earth, and he skulked in her caverns and crevices, brooding on revenge. He climbed twice to the upper world, only to be hurled down again each time. The first time was when Juno, Minerva and Neptune plotted to overthrow Jupiter from the throne of Olympus (see page 153). After rescuing Jupiter, Aegeon hoped for favours, hoped to be admitted into Olympus as an immortal god. But there were to be no favours: the Fates ordained that no giant could ever share the privileges of the gods. Instead of thanking Aegeon, Jupiter banished him once more underground – and this ingratitude led Aegeon to join the giants when they built their stone-pile from earth to sky and swarmed up it to attack Olympus (see page 23). He clambered after the giants, gripping the stone-pile with fifty of his hundred hands and waving swords in the other fifty, roaring defiance at Jupiter with his fifty mouths. But before he could jump into Olympus and begin slicing the gods, Jupiter dashed him to the Underworld with a thunderbolt, and piled ton after ton of rock over him to keep him there.

DIOMEDES (page 105)

Diomedes, son of Tydeus and Deiphyle, was one of the bravest Greek heroes at the siege of Troy. He fought Hector and Aeneas (see page 162), and wounded Venus herself when she went to help her son. When the war was over, instead of returning to his native country Aetolia he sailed to Italy, and founded the city of Argyrippa. He refused to play any more part in wars and battles, and ruled his new people in peace for many years. When he died his people grieved so sorely for him that the gods took pity and turned them into swans, birds which were ever afterwards mute with suffering, crying only at the moment of their own deaths, and whose eyes often ran with tears.

THE LAST BATTLE (page 108)

In Virgil's account of this myth, peace was not so quick or so clear-cut. After the Trojan attack on Latinus' city the Latins rushed to make a treaty. But Turnus' followers, the Rutulians, refused to accept it. They said that they had not been consulted, and that Aeneas' Trojans were so treacherous that there was no guarantee that they would ever keep the treaty-terms, whoever won the duel. Tolumnius, a Rutulian priest, threw a spear into the Trojan army and killed a man, and at once fighting broke out again. Aeneas struggled to stop it, but an arrow wounded him in the leg and he had to withdraw from the battlefield, whereupon Turnus galloped eagerly about, killing a Trojan with every spear-throw: Sthenelus, Thamyrus, Pholus, Glaucus, Ladon, Asbytes, the boxer Dares (see page 163), Thersilochus and many others.

While this slaughter was going on, Mnestheus, Achates and Iulus helped wounded Aeneas into the Trojan camp. He was white with pain, and leaned heavily on a spear for support. Furiously he tried to pull the arrow-head out; but the barbs buried themselves deeper and deeper into his flesh. His men tried widening the wound with a knife, cutting down below the arrow-head, but still had no success. As they worked they could hear the sounds of battle coming closer and closer, as the Rutulians drove the Trojans back across the plain. Soon spears and arrows were falling in the camp itself.

Nothing could save Aeneas but the intervention of a god. And Venus herself, for the last time, took action. She flew to Mount Ida in Crete, and there gathered the sacred plant Dictamnus, a bright-red flower on a leafy stalk, which wild goats chew when they are plagued by arrows clinging in their backs. Veiled in mist,

Venus took this plant to the Trojan camp, and soaked it in the water the doctors were using to wash Aeneas' wound. At once Aeneas' pain vanished, the blood dried up, and the arrow-head came easily away in the doctor's hand. The wound healed in an instant, without a scar, and Aeneas' strength returned as though he had never been injured. Taking up his shield and sword, he strode out through the gates of the camp. Antheus and Mnestheus followed with their men.

As soon as the Trojans saw their leaders they rallied, and surged against the advancing Rutulians. Aeneas moved over the plain like a thundercloud, seeking no one but Turnus, and eager to punish him for his cowardly breach of the treaty.

It would need the pen of a god, Virgil continues, to tell all the battles that followed, as the two sides fought without quarter and without rest. Jupiter had decreed that this last battle was to end their blood-lust forever, to destroy their strength so that all they wanted was for Aeneas and Turnus to fight their duel and for peace to come at last.

Aeneas saw that Latinus' city was lying utterly unguarded, as if the Latins and Trojans had been at peace for years. He called to his men to fetch torches and burn the city: the quickest way to end the war. The Trojans hurried to find fire. Then, forming a wedge, they burst into the city, setting fire to the houses and killing anyone who resisted. King Latinus wandered about the streets plunged in grief, with his clothes torn and dust in his hair, cursing the day he had refused to accept Aeneas as his son-in-law.

Turnus was on the far side of the plain, hunting down stragglers from the Trojan host, when Saces galloped up on a sweating horse, with an arrow-wound in his face. 'Turnus!' he shouted, 'Only you can save us! Aeneas has attacked the city,

and is threatening to burn it unless we surrender. Come quickly, before there is nothing left to save!'

Now Turnus realised at last that the gods were ready for him. There was no way to avoid his destiny. He leapt from his chariot and ran back into the midst of the fighting. The ground was sticky with blood and the air was full of flying weapons. Wildly he shouted, 'Stop the battle! Lay down your arms! It's for me to fight for Latium now! I accept the duel.'

THE FATES   *(page 109)*

The three Fates were the daughters of Night and Darkness or, some say, of the dark waters at the bottom of the sea. They were among the oldest and most respected powers in the universe, feared even by the gods. They sat with distaffs, spinning a thread of life for every being in the world. Clotho began each thread at the moment of birth, Lachesis drew it out for the duration of each life, and Atropos snipped it with scissors at the moment of death. The Fates' decision about the length of each life was irrevocable, and no other being in the universe, not even Jupiter, could change it.

JUTURNA   *(page 109)*

In some accounts, the soldier who gave his spear and sword to Turnus was no mortal man at all, but the goddess Juturna in disguise. Juturna had once been a Rutulian princess, Turnus' own sister. But Jupiter had lusted for her, made love to her and changed her into a goddess of fountains and mountain springs. Although Juno was forbidden to interfere in the battle to save Turnus' life, she told Juturna of her brother's danger, and Juturna flew down to earth, took the appearance of a mortal soldier, and gave Turnus weapons. Jupiter later punished her by banishing her from Olympus and imprisoning her on earth forever, as the spring Juturna which is a tributary of the river Tiber. Her waters were ever afterwards used in sacrifices, and the Romans believed that they had healing power.

ARDEA (page 112)

This myth was probably told simply to explain the Latin word for heron, *ardea*. In some accounts, many of the town's inhabitants escaped the fire, and in due course the gods allowed them to rebuild Ardea as if it had never been destroyed. It was Ardea that Tarquin the Proud was besieging when his son raped Lucretia, the event which began the downfall of the kings of Rome (see page 141).

AENEAS SILVIUS (page 141)

There is confusion over who exactly Aeneas Silvius was. Some say that he was not Lavinia's son at all, but Aeneas' love-child with the wood-nymph Silvia. Others say that the love-child's name was Silvius Posthumus, and that he was born to Silvia after Aeneas' death, at the same time as Aeneas Silvius was born to Lavinia. One writer even calls him Ascanius, the name by which Iulus was known before Aeneas set sail from Troy. This gave rise to another mistaken story, that Iulus and Ascanius were two different people, that Iulus was Ascanius' son.

RHEA'S DREAM (page 115)

In the version of this story by the Roman poet Ovid, Rhea was awakened not only by a lifting of the sleep spell but also by a frightening, prophetic dream. In this version Rhea (or Ilia, as Ovid calls her) dreamed that she was watching the sacred fire of Vesta, brought from the ruins of Troy (see page 156), when her headdress fell to the ground beside the altar. Where it touched the ground, twin palm-trees sprang up, one taller than the other. Their branches canopied the world and their foliage brushed the stars. No sooner were the trees grown than King Amulius appeared and began hacking them with an axe; it was only when a woodpecker (the prophetic bird sacred to Mars) fetched a she-wolf to ward Amulius off that the trees were saved.

AMULIUS' DEATH (page 116)

The Roman writer Livy, in his *History of Rome*, set the capture of Remus on the Palatine Hill, the place where Hercules once killed the monster Cacus (see page 169). Every year, Livy says, the young men of the area used to dance on this hill in honour of Pan, god of flocks and herds, and it was at the Pan-festival, or Lupercal, that the brigands lay in ambush and captured Remus. They took him not to Amulius but to Numitor for judgement – in Livy's account Numitor had been freed from prison after Rhea's murder and the supposed drowning of the twins, and once again shared the kingship with Amulius – and Numitor was so impressed by Remus' royal bearing and his boasting about his twin brother that he began to suspect that the young man was no shepherd but his own grandson, saved by the gods from death. Faustulus the shepherd, too, had long suspected that Romulus and Remus were of royal birth, and now told Romulus the story of their discovery. Romulus took a band of young men secretly into Alba Longa and killed Amulius, and Numitor and Remus paraded with the Alban army before the people to tell them of Amulius' guilt and of the miraculous rescue of the twins.

REMUS' DEATH (page 117)

In another account of Remus' death, its cause was not a misplaced joke but jealousy. Romulus and Remus remembered the trouble caused in Alba Longa by having two joint kings, Numitor and Amulius, and decided that their new town should have a single ruler. Because they were twins, equals, and could think of no way to choose between them, they decided to ask the gods for omens. They took their places, each on one of the seven hills of the new city (Remus on the Palatine Hill, Romulus on the Aventine), and prayed to the gods to send a sign. Six vultures appeared out of a clear sky over Remus' head, and the young man's followers were just about to acclaim him king when twelve appeared over the Palatine, flying high above Romulus' head. A furious argument followed. Remus said that he should be king because his birds had appeared first; Romulus said that because twice as many birds appeared for him, he was the gods' choice. The argument ended in a brawl; Remus was killed and Romulus' followers proclaimed him king.

NEPTUNE, GOD OF HORSES (page 117)

Neptune's connection with horses began at the moment of his birth. He was one of the children of the Titan Saturn (see page 150), and his mother Rhea, afraid that he would be swallowed alive by his father as all her other children had been, covered him in a lambskin, hid him in the sheepfold, and gave Saturn a foal to eat saying that it was her newborn child. Later,

when Jupiter had rescued the gods from Saturn's gullet and he, Neptune and Pluto had led the gods' revolt against the Titans, there was argument over which god should rule which part of Mother Earth. Both Neptune and Minerva wanted power over Attica, the countryside round Athens, and Jupiter decreed that it should belong to whichever of them gave the most useful gift to the human race. Neptune conjured a horse from the ground, and tamed it to carry riders and pull ploughs and carts. But Minerva declared that horses could also be used for war, whereas her gift would bring peace and wealth. Then she planted an olive, and its progeny quickly covered Attica with fruit-bearing, wealth-bringing trees. Minerva was judged the winner and was given Attica to rule; Neptune retired defeated to his sea-kingdom, and turned his horses into the white foam-tips that gallop across the waves. Ever afterwards, he gave horses the power to unlock springs of fresh water by stamping their hooves on the ground. But not even this was enough to blot out the horse's warlike reputation, and Minerva never surrendered her rule over the olive-groves of Attica.

In later Roman times a festival was held each year in the month when Romulus signalled the capture of the women. It honoured Neptune not as god of horses but as a wise counsellor, the overseer of human discussion and debate. His name in this guise was Consus, and the festival was known as Consualia.

TARPEIA (page 120)

In another version of this story, set about ten years later, Tarpeia was a grown girl, daughter of the commander of the Roman citadel, a fortified camp on the

175

Capitoline Hill. She was a priestess of Vesta, sworn to perpetual virginity, but she fell in love with the young Sabine king Tatius and crept out of Rome to meet him secretly at night. It was love for Tatius, not love of gold, which made her betray the citadel, and when the Romans had defeated the Sabines they punished her by throwing her to death from a steep rock on the side of the Capitoline Hill. Ever afterwards, they called the place the Tarpeian Rock, and executed traitors by hurling them from the top.

In still another version, Tarpeia only pretended to betray the citadel. She secretly warned Romulus, and when the Sabines crept in through the opened gate they found the Romans lying in ambush. The Sabines had time only to crush Tarpeia with their shields before they, too, were killed. In this account, Tarpeia was honoured ever afterwards as a heroine of Rome.

HOSTIUS HOSTILIUS   (page 120)

In accounts of this story set ten years later than this one, Hostius Hostilius was the son of Romulus and his Sabine wife Hersilia. In some versions he was not killed in this battle but rescued, and his father rewarded his bravery with a golden crown. In others, he left a baby son, who grew up to be the ancestor of the Hostilii, one of the oldest and noblest of all Roman families.

LACUS CURTIUS   (page 120)

Some say that this myth explains the name of a marshy stretch of land in the Roman Forum: Lacus Curtius or 'Curtius' Lake'. Others, however, explain the name by a different story entirely. About

four hundred years after the reign of Romulus, a huge crack appeared in the Forum, and an oracle said that the only way to close it was to throw into it whatever the Roman people held most dear. A young man, called Mettius Curtius but no relation of the Sabine champion of Romulus' time, realised that the oracle meant life itself. He spurred his horse into the crack, sank into the Underworld and disappeared. His self-sacrifice healed the wound in the ground, which scarred over like human flesh and formed the marshy strip which ever afterwards commemorated Curtius' name.

HERSILIA   (page 123)

After Romulus was taken into heaven and became the god Quirinus, his wife Hersilia was heart-broken. She dressed in mourning and spent her days begging the gods to carry her to Olympus and grant her a place beside her husband. At last Juno agreed. She sent the rainbow-goddess Iris gliding from heaven to earth to stand by Hersilia's side. Without a word, Iris touched Hersilia with one finger, and at once the Fates snipped the thread of Hersilia's mortal life, and her immortal self flew to Olympus, her hair blazing in the sun like a comet-tail. She became the goddess Hora, and was Quirinus' devoted wife and companion ever afterwards, as she had been during his time as Romulus on earth.

The account in this story of Hersilia's hair blazing like a comet-tail fits a possible sighting of Halley's Comet over Italy at some time in the 750s BC, not long after the traditional date for the founding of Rome. Whether the myth arose because of the comet-sighting, or the comet seemed to the superstitious Romans to prove an existing story, who can tell?

HIPPOLYTUS AND ARICIA (*page 124*)

Hippolytus, the son of King Theseus of Athens, was a priest of Diana the moon-goddess, and like all her servants had sworn a vow of chastity. His stepmother Phaedra fell in love with him, and when he refused to make love with her she went to Theseus his father and accused Hippolytus of raping her. Theseus prayed to the gods for vengeance, and Neptune (who had heard nothing of the affair in the depths of his sea-kingdom, and had no idea that Phaedra's accusation was a lie) answered Theseus' prayer and drowned Hippolytus. The other gods were horrified. Aesculapius, god of medicine, flew to the Underworld, revived Hippolytus with ambrosia just as he was stepping into Charon's boat to cross the river Styx, and carried him to the upper world. After this, to safeguard Hippolytus' second life on earth, the gods kept him well away from Athens. Diana carried him in her moon-chariot to Italy, and set him down on the peak of Mount Albanus. Hippolytus founded a settlement on the hillside, and called it Aricia. (Some say that he named it after his cousin Aricia, an Athenian princess who later became his wife: when he returned from the Underworld Diana freed him from his vow of chastity.) He planted a grove of trees on the hillside, and Diana and her nymphs often went there to hunt and to bathe in the Alban Lake. Apart from Diana's presence, the grove was also famous because no horses, the creatures of Neptune (see page 175), would ever set hoof in it.

PUNISHMENTS (*page 129*)

Both Mettius' execution and the destruction of Alba Longa followed examples from Greek myth. Lycurgus, king of the Edonians, went mad and chopped his own son to pieces with an axe; the Edonians punished him by harnessing horses to his limbs and neck and driving them apart. Later, when the Greeks took Troy, they not only smashed the buildings and walls to rubble, but also sowed the ruins with salt so that no one could ever live there again.

The Romans never again executed anyone as barbarously as they did Mettius. But they several times obliterated captured cities as they did Alba Longa. In the second century BC, after a century of war (including the invasion of Italy by Hannibal) they sacked Carthage, burnt it, broke down the walls and ploughed salt into the remains. A few years later the people of Corinth in Greece murdered some Roman ambassadors, and the Romans punished them by enslaving the people, looting Corinth and pounding its remains to rubble.

VENUS AND MARS (*page 129*)

Venus' husband was Vulcan, the lame blacksmith of the gods. Dazzled by love, he gave her miraculous presents: a golden honeycomb exact in every detail, statues with moving legs and arms, tables that ran about of their own accord. But she despised his ugliness: she was in love instead with Mars, the handsome god of war. Vulcan knew nothing of their love-affair until Phoebus Apollo the sun-god, who sees and knows all secrets, told him and urged him to take revenge. Vulcan, reluctant to harm the wife he loved, and knowing that he would be no match for Mars in a trial of strength, decided to punish the lovers by ridicule instead of by force. He made a net of golden threads, stickier than spider's silk and so fine that they were invisible even to immortal eyes, and hung it in the bedroom Venus and Mars used for their love-making. Then he went back to his forge under Mount Etna in Sicily, and waited. That same day the lovers met as usual and jumped into bed, and the net fell on them and trapped them in each other's arms, to the glee of every immortal on Olympus. The shame made Mars and Venus give up their love-affair for a time, but when the scandal died down they began again.

NAVIUS (*page 134*)

One story says that Tarquin was so sure of himself that he even scorned the gods: he took no heed of omens, and did as he pleased without listening to the priests. His madness was stopped by Attius Navius, Rome's leading augur (a man who told the future by the pattern of birds flying overhead). Navius told Tarquin to stop all building-work until the birds gave a sign of the gods' approval. 'Rubbish!' said Tarquin. 'What can birds know that human beings don't?'

'They know – and can tell me – exactly what you're thinking now.'

'Prove it!'

Calmly, Navius sent for a razor and a whetstone. He sharpened the razor, tested the blade, and then with a single slice cut the stone in half. Tarquin was amazed, not so much by the miracle as because he'd been deliberately thinking of the most obscure proverb he could remember: 'Stone blunts blade fears stone'. He never again, or so the story goes, did anything without first consulting the omens – and he put Navius' whetstone, and a statue of Navius himself, beside the steps of the senate house to remind all Romans of the power of augury.

TARQUIN'S CHILDREN (*page 137*)

In some accounts, Lucius and Arruns were not Tarquin's illegitimate sons, and were not brought up secretly in Etruria. They were his and Tanaquil's legitimate children, and it was only because they were too young to succeed to the throne that Servius, Tarquin's adopted son, was named king instead of them. Other versions of the story, concerned that this meant Tanaquil having children at an extremely advanced age, made Lucius and Arruns Tarquin's grandchildren: his son having died when the twins were still babies, he adopted Servius and made him not heir to the throne but regent, with power only till the boys were old enough to rule.

THE FIELD OF MARS (*page 144*)

In their eagerness to loot everything the Tarquins had ever owned, the mob even fell on a field of corn beside the Tiber. They tore the stalks from the ground, threw them into the river and stamped the earth flat so that nothing would ever grow there again. They dedicated the place to Mars, Rome's protector, and called it *Campus Martius*, 'field of Mars', after him. It became one of the main public areas of Rome, and was used for centuries for army-training in wartime and for horse-riding and athletics in peace.

BRUTUS (*page 146*)

Two other outstanding Romans shared the name Brutus. One, in myth, was the grandson either of Iulus, Aeneas' son, or of Ascanius who was Aeneas' son by the wood-nymph Silvia (see page 174). He killed his father in a hunting-accident, and was so ashamed that he went into exile with a shipload of followers. They sailed through the Pillars of Hercules from the Mediterranean Sea into the Atlantic, north along the edge of the waterfall that rims the world, and finally settled in a triangular island in the northern sea. Their descendants called themselves Brutii, or Britii, after Brutus, and their island came to be known as Britain.

The second Brutus, Marcus Junius Brutus, was a real historical person. He was a friend of Julius Caesar, and claimed to be a direct descendant of the Brutus who expelled the Tarquins. When it looked as if Caesar was going to claim royal power in Rome, Brutus remembered his ancestry, and led the conspirators who stabbed Caesar dead in the senate-house on the Ides of March, 44 BC.

THE CAPITOLINE HILL   (page 146)

Some say that the Capitoline Hill was originally called the Tarpeian Hill after Tarpeia, who betrayed it to the Sabines (see page 175). Others say that its Latin name, Capitolium, comes from the phrase *caput Toli*, 'Tolus' head', because the head of a man called Tolus was found there in Tarquin the Proud's time when builders began extending the temple foundations. The hill was large enough to house a fortified village of several hundred people. Its sides were rocky and steep, and when attackers reached the top they found sheer stone walls and defenders hurling down arrows, spears and stones. When the Gauls invaded Rome in 386 BC, the whole Roman population took shelter in the citadel except for the oldest members of the senate, who volunteered to stay below and show the enemy that the Romans were not afraid of them. The senators sat on thrones at

the doors of their houses, and at first their calmness terrified the Gauls. It was only when one of the senators, Marcus Papirius, hit a man who was stroking his long beard in wonderment, that the Gauls killed them where they sat and plundered their palaces. The Gauls' commander planned to follow this by attacking the citadel at night, while the defenders slept. His men scrambled up the Capitoline in the moonlight, passing up their weapons hand to hand. They reached the wall unnoticed, and would have swarmed over and killed everyone inside if Juno's sacred geese had not begun cackling wildly and given the alarm. Marcus Manlius, commander of the guard, held off the Gauls singlehanded until the rest of the defenders ran out and the citadel was saved.

'LEFTY'   (page 148)

When Mucius went back into Rome, with his right hand no more than a bandaged stump, children ran after him and mockingly called him Scaevola, 'Lefty'. The senate were so impressed by his courage and his rescue of Rome from the Etruscans that they gave him the name as a title of honour to use forever, and the Scaevolas later became one of the most distinguished of all Roman families.

SOME · BOOKS
TO · READ

Chapters 1–2

The most enjoyable Roman collection of myths and folk-stories is Ovid's *Metamorphoses* ('Changes'), written at the end of the first century BC. Ovid was fascinated by the idea of living beings changing into other things (for example, nymphs becoming trees), and his account of famous myth-stories is full of bizarre details of that kind. The most famous English translation of *Metamorphoses* – still readable today – was made by Golding in 1567: Queen Elizabeth I enjoyed it, and Shakespeare knew it and used ideas from it in several plays. A sparkling modern prose version is by Mary Innes (Penguin, 1955). A straightforward account of the Greek versions of these and many other myths is in Kenneth McLeish's *Children of the Gods* (Longman, 1983), a companion-volume to the present book. The story of Cupid and Psyche in Chapter Two is beautifully told in Apuleius' novel *The Golden Ass*, published in the second century AD and excellently translated by Robert Graves (Penguin, 1950).

Chapters 3–9

The story of Aeneas is best told in Virgil's *Aeneid* (first century AD), one of the best-known of all Roman books. Virgil wrote in verse, and poetic translations of the *Aeneid* give the best view of it, though they may take several readings to give the full flavour. Good modern verse translations are by C. Day Lewis (Cape, 1940; OUP, 1966) and Robert Fitzgerald (Penguin, 1984); there is a useful prose translation by W.F. Jackson Knight (Penguin, 1956).

Chapters 10–12

All the stories in these chapters, and many others, were told by the Roman writer Livy in his *History of Rome* (first century AD). The stories here recounted come from Books 1 and 2; later books move on to true fact, and tell of Rome's Wars with enemies outside Italy, particularly the Carthaginians and their leader Hannibal. The myth-based part of Livy's book is published as *The Early History of Rome*, magnificently translated by Aubrey de Selincourt (Penguin, 1960). Anyone who enjoys Livy's account of the power-struggles of the Tarquins will find equal fun in two of the most famous of all novels about ancient Rome, Robert Graves' *I, Claudius* (Barker, 1934; Penguin, 1941) and *Claudius the God* (Barker, 1934; Penguin, 1943). They tell of events seven centuries later than the tales Livy tells, but the Tarquins could teach Graves' emperors nothing about craziness, bloodthirstiness or political skulduggery.

1934; Penguin, 1943). They tell of events seven centuries later than the tales Livy tells, but the Tarquins could teach Graves' emperors nothing about craziness, bloodthirstiness or political skulduggery.

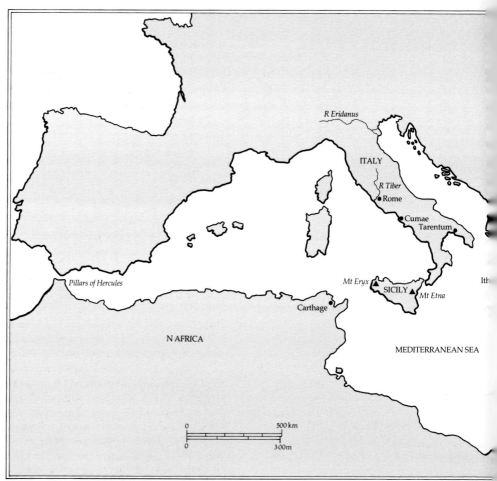

Map of main places mentioned in the stories

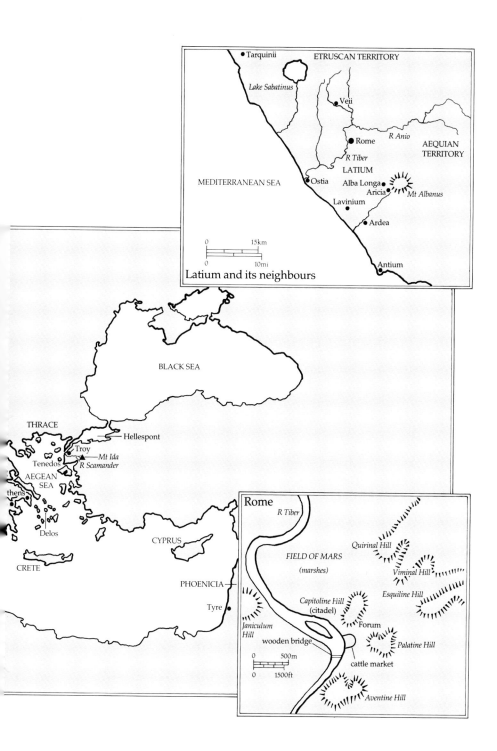

Latium and its neighbours

Tarquinii

ETRUSCAN TERRITORY

Lake Sabatinus

Veii

R Anio

Rome

AEQUIAN
TERRITORY

R Tiber

LATIUM

MEDITERRANEAN SEA

Ostia

Alba Longa

Aricia

Mt Albanus

Lavinium

Ardea

Antium

0   15km

0   10mi

BLACK SEA

THRACE

Hellespont

Troy

Mt Ida

Tenedos

R Scamander

AEGEAN
SEA

thens

Delos

CYPRUS

CRETE

PHOENICIA

Tyre

Rome

R Tiber

Quirinal Hill

FIELD OF MARS

(marshes)

Viminal Hill

Esquiline Hill

Capitoline Hill
(citadel)

Janiculum
Hill

Forum

wooden bridge

Palatine Hill

cattle market

0   500m

0   1500ft

Aventine Hill

183

INDEX

Abaris 92
Abas 54, 101
Acamas 38
Acesta 163
Acestes (king of Sicily) 62, 64, 163
Achaemenides 38, 51–2
Achates 45, 54, 55–7, 66–8, 78, 85, 165, 172
Acheron (river) 68, 166
Achilles 32, 36, 154–5, 157, 162
Acis 160–1
Actor 94
Adrastus 73
Aeaea 168
Aeetes (king of Colchis) 152
Aegeon (Briareus) 70, 102, 153, 171–2
Aegyptus 171
Aello 48
Aeneas vii, 181; and Anchises' ghost 64, 74–6; birth 154; death 113–14; and Dido 56–62, 72; fights Diomedes 162, 172: Greeks 38–9, 162: Latins 84, 98, 102, 104: Turnus 108–10, 125, 173; journeys to Buthrotum 49–50: Carthage 54–5: Crete 47: Delos 45–7: Etruria 87–8, 97: Latium 77–8: Pallanteum 85–7: Scylla and Charybdis 50–1: Sicily 51–2: Strophades 48–9: Thrace 45: Underworld 66–76, 165; leaves Troy 32, 41–3, 155–6; marries Creusa 156: Lavinia 112; and Mercury 59–60; and Sibyl of Cumae 56–62, 72; in storm 53–4; and Tiber 84–5; and Venus 41–2, 55–6, 68, 86, 87–8, 162, 172–3
Aeneas Silvius 114, 174
Aeneid, The 157, 163, 181
Aeolides, The 161
Aeolus 53–4, 161–2
Aequi 140

Aesculapius 177
Aethon 6
Aetolia 172
Africa 162
Agamemnon 35, 36, 38, 40, 154, 158
Ajax 32
Alba (Longa) 84, 114, 116, 122, 125, 127–9, 130, 174, 177
Alban Lake 125, 177
Albanus, Mount 124, 125, 137, 141, 177
alder-trees 8, 168
Aletes 54, 91–2, 94, 97
Allecto 80–3, 169
Almo 83
Alpheus 11–12
Amastrus 106
Amata (queen of Latium) 79, 81
Amathus 99
Ameriola 134
Amphitrite 160
Amulius 114–15, 116, 135, 174–5
Anaxarete 152
Anchises 156; death and funeral games 53, 63–4; father of Aeneas 38, 154, 156, 162; foretells rise of Rome 75–6; as ghost 64; interprets oracle 46–7; leaves Troy 41–2, 43, 155–6; loves Venus 154; in Underworld 68, 71, 74–6
Ancus Martius (king of Rome) 132–4, 135
Androgeus 38–9
Andromache 50, 159–60
Anio (river) 128, 139
Anius (king of Delos) 46, 158
Anna 60, 61, 62
Antaeus 102
Antandros 44
Antemnans 117, 119
Antheus 56, 173
Antiphates 96
Antores 104

Aphidnus 96
Aphrodite 150
Apollo 150, 154, 177; birth 157; builds Troy 153, 155; and Deiphobe 164–5; fights Python 157; rescues Venus 162; speaks to Aeneas 45–6, 66–7
Apuleius 152, 153, 181
Ardea 112, 141, 143, 174
Ares 150
Arethusa 10–12
Arethusa (spring) 11, 12
Arges 170–1
Argonauts 152
Argos 80, 170
Argyrippa 172
Aricia 124, 139, 177
Arne 161
Arruns (brother of Tarquin the Proud) 137–8, 143, 145
Arruns (cavalryman) 107
Arruns (son of Tarquin the Proud) 138, 140–1, 143, 145, 178
Artemis 150
Asbytes 172
Ascanius 156, 174, 178
Astyanax 155
Athene 150
Atlantic Ocean 162
Atlantis 162
Atlas 7, 59, 162–3
Atlas Mountains 163
Atropos 173 see also Fates
Attica 175
Attius Navius see Navius
Atys 63
Augustus (Emperor of Rome) 75
Aventine Hill 131, 170, 175
Aventinus 83–4

Bacchants 156
Bacchus 156, 158
Baucis 27–9
Bellona 150

Beroe 63–4
Bitias 95, 96
Boeotia 162
Boeotus 161–2
Bootes 7
Boreas *see* North Wind
Briareus *see* Aegeon
Brontes 170–1
Brutus (grandson of Aeneas) 178–9
Brutus, Marcus Junius 179
Brutus the Liberator 75, 140–1, 142–3, 144–5, 146
Buthrotum 49–50

Cacus 85, 169–70
Caelian Hill 131, 170
Caeninans 117, 119
Caius Mucius 147–8, 179
Calais 159
Calchas 36
Callirhoe 156
Calybe 81
Cameria 134
Camers 102
Camilla 84, 106–7
Campus Martius 178
Canens (Venilia) 12–14
Cape Misenum 166
Capitoline Hill 119, 120, 134, 140, 146, 170, 176, 179
Capys 156
Carthage 56, 58–62, 162, 177
Carthaginian Wars 163, 177, 181
Cassandra 31–2, 35, 37, 39, 154, 156
Catillus 89
Caulonia 50
Celaeno 48, 49
Cerberus 71–2, 166
Ceres 42, 150, 181; helps Psyche 19, 20; mother of Proserpina 165; punishes Erysichthon 25–6
Chaonia 49, 159
Charon 70–1, 166, 177
Charybdis 48, 50–1, 160
Chloreus 107
Chromis 106
Circe 12–13, 77, 160, 168
Cloanthus 56, 57, 163
Clotho 173 *see also* Fates
Clusium 146
Clymene 5
Clytemnestra 154
Clytius 96, 106
Cocytus (river) 68, 166
Coeus 157
Colchis 21, 152
Collatia 134, 142
Collatinus 141–2, 144
Consualia 175
consuls 143–4

Consus (Neptune) 175
Corcyra 49
Corinth 177
Coroebus 38, 39, 154
Corniculum 134
Corus 89
Corytus (king of Etruria) 158
Crab 7
Crete 46, 47, 66, 151, 158, 164
Cretheus 96
Creusa 41–3, 156
Crinisus 163
Critias 97
Croton 50
Crustumians 117, 119
Cumae 66, 164, 165 *see also* Deiphobe
Cupid 15–22, 57–8, 142, 150, 153
Cures 124
Curiatii 125–7
Curiatius 126–7
Curiatius brothers *see* Curiatii
Cybele 107
Cyclades 167
Cyclopes 4, 48, 51–2, 74, 86, 161, 169, 170–1
Cymodoce 98
Cynthus, Mount 46
Cythera 99

Daedalus 66, 67, 164
Danaus 171
Dardanus 47, 156, 158–9
Dares 163, 172
Deidamia 154, 155
Deiopeia 53
Deiphilus 157
Deiphobe (Sibyl of Cumae) 64, 67–76, 164–5
Deiphobus 73, 159
Deiphyle 172
Delians 158
Delos 45–6, 47, 157, 158
Delphi 140–1, 157, 160
Demaratus 132
Demeter 150
Demodocus 101
Demophoön 106
Desmontes 161
Deucalion 30
Diana 46, 150; birth 157; defends Olympus 23; helps Hippolytus 177; punishes Egeria 125; resents Juno 157
Diana's nymphs 10–11, 124, 141
Dictamnus 172–3
Dido (queen of Carthage) 56–62, 72, 99–100, 162, 163
Diomedes 105, 106, 162, 172
Dis 150
Discord 91, 92, 93, 171
Dolichaeon 103

doves 68, 158
Drances 105–6
Drepanum 53, 163, 164
Dryas 156, 157
Dulichium 49
Dymas 38, 39

Earth, Mother (Tellus *or* Tythia) 2–4, 7, 22–3, 30, 141, 151, 153, 159, 169, 171
East Wind 53–4
Edonians 44, 45, 156, 157
Egeria 124
Egesta 163
Electra (queen of Etruria) 156, 158
Elicius ritual 131
Elis 11
Elysian Fields 68, 74–6, 168
Elysium 73 *see also* Elysian Fields
Enceladus 50, 160
Entellus 163–4
Eous 6
Epaphus 5
Epeus 38, 154
Epirus 48, 155, 159, 160
Erichthonius 156
Eridanus (river) 3, 7, 8, 74, 167–8
Eros 150
Erymanthus 11
Erymas 96
Erysichthon (king of Thessaly) 23–6
Eryx, Mount 62, 65, 163
Esquiline Hill 170
Ethiopia 60
Etna, Mount 50, 51, 52, 86, 160, 171, 178
Etruria 83, 113, 135, 140, 144, 158, 178
Etruscans 87, 140, 144, 146–8
Euneus 106
Europa 166, 167
Euryalus 91–4, 97, 98, 163
Eurydice 166
Evander 84–7, 97, 170
Evanthes 103

Fabaris (river) 124
Fabius 75
Fadus 92
Fates 53, 62, 102, 109, 110, 171, 172, 173, 176
Faunus 79, 80, 109, 150, 169
Faustulus 116, 174
Ferentia, Grove of 139
Ficulea 134
Fidenae 121, 128
Fields of the Blessed 64, 73 *see also* Elysian Fields
Fortuna 150
Forum 120, 131, 134, 138, 144

Forum Boarium 170
Furies 69–70, 72, 74, 81, 110, 143, 148, 169

Gabii 139–40, 143
Galaesus 83
Galatea 160–1
Ganymede 156, 167
Gauls 179
Geryon 169
Glaucus (sea-spirit) 160, 164
Glaucus (Trojan) 73, 172
Golden Age 15
Golden Ass, The 181
Golden Branch 68–9, 71, 74
Golden Branch, Grove of 68
Golden Fleece 21, 152
Gorgas 97
Gyas 57, 163
Gyges 96

Hades 150
Halaesus 84, 101
Halley's Comet 176
Hannibal 75, 163, 177, 181
Harpalycus 106
Harpies 48–9, 70, 159
Harvest 25
Hebrus 103
Hecate 2–3, 151
Hector 32, 38, 50, 155, 156, 172
Hecuba 40–1, 156, 157
Helen 31, 41–2, 73, 99, 159
Helenus 31–2, 49–50, 156, 159–60
Helle 152
Hellespont 152
Hephaistos 150
Herbesus 92
Hercules 155, 160, 163; death 159; father of Aventinus 83–4; fights Cacus 85, 169–70; in Underworld 71–113, 166
Hercules, Pillars of 179
Here 150
Hermes 150
Herminius 146–7
Hermione 160
heron 112, 174
Hersilia (Hora) 120, 176
Hestia 150
Hippolytus 177
Hisbo 106
History of Rome (Livy), 174, 181
Hora 176
Horatia 126–7
Horatii 125–7
Horatius brothers see Horatii
Horatius Cocles vii, 146–7
Hostilii 176
Hostius Hostilius 120, 176
Hours 5, 6

Hundred-Handed Giants 169 see also Aegeon
Hydra 84
Hypanis 38, 39
Hypermnestra 171

Iarbas (king of Libya) 56, 59, 60, 162
Iasius 158–9
Icarus 164
Ida, Mount 44, 91, 98, 151, 154, 158, 172
Idaea (mountain nymph) 158
Idaea (princess) 156
Idaeus (son of Antenor) 73, 94
Idaeus (son of Dardanus) 156
Idalium 99
Idalus, Mount 57, 58
Idamantes 158
Idomeneus 46, 158
Ilea see Rhea, daughter of Numitor
Ilione 157
Ilioneus 45, 46, 50, 54, 56, 57, 78, 80, 84, 90
Ilus 156
Ino 152
Io 5
Iphigenia 36
Iphis 152
Iphitus 38, 39
Iris 27, 89, 90, 176; helps Dido 62; impersonates Beroe 63–4
Iron Age 22–3
Islands of the Blessed 4
Italy 47, 50, 60
Ithaca 49
Iulus 75, 98, 99, 108, 156, 174, 178; crowned 113; fights in Latium 82–3, 172; founder of Alba 84, 114, 129; and Game of Troy 63, 164; impersonated by Cupid 57–8; leaves Troy 41–2
Ixion 73, 167

Janiculum Hill 124, 132, 151
January 151
Janus vii, 2–5, 12, 79, 119, 151
Jason 152
Julius Caesar 75, 179
Julius Proculus 122–3
Junius 140
Juno 62, 84, 85, 112, 113, 115, 150, 176; and Aeolus 53; birth 151; helps Dido 162; and judgement of Paris 31, 155, 158; punishes Jupiter 153: Latona 157; and Trojans 31, 48, 50, 52–3, 58–9, 80–1, 83, 89, 99–100: and Turnus 102–3, 173
Jupiter 8, 15, 64, 112, 116, 122, 134, 140, 145, 150, 153, 171;

arbitrates 99–100, 109–10, 130, 165, 173; and Baucis and Philemon 28–9; birth 46, 151, 175; father of Apollo and Diana 157: of Dardanus 156, 158–9: of Epaphus 5: of Hercules 155: of Minos 166: of Tityus 167; fights giants 23, 73: Titans 23, 73; protects Aeneas 52, 59, 76, 162: Turnus 102: and Psyche 21–2: punished by Juno 153: punishes Aegeon 172: Atlas 162–3: Aeolus 53, 161–2: Apollo and Neptune 155: Charybdis 160: Discord 171: Enceladus 160: human race 26, 27–8, 152: Ixion 167: Janus 4–5: Juturna 173: Lycaon 27: Phaethon 7: Tullus 131; and Styx 166; and Trojan War 31
Juturna 173–4
Juturna (spring) 174

Kronos 150

Lachesis 173 see also Fates
Lacus Curtius 176
Ladon 101, 172
Lagus 100
Lamus 92
Lamyrus 92
Laocoön 35, 37, 156, 163
Laomedon (king of Troy) 153, 155, 156
Larentia 116
Lares 150
Larides 100, 101
Lars Porsena 146–8
Lartius 146–7
Latagus 103
Latins 107, 110, 112, 134, 172
Latinus (king of Latium) 79–80, 83, 105, 108, 112, 168, 173
Latium 4, 47, 77–80, 92, 99, 105, 108, 151, 171
Latona 157
Laurentum 12, 13, 103
Lausus 83, 101, 103, 104
Lavinia 79–80, 81, 106, 112, 113–14, 174
Lavinium 112, 114, 121
Lethe 75, 168
Leucadia see Leucate
Leucas see Leucate
Leucaspis 71
Leucate 49, 159
Libya 56, 59, 162
Lipara 53, 161, 162
Liris 106
Livy vii, viii, 174, 181
Luca 102
Lucius 137, 178 see also Tar-

quin the Proud
Lucius Tarquinius Priscus *see*
Tarquin the First
Lucretia 142–3
Lucumo 132 *see also* Tarquin
the First
Ludi Romani 164
Lupercal 174
Lussin 168
Lycaon (king of Thessaly) 26–7
Lycomedes 154
Lycurgus (king of Edonians)
44, 156, 157, 177
Lynceus 171

Machaon 38
Maenalus 11
Marcus Manlius 179
Marcus Papirius 179
Marica 79
Mars 129, 130, 150, 167, 174;
father of Romulus and
Remus 115, 122, 123: of
Faunus 169; and Trojan War
31; and Venus 86, 177–8
Mars, Field of 178
Meara 26
Mediterranean Sea 7
Medon 73
Medullia 134
Medusa 109
Megaera 81, 169
Megara, Bay of 52
Menelaus 31, 35, 38, 40, 73,
160
Menoetes 163
Mercury 31, 60, 150; and
Aeneas 59, 61; father of
Faunus 169; helps Baucis
and Philemon 28–9: Ulysses
168
Merope 96
Messapus 84, 89, 92, 95, 106
Messina, Straits of 50
Metamorphoses 152, 181
Mettius Curtius 120, 176, 177
Mettius Fufetius 125, 127–9,
130
Mezentius 83, 87, 89, 90, 98,
101–2, 103–4
Midas 158
Mimas 103
Minerva 8, 35, 36, 37, 150;
fights giants 23; helps Ulys-
ses 168; and judgement of
Paris 31, 158; and Palladium
153–4; and Pallas 153; wins
Attica 175
Minos 72, 113, 164, 166–7
Minotaur 164
Misenus 49, 63, 165–6
Mnestheus 50, 96–7, 163, 172,
173

Mucius *see* Caius Mucius
Mycenae 154
Mykonos 46

Navius 178
Neoptolemus 155, 160
Neptune 7, 29, 36, 46, 117–18,
150, 152, 157, 158, 168; birth
151; father of Aeolus 161: of
Charybdis 160: of Messapus
84; fights Titans 4; floods
Earth 27–8, 29, 30; helps
Baucis and Philemon 28–9:
Trojans 54, 78; and horses
175; and Jupiter 155; loves
Scylla 160; and Misenus 165;
punishes Atlas 162: Hippoly-
tus 177; rules the sea 4, 54
Neritus 49
Nessus 159
Nisus 91–4, 97, 98, 163
Noemon 95, 97
Nomentum 134
North Wind (Boreas) 53–4,
159, 161
Numa (Latin soldier) 102
Numa Pompilius (king of
Rome) 124–5, 131, 132
Numitor 114, 116, 174, 175

Oath of the Gods (river) 166
Ocean (Oceanus river) 5, 166
Ocypete 48
Olympia 10
Olympus, Mount 6, 7, 24, 100;
attacked by giants 23, 160
Orestes 160
Orontes 54, 71
Orpheus 74, 166
Ovid 152, 174, 181
oxen, iron-hoofed 7

Pegasus 106
Palamedes 36
Palatine Hill 9, 120, 122, 170,
174, 175
Pales 9
Palinurus 50, 71
Palladium 31, 43, 47, 153–4,
155–6, 159
Pallanteum 84, 85, 87, 170
Pallas 85, 87, 97–8, 100–2, 171
Pallas' belt 98, 101, 108, 110,
171
Pallas (Minerva) 153
Palmus 103
Pan 20, 21, 150, 152, 174
Pandarus 95, 96
Pantagia 52
Pantheus 45
Paphus 56, 99
Paris 31–3, 155, 156, 158
Parthenopaeus 73
Pasiphae 164

Patroclus 32
Pelias 38, 39
Pelops 167
Penates 150
Perseis 168
Persephone 150
Phaedra 177
Phaethon 5–8, 168
Phalaris 96
Pheres 101
Philemon 27–9
Philoctetes 159
Phineus 159
Phlegethon (river) 73, 166
Phlegeus 96
Phlegon 6
Phoebe 157
Phoebus *see* Apollo; Sun
Phoenicia 56
Pholus 172
Phrixus 152
Phrygia 154
Picus (king of Latium) 12–14,
152, 169
Pillars of Hercules 179
Pilumnus 152
Pirithous 166
Pleasure 22
Pluto 150, 169; birth 151;
fights Titans 4, 166; and Pro-
serpina 165, 166; punishes
Tityus 167; rules Under-
world 15, 73
Pluton 150
Po (river) 167, 168
Podarces 155, *see also* Priam
Polites 41, 63, 156
Polydorus 44, 45 157
Polymnestor (king of the Edo-
nians) 157
Polyphemus 51–2, 160–1, 170
Polyphoetes 73
Polyxena 155
Pometia 140, 141
Pomona 9–10, 12, 152
Pompey 75
Poseidon 150
Priam (grandson of king of
Troy) 63
Priam (Podarces) (king of
Troy) 32, 35–6, 37, 40–1, 44,
49, 73, 154, 155, 156, 157,
159, 162
Prometheus 8–9, 23, 30, 151–2
Proserpina 68, 71, 150, 153,
165, 166
Prytanis 96
Prytias 95
Psyche 15–22, 152–3
Pygmalion 60, 162
Pyrois 6
Pyrrha 154 *see also* Pyrrhus
(son of Achilles)

Pyrrha (wife of Deucalion) 30
Pyrrhic victory 155
Pyrrhic (king of Epirus) 155
Pyrrhus (son of Achilles) 38, 40, 41, 154–5, 159–60
Pythian Games 157
Python 157, 167

Quirinal Hill 123, 170
Quirinus 123, 176 *see also* Romulus

Remus vii, 115–17, 135, 174, 175
Rhadamanthus 73, 113, 167
Rhamnes 92, 93
Rhea (daughter of Numitor) 114–15, 174
Rhea (wife of Saturn) 151, 156, 175
Rhegium 50
Rhenea 46
Rhipeus 38, 39
Rhoetes 92
Rome 59, 75–6, 88, 116–18, 134, 141, 148, 156, 179: Seven Hills 170
Romulus vii, 75, 115–23, 135, 156, 174, 176
Rumour 59, 60, 122, 136
Rutulians 84, 103, 112, 172, 173

Sabines 117–18, 119–21, 134, 176
Saces 173
Salentum 158
Salius 163
Same 49
Saturn 5, 150; father of Latona 157; of Neptune 175: of Picus 12, 152; fights gods 4, 8, 22, 151: Sky 151, 169
Scaevola *see* Caius Mucius
Scamander 46, 47, 158
Scamander (river) 158
Scipio 75
Scorpion 7
Scylla 48, 50–1, 160
Scythia 25
senate 122, 143–4
Serestus 96
Sergestus 45, 56, 57, 78, 80, 84, 85, 163
Serranus 92
Servius Tullius (king of Rome) 134–6, 137–9, 178
Sextus Tarquinius 138, 139–40, 141–3
Sichaeus 58, 61, 72, 162
Sicily 11–12, 15, 50, 64–5, 81, 160, 163, 170, 171
Silvanus 145, 150
Silver Age 15, 22

Silvia 82, 114, 174, 178
Silvius 75
Silvius Posthumus 174
Sinon 35–7, 38, 154
Sisyphus 74, 167
Sky (Uranus) 2–4, 151, 169
South Wind 27, 54
Starvation 25–6, 165
Steropes 170–1
Sthenelus 38, 172
Strophades 48, 159
Strymonius 101
Styx (goddess) 166
Styx (river) 3, 5, 6, 21, 61, 68, 70–1, 113, 146, 151, 152, 177
Sulmo 93, 102
Sun (Phoebus/Apollo) 5–8, 12, 15, 130, 131–2, 140–1, 151, 152, 159, 170, 177
swans 172
Symaethus 21

Tanaquil 132, 134–5, 136, 178
Tantalus 74, 167
Tarchon (king of the Etruscans) 87, 88, 89, 97, 107
Tarentum 50
Tarpeia vii, 119, 175–6, 179
Tarpeian Rock 176
Tarpeius 119
Tarquinii 132, 145, 148
Tarquin the First (king of Rome) 132, 133–6, 137, 145, 178, 182
Tarquin the Proud vii, 75, 137–40, 141, 143, 144–6, 148, 174, 182
Tartarus 70, 73–4, 148, 167
Tatia 124
Tatius (king of the Sabines) 119, 121, 124, 176
Tellus *see* Earth
Tenedos 38
Tereus 106
Teucer 158, 159
Thamyrus 172
Thapsus (plain) 52
Thebes 152
Themis 30
Themiste 156
Thersilochus 73, 172
Theseus 71, 166, 177
Thessaly 24, 25, 27
Thessander 38
Thoas 101
Thrace 44–5
Thymber 100
Tiber (god) 13, 84–5, 98, 113, 115, 131, 132
Tiber (river) 9, 77–8, 86, 90, 105, 146, 169
Tisiphone 73, 81, 167, 169
Titans 2, 4, 8, 151, 161, 169
Tithea *see* Earth

Titus 138, 140–1, 143
Tityus 73, 167
Tolumnius 172
Tolus 179
Tritons 54
Trojans *see* Aeneas; Troy
Trojan War 30–43
Tros 156
Troy 44–5, 99; established 153, 155, 158; falls 38–43, 177; game 164; and Rome 75, 110 *see also* Palladium; Trojan War
Tullia 138–9, 143
Tullus (king of Rome) 125, 127, 128, 130–1
Turnus 79–82, 84, 87, 89–91, 94, 96–9, 101–3, 106, 108–10, 171–2, 173–4
Turnus Herdonius 139
Tydeus 73, 172
Tyre 56, 162
Tyrrhus 82, 83

Ufens 84, 94, 95, 102, 108
Ulysses 31, 32, 35, 36, 38, 51, 154, 161, 168
Underworld 2–3, 15, 22–3, 64, 68–76, 113, 159, 166–8, 177
Uranus *see* Sky

Veii 121, 128, 145
Venilia *see* Canens
Venus 58, 59, 115, 150; affair with Mars 86, 177; birth 151; helps: Aeneas 41, 55–6, 68, 86, 87–8, 99–100, 113, 162, 172: Trojans 31, 57; intercedes for Alba 129–30; and judgement of Paris 31, 158; marries Vulcan 86, 177; mother of Aeneas 154, 156; punishes Psyche 16, 20–1, 22, 152–3; wounded 162
Vertumnus 9–10, 152
Vesta 8, 114, 150, 151, 156, 174
Vestal Virgins 156
Viminal Hill 170
Virgil vii, viii, 157, 163, 171, 172, 181
Volcens 93, 102
Vulcan 6, 8, 86, 88–9, 109, 150, 164, 169, 170, 171, 177–8

West Wind 15, 17, 18, 22, 53–4
Whirling Islands 159
Wooden Horse 32, 34–8, 154, 155
woodpecker 13, 152, 169, 174

Xanthus (river) 158

Zacynthus 49
Zetes 159
Zeus 150

189